Reshaping Social Work Series

Series Editors: **Robert Adams, Lena Dominelli and Malcolm Payne**

The **Reshaping Social Work** series aims to develop the knowledge base for critical, reflective practitioners. Each book is designed to support students on qualifying social work programmes and update practitioners on crucial issues in today's social work, strengthening research knowledge, critical analysis and skilled practice to shape social work to meet future challenges.

Published titles

Critical Issues in Social Work with Older People Mo Ray, Judith Phillips and Miriam Bernard
Social Work and Power Roger Smith
Social Work Research for Social Justice Beth Humphries

Forthcoming title

Anti-Racist Practice in Social Work Kish Bhatti-Sinclair

Invitation to authors

The Series Editors welcome proposals for new books within the *Reshaping Social Work* series. Please contact one of the series editors for an initial discussion:

- Robert Adams at rvadams@rvadams.karoo.co.uk
- Lena Dominelli at lena.dominelli@durham.ac.uk
- Malcolm Payne at M.Payne@stchristophers.org.uk

Reshaping Social Work
Series Editors: **Robert Adams, Lena Dominelli and Malcolm Payne**
Series Standing Order ISBN 1–4039–4878–X
(outside North America only)

You can receive future titles in this series as they are published by placing a standing order. Please contact your bookseller or, in the case of difficulty, write to us at the address below with your name and address, the title of the series and the ISBN quoted above.

Customer Services Department
Macmillan Distribution Ltd
Houndmills
Basingstoke
Hampshire
RG21 6XS
England

Spirituality and Social Work

Margaret Holloway

and

Bernard Moss

First published 2010 by
PALGRAVE MACMILLAN

Palgrave Macmillan in the UK is an imprint of Macmillan Publishers Limited, registered in England, company number 785998, of Houndmills, Basingstoke, Hampshire RG21 6XS.

Palgrave Macmillan in the US is a division of St Martin's Press LLC, 175 Fifth Avenue, New York, NY 10010.

Palgrave Macmillan is the global academic imprint of the above companies and has companies and representatives throughout the world.

Palgrave® and Macmillan® are registered trademarks in the United States, the United Kingdom, Europe and other countries.

ISBN-13: 978–0–230–21924–3

This book is printed on paper suitable for recycling and made from fully managed and sustained forest sources. Logging, pulping and manufacturing processes are expected to conform to the environmental regulations of the country of origin.

A catalogue record for this book is available from the British Library.

A catalog record for this book is available from the Library of Congress.

10   9   8   7   6   5   4   3   2   1
19   18   17   16   15   14   13   12   11   10

Printed and bound in Great Britain by
CPI Antony Rowe, Chippenham and Eastbourne

Contents

List of figures and boxes

Figures

Boxes

Acknowledgements

Our grateful thanks are due to the many colleagues internationally with whom we have shared stimulating and fruitful discussions. In particular, we should like to thank Paul Dearey, Wilf McSherry, Leola Furman, Ed Canda, Neil Thompson and Peter Gilbert. Special thanks are due to Andy Bowden, Jo Bowden and Sam Bell for their challenging comments on early drafts. They widened our perspectives immeasurably. Thanks are also due to our respective partners, John and Sheila, for their tolerance and patience as we have sneaked away to write! Likewise, the editorial team at Palgrave have given us the space we needed with just the right amount of nudging encouragement.

chapter 1
Contemporary and historical contexts

Introduction

This book tackles and explores one of the most significant, important and controversial themes to emerge in social work in recent years. Spirituality has 'come of age'. Throughout this book we explore why and how it should be taken seriously by social work practitioners, students and academics, for the simple reason that this is a profession which seeks to make an important contribution to human well-being.

What does spirituality have to do with social work?

This question may well be on your lips as it has so often been the first reaction of students and colleagues when we have raised the subject of spirituality with them. We are two social work academics who have been teaching, writing, researching and discussing the relationship between social work and spirituality for over two decades, as well as thinking about what spirituality means in our society for much longer. We are very familiar therefore with this reaction. Social work is, after all, a secular profession which takes place to a very large extent in secular organisations, and we are proud to belong to it. It is, of course, firmly grounded in a psycho-social model of practice with theoretical underpinnings from the secular disciplines of sociology and psychology, though straying briefly into the realms of philosophy and ethics. But all the while our eyes are firmly fixed on the policy and legal frameworks within which we must work. Although it is true that we are very concerned with the uniqueness of each service user, we are much more concerned with her or his relationships with those individuals around them, whether that be their family, other service users or immediate community, than we are with questions about their relationship with 'God' or some 'Higher Power'. As the authors of this book we both 'sign up' to all of this, except that we are going to suggest that this is not some *either/or* discussion. Far from it. We shall be arguing that our exploration of spirituality will take us to the very heart and spirit of social work. Indeed we believe that this concept provides a powerful and insightful lens through which social work practice can be understood and critiqued.

We also want to suggest at the very outset that you as readers do already recognise something of this reality which we are calling 'spirituality', both for yourselves and in your practice. This is because spirituality (as its root suggests) takes us to the very heart and *spirit* of what it means to be human, to be in relationship with others, and to make connections with each other and between the various parts of our lives. Spirituality is saying something profound that affects each and every one of us, individually and collectively, privately and professionally. It invites us to explore and to articulate the meanings we find *in*, and give *to*, the world as we experience it. The cluster of values and world-views to which the concept of spirituality points us have been around far longer than social work, yet in very significant ways they have always belonged to the heart of social work. For this reason our discussion will be helping us to see with fresh eyes what we have known for a long time, as well as breaking new ground in our understanding and theorising.

So if it's not religion, what is it?

This is usually the second question, and it is fair enough, particularly given the sensitivities which social workers often have towards religion. We are clear that our services should be given free from any religious or other bias. Yet social work is not a morally neutral activity and it purports to respect and nurture the service user's own 'take' on life. That is, except when discriminatory and oppressive behaviours conflict with social work's anti-oppressive value-base and must be challenged. Ironically, one of the earliest 'wake-up' calls to social work in its neglect of the spiritual dimension has come from service users from ethnic minority groups for whom a religious framework for their living is fundamental to their quality of life and approach to problems. For such people, and indeed any who identify religion as significant to both their identity and how they conduct their lives – who they are and how they behave, in other words – religion may well be the main vehicle through which they experience and express their spirituality. It may also be the source of some of their problems, as we shall explore later in this book. For others, however, there may be something which they call spirituality but which has little for them to do with 'organised' religion. As Peberdy remarked,

> People commonly say, 'I am not religious', they do not say, 'I am not spiritual'. (Peberdy, 1993, p. 219)

So before we go much further, let us introduce some definitions which have been suggested by social work writers (see Box 1.1 below).

box 1.1

Defining spirituality

...the human search for personal meaning and mutually fulfilling relationships between people, between people and the natural environment and between religious people and God...Social work practice can be described as a spiritual voyage which involves promoting the growth and fulfilment of user, professional helper, and the wider community. (Patel et al., 1998, p. 11)

...a search for purpose and meaning, and having a moral dimension which reflects a concern with relationships to others, the universe, and to some transcendent being or force. (Lindsay, 2002, pp. 31–32)

...a dimension which brings together attitudes, beliefs, thoughts, feelings and practices reaching beyond the...material. (Lloyd, 1997)

the wholeness of what it is to be human...The spiritual relates to the person's search for a sense of meaning and morally fulfilling relationships between oneself, other people, the encompassing universe, and the ontological ground of existence, whether a person understands this in terms which are theistic, atheistic, nontheistic, or any combination of these. (Canda and Furman, 1999, pp. 43–44)

The first of these, Patel et al. (1998), one of the early publications in the UK to tackle the subject published by the Central Council for Education and Training in Social Work, describes social work practice as 'a spiritual voyage'. Maybe you find yourself subscribing to those feel-good elements like 'meaning' and 'fulfilling relationships', but are not sure why this makes social work a spiritual voyage, since it could be seen to be simply describing good practice. Lindsay's (2002) definition takes us a bit further by adding to some concepts which are familiar to social work – purpose, meaning and relationships – something called 'transcendence', which might seem a little strange to most social workers. In the next definition, developed by one of us to assist people in completing a research questionnaire, spirituality is firmly asserted to belong to a realm beyond the immediate tangible realities of the material world (Lloyd, 1997). So then surely we are talking about God, or some entity 'out there' and we are back to religion again? Not necessarily so, Canda and Furman (1999) assure us, suggesting that it could even be an 'atheistic' or 'non-theistic' concept.

So spirituality is a complex concept and it is still not obvious whether and how it is a *necessary* concept for social work, or whether we could get by without it! Social work has long recognised the importance of the 'search for meaning', particularly in fields like mental health and palliative care, but may have greater sympathy with the idea that this belongs to existential philosophy rather than being in any way 'spiritual' (King et al., 1994).

Perhaps religion is, after all, easier to grasp and to incorporate into our social work assessments, even if as social workers we feel that religious support and intervention should be left to the religious professional. Canda and Furman's definition (Box 1.2) keeps it simple by focusing on what is sometimes described as 'organised religion'. However, in contemporary society few people sign up to organised religion but quite a few more use concepts related to religion, either as metaphors or with a secular twist. For example, people talk about having 'faith in life', or perhaps more often, having lost faith in something, without that implying religious beliefs although it may imply a whole set of other 'beliefs' about life (see Lloyd's definition below). Other writers (see Grainger, Box 1.2) have suggested that religion should be understood as a way of thinking and living, not simply adherence to a set of handed-down beliefs and traditions – in other words, the opposite to organised religion. Grainger goes on to say that we particularly employ this kind of thinking in situations of existential challenge. Dare we suggest that social work has not been very good at engaging with the existential challenges which service users face, much as it has shown itself to be well-equipped, particularly in certain specialisms, to work therapeutically with deep emotion?

---

box 1.2

Defining religion

An organised structured set of beliefs and practices shared by a community related to spirituality. (Canda and Furman, p. 54)

(Faith) Humanistic or religious beliefs which guide the way an individual seeks to live. (Lloyd, 1997)

Religion answers a need for meaning, order, purpose; but it is not itself that need . . . it is one expression of a kind of thinking which is in fact characteristic of human mental processes, but which we become more than usually aware of in situations of existential challenge. (Grainger, 1998, p. 95)

Already we have opened up the complexity of this topic and identified some of the critical questions which we must explore in depth if we are to achieve our objective of reaching a better understanding of a dimension of human existence which social work has for too long largely ignored. Throughout this book we explore the implications of understanding spirituality as stemming from the 'world-view' which we each choose or arrive at (Moss, 2005). Some people, of course, service users and social workers alike, insist that they do not believe in a spiritual dimension and we are concerned to respect that position. Most of all, however, this book aims to explore a social work approach which recognises the service user's spirituality; understands the significance of spiritual issues and needs among the mass of problems with which they may be grappling; and enables the social worker to engage with this aspect at a level and in a manner *and as far as* sits comfortably with their personal belief system. This is not to say that this is comfortable work. Much of it may be distinctly *un*comfortable and a strong theme in this book, contrary to the impression given in much of the contemporary literature, is that spirituality is 'not all sweetness and light' (Holloway, 2007b). So as we begin this exploration, think about the example below – a common scenario for health and social care professionals. How often would the deep spiritual crisis feature in our assessments? Yet whatever else we do to support Joan may have limited impact without some acknowledgement of her spiritual pain as well as her physical and emotional exhaustion.

Example

Joan, aged 83, has been caring for her husband, Jim, aged 87, since he had a stroke 6 years previously. The couple have been evangelical Christians all their lives and in the immediate aftermath of the stroke, Joan insisted that Jim would be healed. The doctors agreed that he had made a surprising recovery to the point where he was able to go home to Joan's care, but despite her feisty spirit, Joan found herself progressively more exhausted and mentally and spiritually worn down. Then one day Jim, normally a very gentle man, had an aggressive outburst directed at Joan, followed by others in which he began to blaspheme. He seems increasingly confused about time and place and incontinence becomes a serious problem. The GP suggests to Joan that Jim probably has dementia. Faced with the disintegration of the person she had known and loved, Joan reflects on her life and the hard times she has survived, supported by her faith, and wonders why it should end like this? The district nurses are very kind and, sensing that Joan is neglecting herself and depressed, refer the couple to social services for home care for Jim. Joan cannot begin to explain to them that, although she might appreciate some help, this isn't really the root of the problem.

The remainder of this chapter will explore some of these questions in greater depth, before placing these contemporary discussions into the broader context of the development of social work from its professional origins to its current international agenda.

The human condition – a good place for social work to start?

Social work, as traditionally understood, deals with all aspects of human life. From the cradle to the grave, social workers find themselves grappling with the complexities of human life. More often than not they also have to deal with the darker aspects of human existence. For every rewarding, life-enhancing moment – sharing the happiness of a successful adoption placement, for example, or of a young care-experienced person making a success of his or her life – there will be far more occasions when the social worker will be working with people destroying their own lives or the lives of others, or struggling with situations which seem to have no hope or possible positive outcome. Admittedly, for most of the time social workers, like others involved in the caring professions, simply get on with the job. They deal with the challenges and the crises that come to them in the people they seek to care for and work with; they use their knowledge, skills and values to achieve the best outcomes possible, which sometimes are woefully disappointing. But there are times when we wonder what it is all about, why do people behave in the ways they do and what is it that we are trying to do as social workers intervening in their lives? Underlying such questions are deeper questions about the human condition, even though for the most part we may not reflect on them. These include:

- What does it mean to be human?
- How can we understand our lives, individually and collectively?
- What sense or meaning can we find in, or bring to, the story of our humanity?

These questions are just as powerful at the other end of the spectrum of human behaviour, where we find, for example, foster parents who never stop taking damaged and disadvantaged young people into their homes and hearts, and succeed in helping them turn their lives around through sheer loving perseverance; people who selflessly love and care for family members; community and faith groups whose sole 'raison d'etre' is about caring and looking after people in need.

Any responses we try to make, therefore, to the challenging questions of what it means to be human will need to acknowledge the extremes of human behaviour and the diversity of human responses in between. Moreover, uncomfortable though it may be for us to acknowledge, we need to recognise that in each and every one of us there is the potential for both. None of us is wholly good or wholly bad; and the factors that predispose or nudge us to move in one direction instead of another in our lifestyle choices, and how we treat other people, constitute an important area of study, not least for social work.

Our starting point for understanding the importance of spirituality for social work therefore is both within us and around us. At least by starting here, we know (or at least we think we know) where we are, who we are and what are the issues that need to be tackled in our lives and in the lives of those around us. This is why social work curricula include core themes such as life-span development, studies in identity development, social policy and the social and political context of social work. But the questions we have just posed take us to a level that social work curricula often do not tackle. Ultimately these questions are profoundly philosophical, and for many people also spiritual. They are questions that seek to tease out and unravel the sense of meaning and purpose we have in our lives, and the extent to which the world-view we each choose to live by and to interpret what goes on within and around us is intellectually, emotionally and spiritually fulfilling and satisfying.

The very fact that we can pose these questions to ourselves and our environment, of course, in itself suggests an important facet of what it means to be human. Emmons (2005) is not alone in suggesting that

> As far as we know humans are the only meaning-seeking species on the planet. Meaning-making is an activity that is distinctly human.... (p. 731)

Thompson (2010) takes this point further when he observes that 'spirituality is fundamentally about meaning making' and suggests that this has a strong link to social work because of the profession's 'strong element of helping people develop more empowering meanings, understandings, or "narratives" ' (p. 142). Thus understood, spirituality can and, as we are arguing, *should* be located at the very heart of the social work enterprise.

stop and think

■ What do you see as the 'heart and spirit of social work'?
■ How does this relate to spirituality?

Religion, secularism and social work

Whatever other criticisms may be made of them, the pursuit of religion and spirituality both enshrine serious and often systematic attempts at meaning-making. However, it is important to emphasise at the outset that while religion is self-evidently raising the possibility of a divine being, however conceived or named, the same is not necessarily the case with spirituality. A secular spirituality would not wish to 'buy into' a theistic world-view, but would nevertheless argue strongly for a world-view that enables meaning and purpose, mystery and awe, to be valid and important concepts. These are issues to which we will return in greater depth in Chapter 2.

It is also important to recognise that the context in which contemporary social work is practised, both in the UK and indeed throughout the world, is *both secular and religious*. As Ford (2004) notes,

> It is, I think, a fairly obvious statement, yet nevertheless necessary to make and often denied in practice... [that] our world cannot truthfully be described simply as 'religious' or simply as 'secular'; it is simultaneously and complexly both. (p. 24)

His comment that this 'truth' about the world is often denied hits home with social work education and practice, as we shall see later in this chapter. The challenges that social work has had to meet in becoming a 'respectable' academic discipline that is recognised and valued in both professional and academic circles have characterised the journey that it has made over the last century or so. One of the by-products of this journey has been the promulgation of a world-view for social work education and practice that is almost exclusively secular in colour and context. Anything that 'smacked' of religion was interpreted as being 'part of the problem' and has either been pathologised accordingly or been relegated to the territory of student-led 'corridor discussions', out of the hearing of sceptical, even hostile, academic staff (Channer, 1998). This is particularly interesting when we note that in the 2001 Census in England and Wales, for example, only 15 per cent of people overall said that they have no religious affiliation, and in some sectors of the community, almost everyone identified with some kind of religion (www.nationalstatistics.gov.uk).

Ford is reflecting on the role of higher education and the responsibilities of universities to provide a safe but stimulating arena in which deep questions and issues can be creatively debated and discussed. His concern is not about social work but for higher education as a whole, where he argues that

> Universities ought to be taking far more seriously than they do their responsibility to contribute to the coming century by engaging with the issues arising from the simultaneously religious and secular character of our world. (Ford, 2004, p. 25)
>
> There are very few settings in our world where the huge range of issues arising out of these differences, relating to every sphere of life, can be thoughtfully and peacefully addressed in ways that allow for fruitful understanding, discussion and deliberation, leading to negotiation of the sorts of settlements that allow religious and secular civil societies to flourish. (Ibid., p. 24)

Social work education internationally is now firmly located within higher education, usually in close partnership with social work agencies and service user and carer groups. Although these professional training courses also bring their own requirements and the assessment of professional competence prescribed by professional bodies, the challenge laid down by Ford is as relevant for social work education as any other academic discipline. This challenge includes all the partners involved in the educational and training process – those practitioners, service users and carers whose active involvement is highly valued for ensuring that social work education stays in touch with 'the real world'. What Ford is saying so compellingly, of course, is that it is the *real world*'s agenda that has to be taken seriously in our education and training, and that we should be challenging each other to take this complex religious and secular world seriously. To what extent are social workers and social work students who themselves belong to faith communities able to explore the implications of their faith and their personal, religiously orientated value-base to work within the secular dimensions of society? How well are social workers and social work students who cleave to a secular world-view equipped to work appropriately with people for whom faith and religious practice is the fundamental 'bed-rock' of their lives? And to what extent are social workers able to understand, as well as radically critique, those faith groups whose values are at odds with professional social work?

These are some of the key questions that can no longer be avoided if social work and social work education are to meet the challenges of our complex societies. Yet a brief overview of the historical origins of social work reminds us that social work's relationship with religion is itself complex.

Philosophical and religious roots

It is easy to forget our roots, but social work in fact grew out of strong religious traditions and values, in a culture which was steeped in Christianity. However, the value-base of respect and caring for others which lies at the heart of social work is often traced back to the work of several key philosophers. Immanuel Kant (1724–1804), for example, proposed his now famous dictum,

> So act as to treat humanity, whether in your own person or in that of any other, never solely as a means, but always also as an end.

Kant was not alone in this thinking. The utilitarian approach espoused by David Hume (1711–76) and John Stuart Mill (1806–73) argued that the benchmark for the morality of any action is the extent to which it achieves more good than harm, and thereby benefits the majority (for a discussion of these themes see Beckett and Maynard, 2005, chapter 2). Such positions are reflected in contemporary professional codes of conduct for social workers and other professional bodies. We are required to treat other people with respect and dignity as befits another human being. Indeed, the whole thrust of anti-discriminatory practice derives its energy from this core value: if individuals, groups or societies act towards others disrespectfully or oppressively, they must be challenged, not least because they fall short of this core benchmark, and in some measure damage the 'common good'.

It is important, however, to note that this fundamental respect for others has a much longer history, especially within religious traditions. The three monotheistic religions, Judaism, Christianity and Islam, all celebrate the dignity and uniqueness of each human being. For these religions, this dignity stems from their belief in a divine Being (referred to by these traditions as Adonai, God or Allah, respectively) whose loving generosity was outpoured into the creation of humanity as the culmination of the created world. For those who belong to these faith communities, therefore, each human being has a 'divine' dignity. They are unique and special in their own right *and also* as creatures of the Divine Being. Other religions would want to make similar claims. Buddhism, for example, has always stressed that all life and all living things are sacrosanct.

The origins of social work in the Western world were heavily influenced by the Christian tradition and the values it promulgates (Goldstein, 1990; Bowpitt, 1998). These values have found a variety of expression, but the words of the founder of Christianity, drawing strongly from his Jewish roots, are often used as the most succinct summary:

> You shall love the Lord your God with all your heart, with all your soul and with all your mind . . . and love your neighbour as yourself. (Matthew 22 vv 37–8)

Without doubt, this religious command has been the motivating force behind many acts of compassion and many of the great humanitarian movements, including, for example, the move to abolish slavery in Britain and elsewhere in the world. It was also the motivating force which took faith communities down the path of social caring in their various localities, and which caused individuals to offer their service in what we now call the medical and caring professions. Not only did their Christian allegiance energise their individual acts of caring and their membership of various organisations, it also informed some of the early theoretical perspectives of social work. Bowpitt (1998) reminds us, for example, that one of the early influential figures in social work, Dame Eileen Younghusband (1964), believed that

> Casework... so far as its principles are concerned is rooted in the Judaeo-Christian and democratic tradition of respect for the value of each individual person. (p. 17)

The seminal work of Biestek (1961), still widely referred to for his articulation of some key principles that underpin what was then called social casework, was undoubtedly influenced by his own underpinning Christian commitment as a Roman Catholic priest (for a recent discussion of Biestek's key principles and their influence on contemporary social work, see Thompson, 2005).

A further dimension to this has been the number of faith-based organisations who have made a significant contribution historically to the development of social care and who continue to be active in this arena. The work of the Salvation Army, the Society of Friends, Jewish Care, together with Roman Catholic, Free Church and Anglican social care and social justice programmes, all provide examples of faith communities undertaking a wide range of caring work in their communities. Often this work focuses on particular areas of need in society: work with homeless people, children and young people, those who are Deaf, or older people, for example. Churches have also played a prominent role in fostering and adoption for many years.

This history formed and shaped the early expressions of what social work was about and the values that were needed to underpin its activity, leading Graham (2008) in his reflections on the connections between religion, spirituality and social work to observe:

> ... we are part of a long tradition. To those colleagues who state that ours is a flash in the pan, that ours is a new and ephemeral way of looking at social work, to those who choose to write us off as guitar-strumming impractical flakes who should not unduly influence mainstream social work, I think we should respond politely (and even not so politely) that ours is the continuation of a long history within social work. (p. 14)

The psycho-social tradition

Alongside this important strand, a counter-balancing influence began to make its mark in ways that contributed significantly to social work's theoretical framework. The emerging disciplines of psychology and sociology, energised by the seminal work of Freud and Marx, radically transformed and deepened our understanding of what it means to be human and to live in relationship to each other. As these disciplines became firmly established in the twentieth century, social work educators realised that they had to respond to the criticism often levelled against them that social work was an activity without a strong theoretical underpinning. If this emerging profession was to stand side by side with the older helping professions such as medicine; if the contribution of social work was to become accepted as a well-informed, well-researched and scholarly contributor to human well-being; and if its analysis of the individual and societal factors that contributed to human misery and suffering were to be taken at all seriously; then it needed urgently and rigorously to earn its place at the bar of academic respectability. To this day, therefore, social work theory applies knowledge drawn from other disciplines, to inform and enhance our practice.

It is widely recognised, however, that the work of both Freud and Marx significantly undermined the authority of the Christian Church and the world-view it offered. In many ways this had already been significantly imperilled by the insights of the Enlightenment and of scientific developments in the field of cosmology, anthropology and by theories of evolution. But the Freudian and Marxist analyses of religion seemed to put the final nail in religion's coffin. Freud and his successors helped people to begin to look deeply *within* for the meaning of what it is to be human, rather than to theological, transcendent 'explanations'. Marx attacked religion as 'the opiate of the people', anaesthetising them to the ravages of human need and abuses of power, instead pinning all their hopes on a better life after death rather than working hard to alleviate human misery in the 'here and now'.

Many people enthusiastically embraced this rejection of religion and saw the potential in rationalism for a new and better way of understanding. Hunt (2002) sums up this mood when he observes,

> Stemming from the Enlightenment, the hope for a secular society began as an academic response to the dominance of the Christian Church and continued as a reaction to religious authority by those who are inclined towards atheism. In good tradition, many sociologists have since viewed religious belief as an intellectual error which the progress of science and rationality would ultimately weaken to the point of disappearance. (p. 14)

For social work education, with its early determination to gain academic respectability, this meant that by and large religion was relegated to the 'trash can of outmoded ideology'. Indeed, if social workers encountered religion in any of the people whom they were seeking to help, it was often seen as being 'part of the problem'. Furthermore, Payne (2005a), in his thoughtful overview of the origins of social work, goes so far as to suggest that

> These trends raise the historical question whether secularism is a necessary condition for the development of social work, and whether the religious or spiritual is inconsistent with social work practice. (p. 156)

This meant that social workers who maintained an allegiance to a faith community were careful to preserve a clear distinction between their personal beliefs and professional identity, lest they be accused of contravening the profession's value-base by engaging in proselytising activities. Yet for many it was the caring imperative at the heart of their faith which had propelled them into social work.

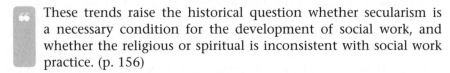

stop and think

- Is secularisation a necessary 'condition and context' for social work to thrive as a profession?
- If so, why?

Postmodernism and consumerism

In contrast to this polarisation of religion and secularism which characterised the early professionalisation of social work, the advent of postmodernism has brought with it a more complex relationship between social work, religion and spirituality which mirrors developments in society more generally. On the one hand, postmodernism's rejection of the 'grand narrative' clearly undermines many traditional religious narratives with their attempts to provide meaningful cohesive world-views. Thompson (2010) draws attention to 'the cynicism of postmodernism with its failure to establish clarity and coherence as a basis for meaning making' (p. 142). On the other hand, 'late modernity' (as sociologists sometimes characterise the late twentieth/early twenty-first centuries) has seen the emergence of more individualistic spiritualities and new age 'religions'. At the same time, consumerism is widely recognised to be a significant feature of contemporary societies and many argue that its influence on the human spirit, at both individual and community levels, has been deeply corrosive.

The significance of these observations for social work is considerable. These societal trends provide both the context for contemporary social work and powerful drivers of its development. It cannot be a coincidence, for example, that health and social care systems the world over have seen the introduction of individualistic tailor-made approaches to service provision where the 'consumer' of services is in the driving seat, as the wider implications of postmodernism and its consequent fragmentation have taken root. Despite the implications in 'personalisation' of valuing and empowering the unique individual, which sit comfortably with social work's fundamental ethos, this approach is not one that social work should accept uncritically, as Ferguson (2007) points out. He draws attention to the 'transfer of risk from the state to the individual' implicit in this approach, and argues that the fundamental issues of poverty and inequality risk being neglected:

> Overcoming powerlessness will involve moving beyond the individualism and market-based solutions of personalisation theory. It will require the development and strengthening of *collective* organisations both amongst those who use services and amongst those who provide them. (p. 401)

This critique resonates strongly with the understanding of spirituality being proposed in this book. However important an individual's spirituality may be, there are wider cultural and societal dimensions to being human, including the fight against injustice that still lies at the heart of social work, which are also core themes in our understanding of spirituality.

Bauman's (2007) ideas about 'liquid modernity' and the impact of consumerism upon our understanding of what it means to be human and to live together in community are also significant for social work and have important things to say about spirituality. Bauman suggests that our modern sense of identity (at least in nations committed to a capitalist ideology) is inextricably linked with what we buy and the range of products we choose to import into our homes. The barometer of personal success becomes the scale of an individual's purchasing power. Bauman is raising significant political, philosophical and spiritual issues about what it means to belong to a particular society; what credentials we need to be members of it; how we treat other people who may be at a similar point, or significantly above or below ourselves on the ladder of consumerist success; and what sort of society we want to create for ourselves and succeeding generations. All of these questions are hugely important as a context for our social work practice.

Bauman has trenchant comments to make about the legacy of individualism and the New Right, and in particular the contribution he suggests it has made to 'the continuing decomposition and crumbling of social bonds and communal cohesion' (Bauman, 2007, pp. 144–145). He also believes that these trends have continued to the point where political apathy and reluctance to engage with communal activity for the well-being of others are now in steep decline; there is a pervasive loss of the sense of belonging and shared responsibility, and as soon as an economy enters a downturn there is a fear that there is nothing left to fall back on. This is echoed by Tacey's warning that as a society, we are 'running on empty' (Tacey, 2003).

These issues assumed an urgency during the serious global economic downturn in 2009, with the impact of the recession being felt worldwide. In what seemed a very short space of time in early 2009 national governments were dealing with banking crises and shrinking pension funds, their impact being felt by individuals facing job losses, reduced incomes and housing uncertainties. The very foundations upon which people had built their lives were beginning to crumble. A world-view founded on consumerism and ever-increasing prosperity suddenly no longer seemed 'fit for purpose' and the questions and issues being raised by the contemporary spirituality discourse assumed immediate relevance. Writing in the *Guardian* newspaper, Ann Pettifor (2008), a political economist, is trenchant in her criticisms of the 'world-view' which has got us into this mess:

> Let us make no bones about it. This financial crisis is a major spiritual crisis. It is the crisis of a society that worships at the temples of consumption, and that has isolated and abandoned millions of consumers now trapped on a treadmill of debt. It is the crisis of a society that values the capital gains of the rentier more highly than the rights of people to a home, or an education or health. It is the crisis of a society that idolises money above love, community, wellbeing and the sustainability of our planet.

This is not a crisis of governments and the well-off only. This consumerist ideology affects the whole of society, including those who struggle financially because they are on low-paid jobs, or because they rely on state benefits for survival. The desire to possess is powerful. Parents who are faced with clamouring desires and demands from their children to have the same goods and designer clothes as their peers often 'give in', irrespective of their capacity to afford. Some may be tempted into crime. Social workers and debt advisers often find that the value-base and consumerist world-view that people choose can easily exacerbate other underlying personal and family difficulties. In addition, social workers frequently find themselves fighting for resources for those who are frail, vulnerable and marginalised, whose only desire is to survive, to be warm and well-nourished, and to receive appropriate medical and hospital treatment when required. These are people who have had to drop out of the consumerist 'race for life' but who are the first to suffer when the consumerist society takes a 'downturn' in its fortunes. At such moments social workers are left powerlessly lamenting the scarcity of resources, and wondering, in Bauman's words, how

> to protect society against multiplying the ranks of the 'collateral victims' of consumerism: the excluded, the outcasts, the underclass. [our] task is to salvage human solidarity from erosion and the sentiments of ethical responsibility from fading. (Bauman, 2007, p. 143)

The resurgence of 'religion'

Nevertheless, there is evidence that the pendulum is beginning to swing back. Firstly, the prediction that religion, religious faith and belief would be in terminal decline has been shown to be mistaken. Even if formal Christian religious observance in the UK may be in numerical decline (Bruce, 1995; Brierly, 2000; Moss, 2005; Glendinning and Bruce, 2006; Crabtree, 2007), there are examples of rapid growth of less formalised house and community churches, especially among young people. Elsewhere in the world, especially in Africa, numbers of Christians are rapidly increasing: some churches in the USA and the Far East report over 10,000 members. Papal visits attract huge attendance figures. In the 2001 Census for England and Wales, 37.3 million people (72 per cent) stated their religion to be Christian. Islam is growing in popularity and influence in the UK and worldwide. Although such statistics need careful exploration to discover their true significance, they are sufficient to justify Ford's assertion at the beginning of this chapter that we live in a society that is both secular and religious. For social work, we cannot make any assumptions about the secular (or religious) orientation of any service user, or colleague, with whom we work. Religion, therefore, is firmly back on the agenda.

Secondly, one of the by-products of the postmodern fragmentation discussed earlier is the escalation of diverse expressions of spirituality. This is evidenced not only in a range of New Age movements, faith-based organisations and an explosion of new religions, but also in the development of secular spirituality whereby people who steadfastly eschew a religious commitment nevertheless feel that the concept of spirituality is important to them. In a similar way Bailey (2002) explores this notion of a secular spirituality through his concept of 'implicit religion'. We will return to these issues in Chapter 2, but at this point it is important to note these developments as part of the pendulum swing against wholesale secularism. For social work, this raises challenges about how to engage with people who may have a very individualised spirituality and world-view but which nevertheless has a profound impact upon how they choose to live their lives.

Thirdly, there is an emerging research literature about the positive effects of religion and spirituality upon health and well-being. Far from being part of the problem, religion and spirituality are being increasingly seen as positive factors that enhance well-being and health. The classic work in this field has been produced by Koenig et al. (2001) in a book which critiques 1200 separate studies in America into the effect of religious and spiritual activities on health and well-being. Koenig's findings are discussed in greater detail in Chapter 4 when we look at quality of life, but, in summary, they demonstrate many positive correlations across a number of health issues, including mental health and physical disorders – a sharp challenge to those who regard religion as an exclusively negative influence upon people's lives. In the UK, the National Institute of Mental Health in England (NIMHE) pioneered important work to ensure that the voices of survivors are heard. Their pilot spirituality projects reveal that religion and spirituality are for many people crucial components in the journey to recovery (Coyte et al., 2007). The Royal College of Psychiatrists has also been highly influential, through their Special Interest Group in Spirituality, in highlighting the importance of this issue. In terms of secular spirituality, the increasing popularity of complementary therapies and treatments may also be seen as a beneficial development (if used wisely) that enhances health and well-being. For social work, these developments present an important challenge both for inter-professional working and in listening to, and taking seriously, people's attitude to healthcare, treatment and the enhancement of their health and well-being as part of our holistic approach.

Finally, faith community leaders are making serious attempts to contribute positively to the debate about health and well-being, social cohesion and the nature of society. The visit of the Dalai Lama to the UK in 2008, for example, demonstrated a thoughtful approach to many of the issues that are troubling people. He reminded those who flocked to his meetings about the efficacy of an inner peace and stillness to their well-being and health. In another instance, The Chief Rabbi, Sir Jonathan Sacks, commented in his visitor's keynote address to the Anglican Bishops at the international Lambeth Conference in summer 2008 at Canterbury on the ways in which globalisation and the new information technologies were fragmenting the world 'into ever smaller sects of the like-minded'. He went on to suggest that a society that has lost its religion also loses a sense of 'graciousness' and risks the breakdown of relationships. Communities can atrophy, and the result is that people feel vulnerable and alone (Sacks, 2007).

Social work's rediscovery of spirituality

In the middle of the twentieth century, recently qualified social work practitioners in the USA began to draw attention to what they perceived to be a major deficit in their education and training curricula. Having moved into the complex multi-cultural and multi-faith contexts of social work practice, they began to experience serious disempowerment as professional workers. They were constantly being challenged to deliver appropriate services to people who practised a wide variety of religious faith and commitment, yet felt themselves ill-prepared even to begin to engage with this cultural diversity. They began therefore to challenge their former teachers and college curriculum designers to ensure that steps were taken to address this serious deficit and to ensure that the 'holistic' approach, which was *in theory* underpinning their training, began to deliver 'what it says on the tin' (Sheridan and Amato-von Hemert (1999); Sheridan et al. (1994)). These argued that a 'holistic' practice that ignores religious and spiritual dimensions was selling practitioners, students, educators and, crucially, the people who needed and used social work services, seriously short.

The following decades began to see a quantum shift in attitudes among social work educators, as Furman et al. (2004) describe.

> The United States has also . . . experienced renewed attention to religiously and spiritually sensitive social work practice. The revised Code of Social Work Ethics of the National Association of Social Workers (1996) includes an understanding of and respect for religious belief as part of the social worker's responsibilities to clients, colleagues, professionals and the broader society. The Council on Social Work Education (CSWE) now recognises that religion and spirituality are vital parts of the cultural diversity of clients and requires that social work curricula on diversity and populations at risk include some content on religion. (CSWE, 1994)

A seminal moment in the development of social work's understanding of the importance of spirituality came in October 2004 when the International Federation of Social Workers (IFSW) and the International Association of Schools of Social Work (IASSW) held their conferences jointly in Adelaide. For the first time, a major stream of papers focused on the topic of spirituality. In the same year, in its revised statement of principles, the IFSW affirmed that social workers should uphold each person's 'spiritual integrity and well-being' (IFSW, 2004). In their jointly formulated global standards, both organisations identified that *spiritual issues are part of the knowledge base needed by social workers to understand human behaviour and development* (IASSW and IFSW, 2004) (our emphasis). Spirituality as a core theme for social work had arrived on the global social work agenda.

The international dimension to these issues was well represented in the First North American International Conference on Spirituality and Social work held in Waterloo, Ontario, in May 2006, where all parts of Canada and the United States, as well as from India and South Africa, were represented. In their editorial reflections on the conference, Coholic et al. (2008) commented that

> If we ignore the spiritual dimension of people's lives, we may be missing an opportunity to help people construct holistic narratives that accurately fit their experiences. (p. 42)

Important work is also being undertaken in Australia, including the significant contribution of Aboriginal perspectives. Rice (2005) reports that

> The Australian Association of Social Workers National Ethics Committee rewrote the Code of Ethics (1999) to include spirituality as a basis for conscientious objection (Section 5.1.3.) [and that] two Australian schools of social work currently offer courses on spirituality in social work.... (p. xvii)

Eastern perspectives find expression in the important work of Professor Cecilia Chan of Hong Kong University through her work on the meeting place between eastern and western traditions (e.g. 2005). Social workers in New Zealand have acknowledged the challenge to their established practice and training models from Maori expressions of spirituality and are working to fully integrate spirituality into their standard approaches (e.g. Nash and Stewart, 2002).

Social work in the UK (with some notable exceptions such as Cree and Davis, 1996; Lloyd, 1997; Bowpitt, 1998, 2000; Moss, 2002; Gilligan, 2003; Holloway, 2005, 2007; Mathews, 2009; Gilligan and Furness, 2005, 2010) has for too long been guilty of neglecting spirituality, and as a result it has a lot of catching up to do with the rest of the social work world if its stated commitment to holistic care is to be taken seriously. Social work in the UK has, however, led the way in developing transcultural and interdisciplinary work in the field (Holloway, 2006; and the contributions of the authors as well as Peter Gilbert to the National Forum for Mental Health in England and the British Association for the Study of Spirituality).

Although some recent findings suggest that in the UK some significant changes of attitude are taking place among social workers, it is not at all clear whether these are also reflected in the views of social work educators (Furman et al., 2004). Building on their experience of a similar survey in the USA (Canda and Furman, 1999; Furman et al., 2005), Furman and her colleagues surveyed a random sample of 5,500 practising social workers from the list of 11,000 strong British Association of Social Workers (BASW), and had replies from 798 members, a 20 per cent response rate. They found that approximately 47 per cent of all respondents thought that it was compatible with social work's mission to include religion and spirituality in their practice (Furman et al., 2004). Clearly it is not possible, or wise even, to seek to extrapolate from this set of findings any broader messages from the profession as a whole, not least because the proportion of social workers belonging to BASW remains fairly low. Nevertheless, Furman found that more than 50 per cent of their respondents felt that using a whole range of religious or spiritual interventions was appropriate – for example, using religious language or concepts; helping service users develop spiritual rituals; discussing the role of religious and spiritual beliefs and assisting people who use services to reflect critically on religion and spirituality; considering the spiritual and religious meaning of current life situations; reflecting on what happens after death. When working with bereaved people, those with terminal illness and foster parents, the majority of social workers in this study felt it *was* appropriate to raise the topic of religion, and that exploring religion or spirituality did not conflict either with social work's mission or with the BASW Code of Ethics. Yet the study reported that

> In the UK nearly 77 per cent of the social workers indicated that they had not received content on spirituality or religion in their social work education, a finding similar to reports in the USA.... This is a cause for concern, because at least half of the social workers in this study were integrating some form of religion and spirituality into their practice without the benefit of training. (p. 788)

These are but a few of the many examples of social work educators throughout the world beginning to engage seriously with the themes identified in this chapter. The international character of these explorations is a timely reminder that there is no single 'system' that can be imported uncritically from one context to another. What 'works' in America, for example, cannot be translated uncritically into the UK context, but that does not invalidate the journey that has to be made in each cultural context, including the context of multi-culturalism. We shall explore this material further in our final chapter. Critically, however, each country-specific work is concluding that spirituality and social work should not be confined to a specialist area of practice but has everything to do with mainstream social work education and practice.

- To what extent has your own education and training so far equipped you to explore issues to do with spirituality and religion in your professional practice?
- What are your main learning needs in this area?

Conclusion

The relationship between religion, spirituality and social work education and practice has historically been tentative, and at times hostile. Social work does not take place in a vacuum but in political, social, economic and philosophical contexts. We have traced some of the influences arising from these contexts and the impact they have had on social work's relationship with religion and spirituality. In identifying some of the contemporary 'pressure points' we have also entered territory in which our understanding of spirituality makes a significant contribution. In particular we have looked at Ford's analysis that we live in societies which are simultaneously secular and religious and the challenges that this presents for contemporary social work. One aspect of this is the role of religion in political conflict. This is an important issue of which social workers in some parts of the world (e.g. Northern Ireland and Israel) have been acutely aware for some time. More recently, the popular linking of Muslim identity with terrorist attacks and the disaffection of young Muslims in countries of the West is an urgent question in which issues of discrimination, religious culture, faith and beliefs are complexly intertwined. We acknowledge the importance of these discussions but do not have the space in this book to do them justice. However, spirituality and fundamentalist religious beliefs is something to which we give some attention.

Against the backdrop of these and other significant challenges, we argue, however, that a focus on spirituality and religion also presents new opportunities for social work. There is beginning to be wider recognition that these issues are not to be relegated to the margins of society so that social work can more or less comfortably ignore them. Instead we are beginning to see that they take us to the very heart of what it means to be human, how we live our lives together and what sort of societies we need to create. This book, therefore, is essentially about the spirit of social work, but it is also challenging us to think about ourselves, who we are and what gives our lives meaning and purpose.

We claimed at the beginning of this chapter that we will arrive in this book at a model for social work practice which facilitates the engagement of every social worker with spirituality, at least up to a point. We call this the 'Fellow Traveller Model'. In one sense this book is all about journeying. Our own personal journeys are embedded in this book, informing but also continuing as we reflect on the past, present and future of ourselves as human beings who have chosen to be social workers. Although both from firm religious backgrounds (sometimes described as 'committed Christian') our own spiritual journeys have taken many turns and loops, tunnelling in the dark as often as we have breathed the exhilarating mountain air! We continue to learn much about spirituality from other spiritual traditions, including secular expositions of concepts which we had assumed belonged to the main religions of the world. We continue to learn much about social work from service users, social work students and practitioners who engage on a daily basis with those scenarios with which we have illustrated our arguments.

So we invite you as readers, from your different starting points, to make your personal journey into the relationship between spirituality and social work. The benefits, we believe, are two-fold. This is a process which will help you to reconnect and/or stay connected with those values and skills which traditionally have been acknowledged as at the heart of social work but which all too frequently feel to be under threat in a climate of technicist responses and measurable outcomes. Just as importantly, understanding how to draw on the spiritual resources both within ourselves and around us helps us to face the new challenges of contemporary social work.

taking it further

- Ford, D. (2004) 'The responsibilities of universities in a religious and secular world', *Studies in Christian Ethics*, 17: 1, 22–37.
- Furness, S. and Gilligan, P. (2010) *Religion, Belief and Social Work: Making a Difference* (Bristol: The Policy Press).
- Gray, M. (2006) 'Viewing spirituality in social work through the lens of contemporary social theory', *British Journal of Social Work*, 38: 175–196.
- International Association of Schools of Social Work (IASSW) and the International Federation of Social Work (IFSW) (2004) *Global Standards for the Education and Training of the Social Work Profession*, p. 6. Available at http://www.iassw-aoets.org/en/About_IASSW/ GlobalStandards.pdf, accessed 21 May 2009.
- Payne, M. (2005) *The Origins of Social Work: Continuity and Change*, chapters 1–4 (Basingstoke: Palgrave Macmillan).

2 Meaning, mystery and social work

Introduction

Chapter 1 highlighted some of the suspicions and antagonisms towards religion that were prevalent in the previous century as social work was seeking to 'come of age' as a profession. In many ways, the hard fought and preciously won battle to establish social work as a secular academic discipline and a respected profession has meant that many social workers will be extremely cautious about re-visiting this territory. They will be rightly suspicious if spirituality emerges as 'religion in disguise'. We looked in Chapter 1 at some major contextual aspects for contemporary social work that imply that social work must take religion and spirituality into account. But more work is needed to tease out the differences as well as any similarities between these two phenomena.

We began the process of seeking to define spirituality and religion separately but soon ran into the complexity of both concepts. We discovered that although there are some obvious differences between them they also have distinctive features in common, such as meaning and mystery. It is important to pursue these discussions rather than slip into using the terms 'religion' and 'spirituality', and their reliance on certain concepts, inter-changeably. This chapter takes the discussion of contemporary understandings and expressions of both spirituality and religion a bit further.

One reason for unravelling some of this is our parallel quest to connect the spirituality discourse with the key concerns of contemporary social work. As Holloway (2007a) observes,

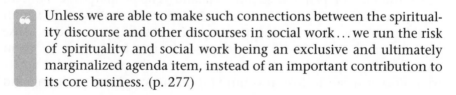

Unless we are able to make such connections between the spirituality discourse and other discourses in social work…we run the risk of spirituality and social work being an exclusive and ultimately marginalized agenda item, instead of an important contribution to its core business. (p. 277)

So this chapter now explores these two concepts not only in order to appreciate the differences between them and the distinctive features they have in common, but also in order to indicate ways in which the spirituality discourse can creatively engage with social work's core business. To facilitate this process, a theoretical framework will be introduced to demonstrate the interconnectedness of these themes, and how they relate to core values and topics in social work education and practice.

Religion and belief

At one level, defining religion and belief might seem to be fairly straightforward, at least as far as religion is concerned. If asked to say what they mean by religion, many people would be likely to respond by naming the ones with which they are most familiar. Christianity, Islam, Judaism and Buddhism might quickly appear on the answer sheet, with perhaps some distinctive strands within them (e.g. Roman Catholics, Anglicans, Methodists, Orthodox and Pentecostals as some of the strands within Christianity). But in the UK they might then struggle to identify the nine major faiths recognised by the Department of Health, let alone those that were identified in the Census for England and Wales (Census, 2001) (for a more detailed analysis of the variations of Christianity in the UK, see Brierley, 2000; Brierley and Hiscock, 2008). In the USA, or in Asia, it is most unlikely that anyone could successfully list the hundreds of religions that attract a significant following. In our pluralist societies it is almost a case of the old Latin tag (suitably upgraded), *quot homines feminaeque, tot sententiae*: there are as many opinions (and perhaps religions) as there are people to hold them. Clearly this is an exaggeration, but nevertheless the sheer multiplicity of religions and new religious movements throughout the world (Richardson, 1995; Hunt, 2002) means that it is no easy task to describe, let alone categorise, what is meant by religion.

This is an important point to have reached. Often religion and spirituality are seen as almost neat and tidy categories, even to the extent that they become polarised along the lines of the gently satirical book *1066 and All That* (Sellar and Yeatman, 1930), with religion being categorised as a 'bad thing', and spirituality as a 'good thing'. The truth of course is far more complex and subtle. Both religion and spirituality have the potential for achieving good and noble ends, as well as the possibility of being used for evil and ignoble purposes. Both of them can have individual and shared/corporate manifestations; both of them can point us to the mystery of transcendence, and a sense of the sacred. Crucially for our purposes in this book, both of them seek to offer responses to the key questions of humanity (who am I? what does it mean to live in community? how can I find meaning and purpose in life?), by means of a world-view that provides a meaningful context for our living and loving, our striving and our searching. For social work education and practice therefore we would argue that both concepts are firmly 'in the mix' and deserve our careful attention whatever our individual views and beliefs may be.

The equally complex issue of belief and belonging is inter-twined with this. The fact that in the Census (2001) in England and Wales such a high percentage of people claimed to believe in God (72 per cent) does not translate into packed places of worship. This phenomenon has led Davie (2004) to suggest that there has been a marked separation of belief and belonging, linked to an individualisation of religious belief in Britain. People may claim to be Christian, for example, but feel no 'social imperative' arising from that belief to link up with other like-minded people for worship, emotional support or social action. Hunt (2002) draws attention to studies in Europe over the last two decades of the twentieth century (Harding et al., 1985; Cook, 2000) the results of which showed that

> under 60 per cent of Europeans regularly define themselves as 'a religious person', some 50 per cent claim that God was significant in their life, and around 50 per cent believe in an existence after death. (p. 21)

Such findings have led Luckman (1990) to conclude that modern societies are witnessing a profound change in the location of religion, away from the supernatural 'great transcendences' concerned with otherworldly matters of issues of life and death, and towards new forms expressing 'little transcendences' of earthly life which involve self-realisation, self-expression and personal freedoms (Luckman, 1990, pp. 129–132). Alongside this data, however, Brierley (2000) suggests that 'the number of people [in Britain] who would describe themselves as atheists or agnostics remained fairly constant at just under 27 per cent' (Hunt, 2002, p. 21).

As an interesting aside to this statistic, Powell, who for a while led the Spirituality Special Interest Group of the Royal College of Psychiatrists in the UK, has noted that

> Whereas in the general population over 90 per cent have a belief in God or a higher power, around only a third of psychiatrists and psychologists hold such beliefs (Bergin and Jensen, 1990). The danger here is that psychiatrists may think that they represent the norm, when it is they who are atypical in this regard. (cited in Moss, 2005, p. 92)

It is worth noting, at this point, the contribution that Bishop Holloway (Holloway, R. [2004]) makes to this debate, and specifically on this issue of the complexity of religious belief. His typology specifically addresses Christian belief, but could be applied equally effectively to any other faith system. Holloway argues that there are four strands or positions that can be identified across the full spectrum of belief. At one extreme, there is fundamentalism, where believers maintain the exclusivity of their 'faith-position' by asserting not only that it is a complete statement of truth, but also that any other faiths must be deemed at best deviant, and at worst heretical. It is important to stress that such a position can be held with honesty, humility and integrity and is not to be identified with (although it *can* certainly lapse into) bigotry and political extremism. This position of course begs the question of how such certainty can be achieved, but those who hold it will claim that this is what has been 'revealed', and that all they are doing is being faithful to this revelation.

The next position Holloway identifies is summed up in the phrase 'to cleave lightly'. This position describes those who would regard themselves as believers, and who may actively participate in the worship and activities of a faith community, and respect its traditions. But for whatever reason, they cannot fully subscribe to the doctrinal tenets of that faith community, or the exclusivity of its teachings. They may feel they are more 'liberal' and would feel distinctly uncomfortable with any fundamentalist expectations.

The third position is 'religion without religion' which is a somewhat more difficult position to describe, but refers to people who are able to identify with a religious culture but do not themselves have a specifically religious personal faith. Such a position might well apply, for example, to people who attend harvest festival and Christmas celebrations at their local church, and feel that these are important community events, but do not feel themselves personally challenged to make any deeper commitment. A similar position might also describe some members of the Jewish community for whom their 'Jewishness' is an essential cultural ingredient of who they are, but for whom religious ritual and worship may feature hardly at all.

Holloway's final position, at the other extreme on the spectrum, is 'homeless humanism'. This represents a cluster of humanistic beliefs that may or may not be susceptible to being classified into a belief system, but which specifically reject any religious creeds and have no need to make any commitments to 'belonging', 'gathering together' or 'setting up home' with like-minded people.

Example

James and Liz lost their baby daughter at the age of 9 months to a congenital disorder. They attended a bereavement support group run by the social workers at the Children's Hospital.

Neither held any religious beliefs – James declared himself an atheist and Liz said she was agnostic – yet both described their meaning-making in spiritual terms, Liz even using the term 'spiritual bonding'. Liz described how she had learnt to 'go with the flow' and James talked about the 'connection' he felt every time he typed in his daughter's name as the password on his computer. Perhaps most significantly, James described how this experience had made him a 'slightly better person':

> Things happen and some of them are upsetting and some of them are incredibly invigorating and uplifting, and you've got to try to take whatever you can from that (and I don't just mean on an individual basis) and then distribute it...It's a peculiar mix of getting on with it but also thinking about others who perhaps will never impinge on your life, and, technically, it is almost a sort of religious attitude. (quoted in Lloyd, 1996, p. 305)

Holloway's typology is a helpful reminder to social work educators and practitioners, who might be tempted to feel that 'all Christians do 'x' and believe 'y', or that all Muslims do not do 'z'. It underscores the importance of finding out what a person really does or does not believe, and the impact that these beliefs have upon their chosen world-view and their patterns of behaviour.

So far, our discussion has not got us very far in our search for definitions, except to realise that even to dip a toe into the waters of the sociology of religion (which is all we have done) reveals the complexity and far-reaching nature of the debate about what constitutes religion and the extent to which people are still 'buying into it'. It is perfectly legitimate, therefore, to pose the question 'what do you understand and mean by the term religion?' to social work academics, students and practitioners who seem fearful about this topic. While it is easy to catalogue some of the negative impacts of religion, similar accusations could just as easily be made against several secular political movements and ideologies. Instead, we need to delve beneath the surface a little to understand what function or purpose religious beliefs fulfil for those who espouse them.

Once more, this is not as straightforward a question as some might think. Nevertheless, 'at root' the issue around religion may boil down to the fundamental question about the existence of the Divine Being or the Higher Power, however conceived or named. In broad terms, religion seeks to take the concepts of transcendence, sacredness and holiness one major step further than secular expressions of it, and to regard them as pointers to the Divine Being who, in the belief of Christianity in particular, has chosen to reveal some 'self-aspects' in the human arena. It is probably true to say that misgivings about religion come into much sharper focus with regard to revealed religions such as Christianity than they do with some other apparently more diffuse expressions such as Buddhism or Shamanism. This is because it is one thing to respect the creative *human* spirit that is constantly reaching out, seeking for meaning, healing and fulfilment; it is another thing altogether to believe in some higher or *divine* Spirit who seeks us out and invites relationship, forgiveness and worship. Although the function of organised religion with its sense of belonging and tradition is still important – it provides opportunities and rituals for community solidarity and cohesion at moments of celebration or grief; it is able to formalise rites of passage; and it provides contexts and traditions in which some of the deep questions of humanity have been grappled with, sometimes for generations – it is this central issue of a divine Being that is crucial for our discussion. This is perceived as the great divide, and the question that flows from it is whether the spirituality discourse necessarily involves belief in a divine Being.

We have briefly explored some facets of what we may understand about religion, and the complexity of this topic. We have argued that any narrow stereotyped views about religion do not do justice to its complexity, and that social work educators, students and practitioners need to take it seriously as part of their commitment to understand various human attempts to find meaning and purpose in people's lives.

From this discussion of religion we now turn to the issue of spirituality to explore it from a secular perspective.

Secular spirituality

It is perhaps useful to begin with a 'sign-posting statement'. Echoing the sentiments identified at the beginning of Chapter 1, Wright makes a firm assertion about human beings' innate spirituality:

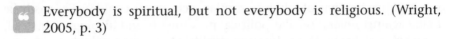 Everybody is spiritual, but not everybody is religious. (Wright, 2005, p. 3)

This is but one of several ways of saying that the spirituality discourse can be both religious or secular, and that a secular spirituality without a belief in a divine Being can have just as powerful a validity and value as a religious spirituality. There may be similarities and common themes that they share, but a secular spirituality must be seen not as second best or as a watered down version of something else, but as having strength and potency all of its own.

This assertion may appear controversial, especially for those who regard spirituality as belonging exclusively to the territory of religion. They would want to argue that the spirituality discourse must have and maintain a distinct religious framework, in which prayer, worship, contemplation, fasting, meditation, the acknowledgement of mystery and selfless devotion to the welfare of others are key components. To claim otherwise, they would argue, would be to drain the life-blood from the concept which they claim draws its energy, vitality and *raison d'etre* from the Divine Being and the relationship established with the believer or follower.

The argument for a secular spirituality, however, does not seek in any way whatsoever to detract from a religious spirituality. Instead it argues that spirituality needs to be understood in a much wider context, and that it has some important things to say about what it means to be human. Spirituality is thus is to be understood as a common shared aspect of our humanity, whether or not we *additionally* choose a religious world-view that brings with it some distinctively religious spiritual beliefs and practices at the individual and faith community levels. The question about spirituality therefore involves inclusivity and exclusivity: is it an *exclusively* religious activity and mindset, implying that the concept should only be used in that context; or is it an *inclusive* term that touches the lives of everyone by raising issues that illuminate what it means to be human, and includes, but is not constricted by, religious world-views?

It would perhaps be more comfortable for those social workers, educators and practitioners who remain hesitant or resistant to the issues of religion and spirituality being brought into mainstream curricula and practice, if an *exclusive* definition of spirituality held sway. They could then argue that the value-base of social work education and practice is robust enough to deal with such issues as part of a culturally competent, values-based approach to social work practice. But the track record of this approach has been to marginalise these themes, leading to social work students complaining that the deep issues of religion and spirituality are simply not on the agenda of their social work education and practice.

This chapter therefore argues for an inclusive approach that somehow helps us to engage with core questions and issues about what it means to be human. This approach may be represented diagrammatically as in Figure 2.1. In this diagram 'S' represents an inclusive understanding of spirituality, incorporating, but not being restricted to, a religious world-view ('R'). The boundaries around the religious world-view (R) are necessarily porous for reasons we have already discussed: there are religious dimensions to spirituality, but the secular dimensions are much broader and all-encompassing. To enrich our understanding of secular spirituality we can add a further 'encircling' theme to indicate some of the issues that spirituality raises. These include the issues of meaning and

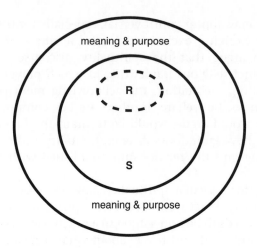

Figure 2.1 Spirituality as an inclusive concept

purpose, terms that also resonate with, and are strongly owned by, people for whom a religious world-view is not meaningful.

Spirituality and meaning-making

The use of the term 'meaning' is significant in our discussion about spirituality, not least because it raises the complex question of what meaning to give to the term itself. Readers may be familiar with Shardlow's (1998) 'slippery fish', a metaphor he used to describe the difficulty of pinning down the term 'values' to a precise set of meanings. Pinning down spirituality seems to be an even greater challenge, with almost every book on the subject coming up with its own definition. This was perhaps inevitable, given the explosion of interest in various aspects of spirituality and New Age movements in the 1960s. As Robinson (2008) notes,

> Beginning in the 1960s, this was a loose collection of different movements and ideas that asserted many different spiritualities. They generated a real sense of excitement and inspiration focused on the idea that each person can discover, control and develop his or her own spirituality in their own way. A common theme throughout this movement is asserting freedom from a view of spirituality that had been imposed by patriarchal institutions and authorities. (p. 19)

With everyone being free to choose their own spiritual path (Perry, 1992), it is no surprise that, as we noted with the proliferation of religions earlier in this chapter, spirituality has many varied secular, as well as religious, expressions. Is spirituality, therefore, merely an expression of individual 'quirkiness', important no doubt for getting the 'feel' for someone's unique individuality and sense of identity, but no more than that?

Let us return to Edward Canda's approach to defining spirituality. Canda has been at the forefront of the drive to incorporate spirituality into social work theory and practice, certainly in America. He suggests a way forward here when he writes,

> Spirituality...refers to the human search for a sense of meaning, purpose and morally fulfilling relations with oneself, other people, the universe, and the ground of being however that's understood (such as theistic, non-theistic, animistic...)...Spirituality is a larger concept that can be expressed in religious or non-religious ways...spirituality is [not] just an individualistic thing. Spirituality can be shared and in fact, in some ways it must be shared, because it impacts our relationships and our connectedness with others. (Canda, 2008, p. 27)

Several themes emerge from this. First, Canda re-emphasises the importance of an inclusive understanding of spirituality if it is to be a useful concept in social work or in the discourse of any other helping profession. Second, the inevitable individuality of spiritualities does not rule out a corporate, shared dimension. Indeed, for Canda, the dimension of connectedness and morally fulfilling relationships are central. This is a topic to which we will return in Chapter 7 when issues about spirituality and social justice will be explored. Third – and this takes us back to our diagrammatic representation – the themes of meaning and purpose lie at the heart of the discussion about spirituality, whether this is conducted in religious or secular terms.

In social work practice (although as a profession we are not alone in this) questions about meaning and purpose are always implicit, and sometimes explicit, in the work we undertake with people, especially in times of crisis. The big questions – *why?*; *why has this happened to me/them?*; *what sense can I make of what has happened?* – are easy to ask, but notoriously difficult to answer. In fact, answers, as we normally understand them, may be impossible. Nevertheless, they serve as pointers to the world-views we have chosen to hold. The deep-seated need within us to find a meaning and sometimes a purpose in what has happened to us points us to the ways in which we interpret the world. The 'answers' – however partial and incomplete they may be – that we give to these searching questions will either confirm or cause us to reshape or even change the world-view we have chosen.

Let us explore this through one of the most challenging personal experiences in which the search for meaning is commonly strong (Holloway,

2007c). The experience of personal tragedy can have a profound impact upon our world-view, whether this is secular or religious. By its very nature the tragic event stops us in our tracks and compels us to think about the extent to which this event can in any way 'fit into' the world-view we have chosen, or whether we need to re-think it. Some people who hold religious beliefs, for example, may find their faith shattered as a result of the tragic event, whereas others (such as Bertrand Russell) who were previously strongly atheist in their approach to life may experience a religious conversion. In all these situations, the tragic event causes people to re-examine their previously held beliefs because the tragedy makes them begin to see the world differently.

It is worth exploring this issue from a faith perspective in a little more detail so that we can better understand its complexity. Within several faith communities a response to a personal tragedy will be to say that in some mysterious way this is the will of God (DV: *deo volente; Insh'Allah*).This may be interpreted, and responded to, in several ways. It could be taken to mean that the tragedy was the *direct* result of God's action and intention: we may not agree with it or understand it, but God is God and we cannot expect as human beings to fully grasp such things. A person belonging to that faith community can choose whether or not to accept this statement at face value theologically, and to allow it to strengthen the faith that they hold. Another response might be to say that their understanding of God is such that to attribute such an intentional act goes against the grain of their own moral beliefs, let alone their theological understanding. Therefore, perhaps in the spirit of Holloway's 'cleaving lightly', they may choose to modify that understanding of the Divine Being, and re-shape their faith and belief in the light of their painful experience. And finally, they may find that any belief in a divine Being is so 'out of kilter' with what has happened to them that they reject this world-view altogether, and replace it with something else. They now see the world altogether differently.

The point of this example is not to argue the 'truth claims' of a religious or secular world-view one way or another, but to show that there *is* a world-view underpinning each of the positions people choose to adopt. We all have chosen, consciously or by 'absorption' from our family or other dominant influences, a world-view that by and large we find satisfying for our day-to-day living. It informs our understanding of who we are, how we interpret the world and the contribution that we seek, or neglect, to make to its well-being. It is our world-view that represents our search for meaning, and our response to the question that Morgan (1993) posed,

> How can you make sense out of a world which does not seem to be intrinsically reasonable? (p. 6)

It is for this reason that in Figure 2.1 the encircling themes of meaning and purpose encompass, and also provide a context for, the concept of spirituality.

The search for definitions

We have already been engaging in the search for definitions of spirituality, not least in referring to Canda's approach to this challenge. Before we look at some other approaches, however, it is worth entering one caveat. Definitions are important to help us identify the territory we are exploring and the themes and topics that are included or excluded from the discussion. But some aspects of our human experience are not easily circumscribed. Concepts such as truth, passion, love, beauty, wonder, mystery, awe, creativity and justice, for example, are all important, and we sense that we know what we are talking about when we refer to them, but they present some challenges if we try to pin them down with exact definitions. So too with spirituality: it has become increasingly popular, but it consistently resists the challenge to find a universally agreed 'definition'. As Burke (2007) notes, 'there is no definition on which all can agree, but many definitions in which all can share' (p. 3).

We have noted that spirituality is a broad concept that encompasses religion but is not reduced to it; indeed, it has a powerful, secular appeal that can genuinely be described as universal. It may be more helpful therefore to regard it as a 'gateway' word, or, as Coleman suggests (2006, p. 45) following Wittgenstein, a 'cluster concept' that *points us towards* some key themes, rather than being a watertight category that can be pinned down and analytically dissected. Social work claims to deal holistically with people, and to know something about the human spirit. In this regard at least it may have much more in common with art and music than we realise. We work with people in whose lives great themes of love and hate, passion and power, searching and change, meaning and purpose are played out. We would argue therefore that it is to this cluster of themes that spirituality, as a gateway word, points.

It would be counter-productive, even tedious, therefore, to explore too many of the definitions of spirituality in the literature. It is useful, nevertheless, to look at least at a few of them to identify a cluster of common themes that are emerging. We have already looked at some of the work of Canda (2008, p. 27, see above) who paints his definitions on a very large canvas. Moss (2005), by contrast, offers a much briefer definition in suggesting that

> Spirituality is what we do to give expression to our chosen world-view.

Here the emphasis is upon human behaviour, and what people *do* and how they behave as a result of how they see the world, and the consequences that flow from it. This definition offers a very 'down to earth' approach that easily resonates with contemporary social work practice and the assessment and intervention skills at the heart of our praxis. It poses the social work practice question: if a person is acting and behaving in this sort of way, what world-view does this flow from? And what does this therefore tell us about this person's spirituality?

In a similar vein, Patel et al. (1998) talk about spirituality as

> the human search for personal meaning and mutually fulfilling relationships between people, between people and the natural environment, and between religious people and God. (p. 11)

As Holloway (2007a) observes, the first part of this

> is indistinguishable from social work literature which ... addresses the search for meaning and purpose, re-valuing, and achieving personal growth and maturity. (p. 274)

stop and think

- How important in social work practice are issues to do with meaning and purpose?

Social work has tended to look at meaning and purpose as an individual search or need. Other professions have located questions of meaning and purpose within a wider scheme. From a nursing perspective, McSherry (2006) cites Murray and Zentner (1989) suggesting that spirituality is

> a quality that goes beyond religious affiliation, that strives for inspirations, reverence, awe, meaning and purpose, even in those who do not believe in any god. The spiritual dimension tries to be in harmony with the universe and strives for answers about the infinite, and comes into focus when the person faces emotional stress, physical illness or death. (p. 259)

Mayers and Johnston (2008) have provided a review of some of the definitional literature around spirituality from a healthcare practice perspective, suggesting that the lack of consensus about what spirituality is has been unhelpful to practitioners seeking to offer spiritual care. They too emphasise 'the search for meaning and purpose in life, which may or may not be related to a belief in God...'(p. 273) and draw attention to the work of Stoll (1989) who distinguishes between 'the vertical and horizontal components of spirituality' (p. 268) whereby

> The vertical component involves a person's relationship with a higher power...and the horizontal component which is ones relationship with self, others and environment.

This distinction between the vertical and the horizontal is important and helpful, especially when thinking about religious and secular approaches to spirituality. It clearly resonates with the diagrammatic representations being offered later on in this chapter.

The final example we have chosen is from Robinson (2008) who offers a working definition of spirituality that has three themes:

1. developing *awareness* and *appreciation* of the other (including the self, the other person, the group, the environment and, where applicable, deity);
2. developing the capacity to respond to the other. This involves putting spirituality into practice, *embodying* spirituality, and thus the continued relationship with the other;
3. developing *ultimate life meaning* based upon awareness and appreciation of, and response to, the other (p. 36).

The emphasis here is upon an active approach to spirituality. It is not a static or fixed concept so much as an activity that we engage in as human beings of all ages, where we are seeking to develop these important capacities and insights. As the root word 'spirit' suggests, there is an aspect of seeking, searching and restlessness which this idea of spirituality also seeks to capture, an aspect which underlies many of the definitional attempts we have briefly explored.

There are three further points which we should note before leaving the subject of definitions. First, each of us needs to decide for ourselves the extent to which we feel we need a concrete comprehensive definition. It may be that the very attempt to pin down spirituality with a watertight definition will always fail because of the territory that spirituality occupies in our human endeavours. To have pointers, signposts and gateways may ultimately be more helpful if they enable us suddenly or gradually to see things differently. Second, some of the definitions seek to widen the scope of spirituality to include relationships with the environment, an emphasis that has only recently been explored in any detail in the social work literature (e.g. Coates, 2007; Zapf, 2007). This we believe is an important development to which we will turn later in this book. Third, there appears to be no room in some of these definitions for *negative* aspects of spirituality. It is to this important dimension, therefore, that we must now turn.

■ What fresh approaches to social work practice does spirituality as a 'gateway word' open up for you?

The dark side of spirituality

It was argued in Chapter 1 that Ford's (2004) observation about today's societies being complexly both secular and religious is an important context for contemporary social work education and practice. We need now to develop that observation by suggesting that religion and spirituality are each complex phenomena, containing within them the power for good or evil, and having potentially positive or negative impact on people's lives – usually, in fact having some elements of each. Many of the great mystics and faith leaders – past and present – attest to this, describing their inner struggles and wrestlings as much as their moments of enlightenment. Religious and spiritual impulses can be creative, generous and awesome, but at the same time they can be destructive, oppressive and awful. They have been in the forefront of artistic and musical flowering and humanitarian relief, and they have also been at the root of unspeakable violence, wars and internecine conflicts. Etymologically, the word 'spirituality' is derived from the Latin root *spiritus*, meaning 'breath', in a similar way to the Hebrew *ru'ach* (Cook, 2004; Gilbert, 2007; Robinson, 2008). But breath, wind and spirit can be destructive as well as benign. Furthermore, as Robinson (2008) points out in connection with New Age Movements (but the comment is just as apposite for religion and spirituality in general),

> If all forms of spirituality are acceptable, then there can be no common criteria for how to judge the claims and the worth of any particular spirituality. (p. 20)

From social work's perspective, we need a framework that contextualises this complexity and addresses these issues from the value-base of social work, with its strong commitment to anti-discriminatory and anti-oppressive practice. The value-base of social work, with its celebration of diversity, continues to challenge and resist oppressive systems and behaviours. Social work has always taken seriously the capacity of human nature to change for the better, as well as its tendency to hurt, injure and harm, although we probably do not, as a profession, have a clear view about whether we believe human nature is, or is not, intrinsically good. Our curricula do not help us understand various world-views, for example, that talk about the conflicting 'pull' of good and evil within ourselves, both individually and at wider levels. What we are much better at doing is to recognise that oppression and discrimination can and do operate at cultural and societal levels, as well as at the individual level. Thompson's (2006) personal, cultural and structural analysis (PCS) has been particularly helpful here in highlighting the complexity of oppression and its impact. As a framework it can also be used to highlight and emphasise the ways in which positive outcomes at all levels can be achieved. It can be particularly relevant in this discussion, therefore, not only in highlighting ways in which religion and spirituality can be forces for good at the individual, cultural and societal levels, but also as negative, even destructive influences.

Philosophers, theologians and psychologists have grappled with issues of good and evil and what these concepts say about the world-views we hold. In the 'helping professions' social work is not alone in having to meet 'head on' some of the powerfully destructive behaviours that people inflict upon themselves and others, but we have perhaps fought shy of labelling this as 'evil'. In part this is because we are rightly cautious of the value judgements which come into play when criticising another person's ideology, lifestyle or behaviours. Yet as we have already identified, social work is not a morally neutral activity; there are some people whose lifestyle actually cultivates the practice and development of attitudes and behaviours that from a social work perspective we would roundly condemn.

In summary, there are probably three angles to this darker side of spirituality which, for social work purposes, are important to distinguish. First, we need to acknowledge that not all religions and spiritual expressions are benign in their human intent. Satanism and the Nazi exultation of the music of Wagner are two examples which we would put into this category. Second, religious adherence may have oppressive or destructive consequences for the individual and also a wider community or society, both intended and unintended. A religious doctrine which subjugates women, for example, could lead to women being submissive and unfulfiled, or it could result in outright cruelty towards women by men who use the religious doctrine as an 'excuse' for violent behaviour; the former would be an intended consequence of the religious doctrine, the latter an unintended consequence arising from the way in which its precepts are applied. Third, within every spiritual journey (both individual and communal) there will be experiences of light and experiences of darkness. The consequences of unrelieved spiritual pain may be considerable and at the root of many other problems.

The following provides an example of a type of situation in which a social worker may encounter the first category, where the spiritual expressions and practices may be far from benign. In this example, it is crucial to the well-being of the children concerned that the social workers are able to distinguish between a culture which they find alien and disturbing because it is outside of their world-view and one which may be putting vulnerable parties at risk.

> **Example**
>
> Gina is a social work student on placement with a children and families team. She makes a home visit, accompanied by an experienced colleague, to a new family about whom some concerns had been raised by the health visitor. They find two toddlers playing in the sitting room with their pet rabbit. They seem happy and well cared for, but the atmosphere in the house feels (to use Gina's words) icy cold and frightening. There are Satanist pictures and images all round the walls, with pictures of animal sacrifice. The children's mother dismisses their concerns saying that it is her partner's hobby and is harmless enough, although he did do some strange things with his mates from time to time. Gina feels very worried. However, her supervisor points out that there is no evidence that the children are anything other than well cared for, and this has to be her only concern as a social worker. A few weeks later, however, the office receives another referral on the family from the school of an older child. He had drawn some disturbing images of men in Satanist masks during the painting session, and, when asked about them by his teacher, had got very distressed, but would say only that he didn't like it when his dad's friends came round.

In the next example, a different set of issues emerges, where people who belonged to a faith community had interpreted its teachings in such a way as to demean and devalue their child, and to deny to that child many of the basic rights and opportunities that they would have willingly granted to one who did not have learning disabilities (perhaps). Here is an example of a religious faith being (in our view) distorted, and used in an oppressive way against another human being.

> **Example**
>
> Ishfaq was an experienced social worker in an inner city team that worked with people with learning disabilities. He enjoyed his work and got a real 'buzz' from seeing how the people he worked with responded to his trusting and respectful approach,

and blossomed in confidence as a result. He felt dismayed therefore when working with a new family who had just been referred to him. They were strongly religious, and felt that their child and they themselves had been cursed by God – what other explanation could there be for having a child 'so clearly lacking in perfection'. He recognised this thinking from his own upbringing – it was part of the background he had tried to get away from, seeing it as superstitious ignorance.

It is our contention that the third category – unrelieved spiritual pain – features far more widely in social work practice than is commonly recognised and we illustrate this throughout the remaining chapters. These brief examples illustrate the complexity of understanding religion and spirituality and their interface with social work. We must be open to the possibility of spirituality itself not being value neutral, but that, just like religion, its influence is not necessarily for good and may even be destructive. When we come to integrate spiritual and religious perspectives with social work practice, therefore, we need an interpretive framework that allows us to take account of all sides of human behaviour in all its complexity.

stop and think

■ How do you understand and face the 'darkness' in your social work practice?

A conceptual framework for social work practice

It is perhaps because of the problem-centred nature of social work and the side of life with which it so frequently deals (even though we have as one of our key objectives enhancing the quality of life of the service user) that we are emphasising the importance of using concepts and models which encompass the darker sides of spirituality as much as they celebrate its creative and enhancing potential.

The following diagram builds on Figure 2.1, but makes two important additions. First, it introduces another encircling theme of mystery and awe, which we argue are common to our human experience whether or not we interpret them in a religious context. It is important to emphasise at this point that we are including children and young people in our discussion of spirituality. Spirituality is not an aspect of becoming adult which somehow we begin to experience or be aware of once we reach 18 years of age. Spirituality is about our humanity, irrespective of our age. This important point is emphasised by the National Occupational Standards for Youth Work in the UK (NYA, 2005) which state that

> Youth work addresses the development of the whole person, including the social spiritual, emotional, physical and intellectual...(p. 5)

In a similar way, Hyde (2008) suggests that

> children are natural philosophers who frequently wonder about the larger existential questions of life. (p. 57)

Hyde argues that 'experiences of wonder act as a corner stone for a spiritual life', which links closely with the concepts of awe and mystery we are discussing in our framework. Indeed, specialists in the topic of children's spirituality argue that children are more intuitively attuned to wonder and awe. Children and young people, therefore, populate our discussions and examples and belong within our theoretical framework just as much as adults. In chapters 3 and 5, we build on a model for spiritual development which is linked to chronological age and maturation, but not wholly coterminous with either.

The second addition in Figure 2.2 is the attempt to depict the points at which spirituality begins to engage with some of the core themes of social work.

This diagram immediately reflects the observations already made in this chapter, that both religion and spirituality have the potential for good

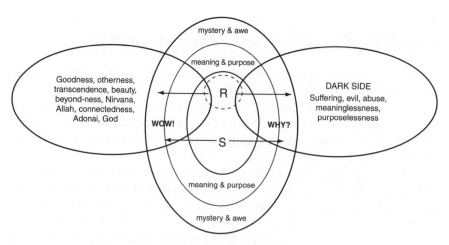

Figure 2.2 Meeting points for spirituality and social work

and evil outcomes, but just as importantly, there is quite a lot of middle ground. As far as spirituality is concerned, with its emphasis upon meaning-making through the world-views that each of us chooses to adopt, it does not matter whether a religious or secular spirituality is being considered. Both demonstrate, as we have argued, the capacity for good or evil outcomes; both have the capacity and strong desire to recognise and respond to mystery and awe. The only difference is that religious spirituality would want to push the boundaries of mystery, awe and transcendence in the direction of acknowledging and responding to aspects of the Divine Being or Higher Power.

Diagrams are useful in showing relationships and the interconnectedness of key themes; in this instance, they are useful by helping to build up a framework that demonstrates first of all how spirituality can and does engage with core human themes in both positive and negative ways. In this diagram, these themes are clustered together in positive and negative groupings. But the *Why?* question that seeks to make sense of meaningless events bedevils our attempts at creating neat and tidy world-views which automatically produce good outcomes. By contrast, another cluster of concepts reminds us that from time to time we experience moments of wonder, beauty and a sense of what John Barry calls '*the beyondness of things*', which break into our routine attempts at meaning-making. Such responses are encapsulated by the exclamation in our diagram, **Wow!** Admittedly between these two strong reactions– why and wow – there is an ocean of ordinariness and the mundane struggle to survive, to get on with things, to earn a 'crust', to pay the mortgage or to struggle to make ends meet on welfare benefits. T.S Eliot (1944) was probably right when he suggested that as human beings we cannot bear very much reality (p. 14). Nevertheless, spirituality needs to be able to address these extremes, or at least to be able to include them within its purview if it is to be a concept that has value and usefulness, not least as a lens for understanding social work.

The 'down side' of such pictorial representations, of course, is that they cannot do justice to the subtlety and complexity of human living. Nor can they adequately capture pictorially the dilemmas facing social work practitioners, where often the situations they are engaged with are not starkly 'either-or' but a complex blending of 'good', 'not so good' and the downright 'bad'. Nevertheless, as we shall see in Figure 2.3, it is possible to demonstrate some specific connections between spirituality and core social work themes.

If we concentrate initially at the individual level we note that, at the left hand side of the diagram, there is a cluster of human qualities that are important to living successfully, and also lie at the heart of the core value-base of social work. This reflects the capacity of both spirituality and religion to bring the best out of people and to seek the best in others. By

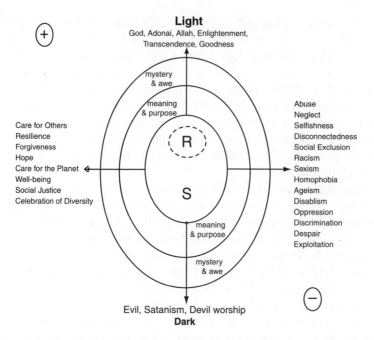

Figure 2.3 A framework for conceptualising spirituality and social work

contrast, the right hand side of the diagram focuses on the ways in which human nature can become abusive, destructive and inward-looking, a 'territory' with which we, as social workers, are all too familiar in our dealings with people. Sometimes, as we have discussed, spiritual and religious experience contributes to this process.

Similarly, the search for meaning and purpose can be interpreted in selfish or unselfish ways: we can put our needs above the needs of others and, indeed, trample on the rights and needs of others in our scramble to get on top. Or they can be much more outward-looking where meaning and purpose can be found in the welfare of, and our care for, others. It all depends upon the world-view we have chosen and the impact that our spirituality has upon how we view ourselves and others, and our behaviour towards them. We would also argue that this framework of understanding for spirituality not only informs our personal, individual life-styles but also lies at the heart of our professional social work values and practice. This is why the concept of 'world-view' is so important, because it determines so many other things. How we view the world as individuals and as professional social workers impacts hugely upon our practice. It is this insight that underlies the definition offered by Moss (2005) who argues that *spirituality is what we do to give expression to our chosen world-view.*

There is clearly more to spirituality than what we *do* – awe, wonder and mystery, for example, are what we experience – but it is by our *behaviour* above all that we are judged – by ourselves, by others and (some would suggest) also by the Divine Being. Yet even awe, wonder and mystery can have a powerful and positive impact upon how we behave, although it is not inevitable, as the music-loving Third Reich revealed. We do have the capacity to compartmentalise our lives, but again this can be both positive and negative. The ability to switch off and concentrate totally on the task-in-hand can be life-enhancing, and at times absolutely necessary; but on the other hand it can also allow us to abuse, oppress and despise other people while 'carrying on as normal'. Thus the darkness of fragmentation is essentially an absence of wholeness and lack of relatedness.

The starkness of the diagram – positive and negative; light and dark; good and evil – is not meant to suggest that life is that simple. But it does highlight the ways in which social work is caught up in wider, powerful struggles at individual, cultural, societal and structural levels. Some of the forces at work in our communities, often encapsulated by the wide range of 'isms' (racism; sexism; disabilism, for example), are hugely powerful and destructive. Social work's commitment to anti-oppressive, anti-discriminatory practice is nothing less than an alignment of our energies and strategies to tackle the darkness of oppression and to fight for a more just and compassionate society, with and on behalf of people who have been marginalised and dispossessed. Whether such approaches are driven by a secular or religious spirituality, the impact is the same: people will want to work together in a variety of organisations and through politics to strive for a better, fairer society where discrimination, oppression and corporate abuse are eradicated. They will want to challenge the disconnectedness and fragmentation that widen and stretch the threads of the social fabric so that the weak, the marginalised and the poor 'slip through the net'.

It is difficult to discuss such themes from a social work perspective without a burning sense of zeal and passion bursting through the words we use. These are great issues that have gripped the heart and mind of social work from the earliest days, and which we lose at our (and society's) peril. This is not to claim a unique role for our profession in its fight against oppression. We have many allies sharing the struggle with us. But it *is* insisting that these issues *really matter*. They shape the sort of society we live in, and they enliven the vision we have for the sort of society we believe has yet to happen. They remind us of the insidious and stealthy progress of oppressive ideologies such as racism and sexism and many more, which have the capacity to flourish when they feed on fear, greed and hate, and *will* flourish if they are not challenged and confronted, or are simply ignored.

This chapter is arguing that this life-enhancing, diversity-celebrating and anti-discriminatory profession known as social work has a proud 'spirit' that is both secular and religious, as is the society in which it undertakes its work. As a profession it is united in its quest for a better society for everyone. To some, though not all, this is a deeply spiritual quest. Indeed, we shall see in Chapter 7 that some definitions of spirituality insist on a concern for social justice as an intrinsic element. Whether from a secular, spiritual or religious perspective, there needs to be a passion behind the paradigm. If social work loses its passionate heart, then we will indeed sink into a tired, dark and disheartened bureaucratic agency of the state.

Conclusion

In this chapter we have been wrestling with conceptualising the phenomenon of spirituality that is increasingly recognised in contemporary culture, but which consistently resists the challenge to find a universally agreed 'definition'. Its relationship to religion has also been explored, during which we discovered that as a concept and a phenomenon it too resists clear definition, with a multiplicity of religious beliefs, organisations and practices being evidenced. Along with many others, we argue that spirituality is a broad concept that encompasses religion but is not reduced to it; indeed, it has a powerful, secular appeal that can genuinely be described as universal. We also argue that too heavy an emphasis upon finding the right definition may be counter-productive to understanding and experiencing the cluster of concepts to which spirituality is a pointer, a signpost and a gateway word.

Perhaps more productive then than the search for a consensus about definitions is to find a conceptual framework for social work practice which accommodates plurality of belief and the many shades of spirituality and finds meeting points between the key elements of spirituality and the core concerns of social work. Our quest throughout has been for a comprehensive framework that does justice to both positive and negative aspects of spirituality, that provides an overview for our education and practice and serves as an interpretive lens through which our theory and practice can be undertaken and evaluated.

One further point deserves mention. In this chapter considerable emphasis has been placed upon the importance of meaning-making. But neither spirituality nor religion can be packaged neatly and tidily as some meaning-making 'fix'. In both secular and religious ways we are also pointed 'beyond'. Mystery, awe and transcendence are all meaningful terms to us whether we approach life from a religious or secular standpoint. Burke (2007) refers to the words of the theologian Karl Rahner who wrote:

> Even if the term God were to be forgotten...and those realities which we call religions were totally to disappear...the transcendental, inherent in human life, is such that we would still reach out towards that mystery which lies outside our control. (p. 5)

Herein lies the richness, the challenge and the frustration of this term spirituality. It reminds us that there is always 'more', always 'something beyond' that we cannot 'put our finger on', but is nevertheless tantalisingly witnessed to by the 'ache' within. Some might refer to this as 'spiritual need', a term that has yet to appear in our discussions. It is to this, therefore, that we now turn in Chapter 3.

taking it further

- Gilbert, P. (2008) *Guidelines on Spirituality for Staff in Acute Care Services* (Staffordshire University/Care Services Improvement Partnership/National Institute for Mental Health in England).
- McSherry, W. (2006) *Making Sense of Spirituality in Nursing and Healthcare Practice: An Interactive Approach*, 2nd edn (London: Jessica Kingsley).
- Thompson, N. (2006) *Anti-discriminatory Practice*, 4th edn (Basingstoke: Palgrave Macmillan).

3 Spiritual need

Introduction

Our discussion so far has been concerned with the broad dimension of spirituality, incorporating both positive and negative influences. Social work, however, is primarily concerned with problems and needs. Indeed, the concept of need is at the heart of social work. The ability to undertake an assessment of the 'problem' and intervene on the basis of that assessment marks the beginnings of the professionalisation of social work. Contemporary social work practice is very much concerned with the knowledge and skills required to undertake a needs assessment; the relationship between the social worker and service user in arriving at that assessment of need; and the matching of those needs with appropriate services and interventions. The questions which concern us are around how to undertake a genuinely needs-led assessment when constrained by the type and level of services available in the context of limited resources. Little attention is paid to the notion of need itself and *why* 'meeting needs' is an important aspect of social work. Possibly for this reason, social work has barely considered the dimension of spiritual need and its relevance to social work assessment (Holloway, 2007a).

Yet social work does pay lip-service at least to the idea of holistic assessment. It has proudly guarded its psycho-social tradition, with a tendency to imply that this in itself is 'holistic'. Only in the field of palliative care has there been a recognition from the outset that holistic care also implies spiritual care. Even here, the term 'spiritual need' has often been used with little clarity or consensus about its meaning or how such need may be identified (Satterly, 2001). Nevertheless, social workers working with people who are dying or bereaved do, in surprisingly large numbers, acknowledge spiritual need among service users (Lloyd, 1997; Furman et al., 2004).

Yet there is both confusion and contradiction in our practices across the globe. In Northern Europe we see a secular profession cautious of raising the topic of spirituality lest it be seen to trample on religious sensibilities. Sometimes there is even some continuing hostility to religion and suspicion of spirituality being 'religion under a contemporary guise'. Meanwhile, African and Indian writers point out that 'the spiritual' is an integrated dimension of their culture and therefore their practice (e.g. Sacco, 1994). In New Zealand and Australia, the influence of beliefs and practices from indigenous peoples sits alongside a western secularised perspective (e.g. Nash and Stewart, 2002). So we need to ask what is going on if social workers acknowledge spiritual need, but are less than clear about whether, when and how a spiritual component is their concern. Part of the problem may lie in the way in which we have theorised assessment practice, so as to assume that 'need' is a given, while paying very little attention to what it is, how it manifests itself and what might be required of us, individually and as a profession, if we are to respond to deep human need. So in this chapter we shall arrive at a consideration of spiritual need and spiritual pain, through first exploring the concept of need and its relationship with social work practice. Only then will we look at models for assessing spiritual need and their relevance for everyday social work practice.

Social work and the concept of need

Despite the fact that many social work writers will assert the central importance of good assessment in effective social work practice, and will refer to the assessment of need, surprisingly few dwell on the concept of need itself. This is the case even where 'needs-led assessments' (formalised in the UK under the National Health Service and Community Care Act [NHSCCA] 1990) are the subject. Those writers who do make connections to underpinning theories of human need generally refer to Maslow's hierarchy of need (1970), Bradshawe's taxonomy of need (1972) and the sustained treatment of the subject, building on these earlier categorisations, provided by Doyal and Gough (1991).

Broadly speaking, the social work literature is interested in 'need' in terms of its perceived relationship with 'problems' on the one hand, and 'resources' on the other. There is a tendency in earlier texts to speak as though the service user's needs *are* the problem (e.g. Butrym, 1976; Howe, 1987). Only in more recent times have we begun to talk about *unmet need* as the problem (e.g. Thompson, 2005; Coulshed and Orme, 2006). Payne (2005b) points out how easily social work assessment of need can be turned into a service rationing exercise – hence the arguments about whether a needs-led assessment is in fact a service-led assessment, both in terms of the type and level of response to meeting need. It is increasingly argued that social work is in danger of losing

sight of the holistic assessment of need as it is sucked into technicist responses (e.g. Lloyd and Taylor, 1995; Lymbery, 2001). Probably
Bradshawe's taxonomy has had the most influence on thinking about
service delivery. Bradshawe defined *normative need* as that defined by the
expert or professional; *felt need* as broadly equated with what the person experiencing the need wants; *expressed need* as a demand made on
the provider or helper; and *comparative need* as that which is defined relative to the situation of others. This way of describing and categorising
need does not sit easily with what we instinctively feel 'spiritual need'
is all about; nor, indeed, does it sit easily with the concept of holistic
assessment.

Lloyd and Taylor (1995) analyse the emergence of an assessment stage in
the social work process with its accompanying skills, as a key part of social
work's drive for professionalisation. Thus, social work assessment at any
one point in time will reflect the dominant influences on the profession.
Probably the key emphasis currently in social work assessment is that the
assessment of need should be *user-centred* with needs defined jointly by
the service user and the professional. In this climate, for social work to
recognise the importance of spiritual need and the relevance of this for
its assessments, the case must be made that spirituality and spiritual need
are intrinsic to the lives of, and contexts of, those who use social work
services. Moreover, this case must be articulated by service users themselves. It is in fact the service user voice in mental health services which
has been raised to assert that their spirituality, and hence their spiritual
needs, is integral to who they are and hence an essential component in
any assessment (Nicholls, 2007).

Spiritual need

So we are back to grappling with those questions posed in Chapter 2.
What does spiritual need look like; how, in social work terms, does the
problem present itself? One of the problems in identifying spiritual need
is that, in the same way as definitions of spirituality range from those
which have clear links to a religious sense, to those which are virtu-
ally indistinguishable from emotional and psychological dimensions, so
understandings of what can be termed a 'spiritual need' vary. Indeed,
Paley argues that stretching the concept of 'spirituality' allows almost any
need to be defined as 'spiritual' (Paley, 2008). However, the need to find
meaning and to experience peace and reconciliation in life in general and
in particular circumstances and relationships, features as a central spiritual concern in almost any definition, and this is an area with which
social work is very familiar.

One way in which researchers have approached this issue of definition
is to allow respondents to identify what for them constitutes a spiritual

issue or need. For example, Lloyd (1997), in her study with dying and bereaved people, asked broad questions such as 'Has this experience made you think differently about life and death' and 'What things are important to you now?', leaving the definition of these as belonging to the spiritual or religious domain to the respondent. Similarly, Ross, in her study of older people in a hospital assessment unit (Ross, 1997), explored their 'thoughts on spiritual matters and their experiences of spiritual needs' through such questions as 'People seem to have different ideas about spiritual things. What do you think of as spiritual things?' (p. 711). Ross (1997, p. 712) identified five categories of spiritual need experienced by her respondents:

1. Religious needs, such as to attend church or pray;
2. To make sense/find meaning in life;
3. Love/belonging needs;
4. Needs related to death and dying;
5. Need for moral standing, for example, doing the 'right thing', fulfilling responsibilities.

When we look at these carefully, we see that all but the first category – specifically religious needs – could be covered, where relevant, in any comprehensive social work assessment. However, social workers (whatever their religious persuasion) would not necessarily identify these as 'spiritual'. Yet the service users might very well do so.

stop and think

- Are there situations in your practice where the assessment tool or approach which you use does not seem fully to address the problem?
- Could these needs be spiritual? Go back to Chapter 2 and re-think Joan's assessment.

Spiritual pain

It does not take long in social work practice before we find ourselves dealing with the 'sharp end' of life – the really problematic situations, or the extreme manifestations of a phenomenon or behaviour. In the spiritual dimension this moves us on to look at spiritual pain.

The terms 'spiritual pain' and 'spiritual distress' in fact have been in use in the helping professions much longer than the concept of spirituality. Ledger suggests that in general nursing, the nurse 'very occasionally...meets a patient who appears to be spiritually distressed' (Ledger, 2005, p. 224). Surprisingly, there have been relatively few attempts to define spiritual pain or distress. Satterly (2001) states that even religious professionals use the terms 'religious pain' and 'spiritual pain' interchangeably and with no real attempt to define what they mean. One exception is found in Burton's discussion of the origins, nature and management of spiritual pain:

> ...spiritual pain might best be described as pain operating at a deeper level of consciousness...manifest in a wide variety of symptoms such as constant and chronic pain; withdrawal or isolation from spiritual support systems; conflict with family members and friends; anxiety, fear or mistrust; anger; self-loathing; hopelessness; feelings of failure...unforgiveness; despair; and fear or dread. (Burton, 2004, p. 4)

Given the nature of the problems and issues with which social work routinely engages, it might be expected that social work would have paid rather more attention to spiritual pain and distress than routine spiritual care. However, there is again a dearth of literature. In the context of palliative care, Heyse-Moore (1996) suggests that carers need 'bi-focal vision', seeing symptoms both 'literally and symbolically', in order to recognise spiritual pain. Another way of distinguishing where pain operating at a 'deeper' level (as Burton describes it) is 'spiritual' rather than extreme emotional distress, is that spiritual pain stems from a spiritual or existential source. Three sources may have particular relevance for social work:

1. alienation, dissonance or deep conflict in the inner self;
2. the 'dark night' (May, 2004; also see the writings of St John of the Cross) or 'groanings' of the soul (Psalms 37 and 38);
3. loss of faith (Holloway, 2007b).

To take the first of these, a number of writers have arrived at this way of looking at spiritual pain. Satterly's quest to understand the concepts of what he terms 'religious pain' and 'spiritual pain' through his contacts with hospice patients as a pastoral visitor led to the conclusion that spiritual pain arose from profound difficulties in a 'person's relationship with the source (God) of his or her life' (Satterly, 2001, p. 34). Presumably the definition of 'source' can be understood as the core of one's being in nontheist as well as theist terms. Skalla and McCoy (2006) also assert that spiritual distress occurs when 'conflict exists between individuals' core beliefs and their personal experience' (p. 745).

Alienation, dissonance and inner conflict should be recognisable to social workers whatever their field, but particularly, perhaps, those working in mental health and with troubled young people. In broad terms, grinding levels of socio-economic deprivation, long-term abuse and repeated experiences of racism or other forms of discrimination can lead to the sort of alienation and distress which strikes at the core of the person's being. From a psychiatric perspective, Parker (2004) argues that this type of pain may be significant in religious and non-religious people alike. Attig (2001) suggests that spiritual pain is both a cause and a consequence of losing motivation to soar above the mundane and, also, to struggle with adversity. Social workers are familiar with situations such as long-term caring, coping with chronic illness, in which people wonder whether they can go on, often experiencing deep inner conflict about their situation. 'Maintaining the spirit' (Lloyd, 2002) is as important as any other support which the social worker may offer in these situations, and we shall look in Chapter 5 at the potential within the notions of transcendence and transformation for enabling people to 'soar above the mundane' as Attig suggests.

Example – Leroy

Leroy, aged 10, is the fourth of five siblings in an Afro-Caribbean family. His parents settled in England when their two eldest sons were small; a daughter Sharon was born soon after and then after a gap of some 10 years, Leroy and Robbie arrived in quick succession. When Leroy was 3, their mother left the family and their father requested that Leroy and Robbie be taken into care. The two little boys were placed in foster care until one day Robbie was discharged home. The case records show that Sharon, then 15, was to play a major role in the care of Robbie, but neither she nor their father felt able to take both boys and Leroy's behaviour was in any case quite disruptive and the social workers felt that he needed a firmer environment. Although this was explained to Leroy at a later date, contact with his family became less and less, and he still doesn't really understand how his family could leave him behind. It isn't as though Leroy objects to his foster family. His foster parents are kind and patient with him – and Leroy knows that he does 'push it' sometimes. He likes his foster brothers and, to be honest, has more fun with them than he used to have with Robbie when his family visited. It's just that sometimes he feels like an alien, out of sorts with himself and disconnected from everything going on around him. When that happens he wants to destroy things because he doesn't understand what his life is all about and he certainly can't explain how he feels to his social worker. One day, he sets fire to the house. He is moved the next day to a temporary place in a children's assessment unit.

The second category – the 'dark night of the soul' – is more usually associated with a specifically spiritual/religious crisis. It is likely that a social work service user manifesting this type and degree of spiritual pain will be dealing with a complex web of issues and problems – for example, in cases of sexual abuse or violence where either the perpetrator or the victim is a religious believer. Some of these may be appropriate for social work intervention and some better referred elsewhere. We shall return to this discussion in Chapter 5 when we look at a model for spiritual care which we shall call the 'fellow traveller'.

Kate Maguire, a psychotherapist who works with survivors of torture and extreme experiences, describes her own 'dark night of the soul' for which nothing in her training had prepared her (Maguire, 2001). Her work required her to engage with her own 'self' and thereby discover her spirituality. Her path was through the darkness of suffering rather than the popular concepts, as we discussed in Chapter 2, of mysticism and beauty. In fact, an important aspect of the 'dark night of the soul' is discovering a renewed sense of self through the stripping away of ego and pretence. It is important to remember the potential for spiritual and personal growth in experiences of darkness:

> Light in light is invisible ... but light in darkness gives great light and hope. (Indian guru quoted in Maguire, 2001, p. 136)

Similar thoughts are expressed by the Christian theologian Hans Kung:

> ... resurrection-faith is not to be had by passing over suffering, concrete conditions, opposition and antagonism, but only by going through all these ... The cross is 'surmountable' only in the light of the resurrection, but the resurrection can be lived only in the shadow of the cross. (Kung, 1984, p. 147)

As we have already suggested many times, social workers have to find a way of dealing with the darkness they encounter, if they are not to risk burn-out and disillusionment, both as individual practitioners and as professionals seeking to hold onto core values and approaches which are at the very heart of social work.

The third category – loss of faith – may well be part of 'the dark night of the soul' but it should be considered in itself. Its significance and impact on the well-being of the service user is in danger of being overlooked by social workers unless they themselves are, or have been in the past, associated with a faith community. However, there is a parallel in the loss of a secular world view which has assumed the guiding status of an ideology. It was not uncommon, for example, for people of left wing persuasion to be deeply affected by the collapse of communism in Europe, bringing with it disillusionment and the smashing of their political dreams. The common feature is that the loss of 'faith' strikes at the core of the person's being, and all other problems are seen as incidental or part of the wider angst.

Example

Jackie's husband, Dave, had committed suicide in particularly traumatising circumstances. A coal miner who became deeply depressed during prolonged strike action and whose colliery was one of the first to close, he eventually doused himself in petrol and set fire to himself in front of his wife. As well as the loss of her partner and childhood sweetheart, Jackie had to deal with the horror of those memories, her guilt that she had been unable to save him, her anger with him for voluntarily giving up on it all, but at the same time her sense of rejection. She was left with four young children to bring up, coping with the financial, practical and emotional problems in their family life with very little support from family and friends, since she was alienated from the miner's cause by hers and Dave's experiences. Three years on, she was still seeing a bereavement counsellor and repeatedly returned to the loss of her Catholic faith – which she felt had failed both her and Dave – as being at the centre of her problems: 'I can't go back to what I was but it's how to deal with who I am now' (quoted in Lloyd, 1995, p. 18).

Other writers have defined spiritual pain as 'a desolate feeling of meaningless' (Saunders, 1988, p. 3) and 'a total inability to invest life with meaning...(which) can cause anguish to the sufferer' (Burnard, 1987). This relates to what more contemporary writers would describe as 'existential' pain. For example, Heyse-Moore (1996) refers to 'existential anguish' as complete desolation and a profound sense of meaninglessness. Parker (2004) describes the core phenomena of 'existential distress' as hopelessness, helplessness, powerlessness, loss of a sense of control and a sense of meaninglessness. Unrelieved spiritual pain may, particularly for the person who has no spiritual belief system through which to engage with the spiritual pain which they are experiencing, move into a profound despair about the grounds for one's being and framework for living (Holloway, 2007b).

Social workers work with two groups in particular where it is important to recognise existential despair. Rates of suicide in the developed world are disproportionately high among younger people (between the ages of 17 and 25), especially young men. If we add in figures from deaths because of drug overdose, on the assumption that a significant proportion are non-accidental, suicide accounts for the highest number of deaths of all younger people in the UK over the past decade (Shaw et al., 2008).

Example – Leroy again

Leroy has spent most of his life in care. After frequent changes of care placement, in which his own behaviour contributed to the breakdowns, Leroy ended up in a leaving care facility. For the first time he forms a close relationship with a young black male student social worker, who helps him move into a flat. However, shortly after that the student finishes his placement and the case is closed, on the basis that Leroy is over 18 and settled into the community, Leroy finds himself lonely and adrift. He loses his job because of poor time-keeping and finds managing on benefits impossible; he is frequently without food. Leroy gets back in touch with his mother and asks if he can live with her but she refuses. He then returns to the last hostel he was in, but they are also unable to take him because he no longer fits their criteria. Leroy continues to drift, gets into bad company and starts to steal to fund his growing drug habit. Leroy is now 19 and up in court on a burglary charge. The Probation Officer warns him he could go to prison. Leroy doesn't really care what happens to him. He regards his life as over before it ever got going. He feels alienated from everyone and everything. He has no self regard and no aspirations. His mates warn him about the risks of overdosing; sometimes he thinks that would be the easiest way out of his dead-end life.

The other group for whom suicide rates are disproportionately high is older people. These suicides (and also suicidal feelings) appear to be associated with depression, alcoholism and existential issues such as feeling cut off from the rest of society, feeling useless, helpless and not valued by their families, rather than being associated with terminal illness, as might be imagined (Kissane and McLaren, 2006). A recent UK-wide health care services review found that one in four attempted suicides by those over the age of 65 is successful. 'Spiritual despair' was identified as a contributory factor with sudden or renewed church attendance being an indicator that the older person may be struggling with such issues and at risk of becoming suicidal (Beeston, 2006). Because social workers work primarily with older people who are marginalised in the ways identified above, we need to take seriously the possibility that spiritual pain and despair are significant contributors to their unmet needs.

stop and think

- How do you explain despair?
- What do you offer when a service user seems to be in despair?

Assessment of spiritual need and spiritual distress

We might conclude from the discussion so far that a spiritual dimension should be included in a social worker's assessment, but the question of how to go about it is complex and there are markedly different approaches and models available. With the exception of the US, where the topic of spirituality has been pursued for some time in the social work literature, most of these tools come from other professions.

There are essentially four approaches taken to spirituality assessment in the literature of the 'helping professions'. The first takes a generic approach which emphasises the importance of acknowledging a spiritual dimension in the service user's life, including the potentially spiritual nature of the service user's problems. The second seeks to systematically measure the degree and significance of spirituality which the service user exhibits, including the significance of spiritual need and spiritual resources to their individual coping. The third takes a biographical approach to illuminating the individual's spiritual life and development in the context of their overall personal narrative. The fourth takes a holistic approach in which the service user's situation is assessed within separate but interacting and overlapping 'domains' such as the family. The degree of emphasis given to spiritual need and, more especially, spiritual pain varies according to the approach taken.

Recognising spirituality

This approach is mainly concerned with identifying when, where and how spiritual and religious issues feature for the individual within the routine encounter. It takes an open-ended approach which allows the service user to identify spiritual or religious needs and/or supports, or not, as the case may be. It requires that the practitioner be spiritually aware and alert to the spiritual or religious need which the service user may be expressing, but it does not purport to undertake a detailed assessment of the person's 'spiritual state', nor does it lead to focused spiritual interventions or care.

The practitioner may, however, suggest specific spiritual supports to the service user and, with their permission, make a referral to a religious or other professional able to provide this help.

An assessment tool which takes as its starting point the spiritual needs which emerge in more general discussion is the HOPE questions. Developed in the US for family doctors to assess spiritual need in the routine encounter, its authors stress that it has not been validated as a research instrument but grew out of their own considerable clinical practice (Anandarajah and Hight, 2001). The authors claim that the HOPE tool 'serves as a natural follow-up to discussion of other support systems' (p. 85), but does not focus on either spirituality or religion unless led to do so by the patient. The purpose of such an assessment is to 'evaluate whether spirituality is important to a particular patient and whether spiritual factors are helping or hindering the healing process' (p. 84). The authors further claim that this approach allows for meaningful discussion with people who have been alienated from religion and those whose spiritual experience is outside of traditional religious understandings. Potentially, therefore, such a tool should be adaptable to social work contexts, since social work is also a secular helping profession which purports to employ core holistic assessment skills in both generic and specialist settings, and where the starting point is needs and problems.

The HOPE questions flow from the four areas denoted by the mnemonic:

H: *Sources of hope, meaning, comfort, strength, peace, love and connection*
O: *Organised religion*
P: *Personal spirituality and practices*
E: *Effects on medical care and end-of-life issues.*

Sources of hope, meaning, comfort, strength, peace, love and connection are assumed to constitute the person's core spiritual resources. Questions about organised religion and personal spirituality and practices – if indicated from the initial discussion – are designed to elicit the extent to which, and in what way, these are helpful, may be hindering problem solution, or in some cases may be destructive of the person's well-being. 'Normalising' statements such as '*For some people, their religious or spiritual beliefs act as a source of comfort and strength in dealing with life's ups and downs. Is this true for you?*' are suggested as non-threatening ways of introducing these topics (Anandarajah and Hight, 2001, p. 86). The final set of questions focuses on the effects and implications for care, of the person's spiritual beliefs and practices. In social work contexts, the specific application of this would depend on the setting and user group. For example, care planning choices for an older person requiring high levels of support should facilitate practices which are desirable for the service user, such as private prayer and church attendance, and avoid environments dominated by activities which may cause offence, such as card-playing and bingo. For someone going through a divorce who believes strongly in the sanctity of marriage, the counsellor may need to recognise that the spiritual crisis instigated by the divorce is of greater or equal severity to the emotional effects of the relationship break-up and should be afforded primary focus. For the young person with a fundamentalist religious background who has been convicted of a criminal offence, punishment (combined with seeking God's forgiveness) may be desired, where participation in a cognitive behavioural therapy group, designed to explore their offending behaviour, may be resisted.

Ruth Stoll's work has been pioneering in the development of spiritual assessment tools. Stoll developed a template using questioning focused on four areas:

1. concept of God or Deity;
2. sources of hope and strength;
3. religious practices;
4. relationship between spiritual needs and health (Stoll, 1979).

Stoll advocated routinely undertaking a full spiritual assessment in any contact with the service user. In this respect her work does not entirely fit with the generic approach described here. The issue is whether the approach of comprehensive questioning concerning religious and spiritual issues, used routinely, is appropriate. Mohr (2006) suggests that it is not appropriate for nurses to take a spiritual history with every patient, but advocates asking seriously ill patients whether faith is important to them now or has been in the past, and whether they have someone to talk to about religious matters or would like someone with whom to explore religious matters. The assumption here is that facing one's own death (and presumably this approach might reasonably be extended to close relatives facing bereavement) is a situation of existential challenge (Thompson, 2007a) which justifies opening up the topic of spiritual need or pain. Perhaps more in line with social work's ethos, however, is whether the practitioner should only do so if led by the service user in response to general questioning. Although this may appear to better fit the ethos of contemporary practice, it is worth noting that contemporary social work practice has gone down the line of routine comprehensive assessment of need when the intervention required is either continuing and/or multi-agency. 'Comprehensive' assessment has not, however, generally encompassed spiritual need.

Measuring spirituality

The approach taken here is to measure or rate the spiritual and/or religious traits (sometimes termed 'religiosity') which the individual exhibits. It is strongly influenced by the psychology of religion and psychometric testing and has led to the development of a number of spirituality scales and assessment schemas; although most of these are quantitative measures, qualitative tools also exist. Among the professional disciplines, nursing has been foremost in both developing these and evaluating their utility in practice. Social work, by contrast, is ambivalent about the use of quantitative approaches. For example, Nocon and Qureshi (1996) argued that the UK government and service managers favoured quantitative measures and performance indicators when evaluating the implementation of the 1990s community care changes, whereas front-line social workers and service users valued qualitative information. However, social work in the US has been much more inclined towards quantitative measures and assessment scales. McSherry and Ross (2002) provide a review of a range of spiritual assessment tools utilised in health services which they categorise as *Direct Questioning*, *Indicator-Based*, *Audit* and *Value Clarification*. Audit tools appear to be concerned more with identifying the extent to which spiritual care is provided within health-care agencies, and will not be discussed here. The other three approaches, however, all offer tools for undertaking some form of spiritual assessment with the individual. The two categories which most specifically seek in some way to quantify the service user's spirituality and spiritual need are 'indicator-based' and 'value clarification'.

Indicator-based models are designed specifically to focus on spiritual *need*, including deep spiritual *distress*. McSherry and Ross suggest that there is a degree of overlap and possible confusion between psycho-social and spiritual indicators. The approach is similar in its starting point to the generic approach which acknowledges the significance and impact of spirituality in the life of the service user. However, it differs significantly in terms of assessment practice, in that it attempts to quantify the *degree* of need or distress rather than explore its nature or source. Moreover, all questions in the scale will be addressed, rather than the assessment being led by the areas which the service user raises as part of a generic assessment.

Value clarification tools, likewise, attempt to quantify the spiritual state of the individual, commonly through the use of Likert scales in which the respondent identifies the degree to which they agree or disagree with a particular statement, or 'item'. McSherry and Ross cite the Ellison Spiritual Well-being Scale (ESWS) (Ellison, 1983) as one established tool which refines the use of a Likert-based questionnaire to generate an overall well-being 'score'.

One of the problems of questionnaire-based assessment scales is that they have more obvious applicability as research tools than in direct practice with service users. Narayanasamy (1999) has developed a framework which he suggests can be used by the nurse to identify when there is a priority need for spiritual care in a given situation. The Actioning Spirituality and Spiritual care in Education and Training (ASSET) model offers a 'spiritual assessment guide' with suggested questions to assess the following needs:

- meaning and purpose
- sources of strength and hope
- love and relatedness
- self-esteem
- fear and anxiety
- anger
- relationship between spiritual beliefs and health.

Since Narayanasamy advocates a problem-based approach to nursing care, he is by definition focusing on unmet or problematic needs rather than an overview assessment of spiritual well-being. However, it is questionable whether the assumption of total overlap between psycho-social and spiritual need contained within his framework should be made. While some of the broader definitions of spirituality looked at in chapters 1 and 2 would be perfectly comfortable with this, others (and we include ourselves in this) would argue that assessment of spiritual need must indicate something more than that which a standard psycho-social assessment would encompass (Holloway, 2007a). In a review of the nursing literature on spiritual assessment and spiritual care, Ledger (2005) gives more detailed attention both to specifically religious needs and to the dimensions of 'reverence' and 'awe' and beliefs about the universe, including its 'sustaining power', the 'source of life' and its 'higher purpose'. She quotes Burkhardt's (1989) assessment tool, which, while taking similar starting points concerning meaning and purpose in life as do those tools which tend to conflate psycho-social with spiritual need, goes on to distinguish between responses which point to a spiritual or religious dimension and those which do not. A similar approach is taken by researchers at Brown University in the US, who list what they term 'Spiritual Identifiers':

- Is there purpose to the person's life?
- Are they able to transcend their suffering?
- Are they at peace?
- Are they hopeful or do they despair?
- What nourishes their sense of self-worth?
- Do their beliefs help them cope?

It is the *way* in which the person approaches these issues that determines the significance or not of spirituality in their life. If spirituality *is* indicated, the specific answers will indicate whether or not they might benefit from a fuller spiritual assessment (www.chcr.brown.edu/pcoc/spirit.htm).

In summary, 'measurement' approaches assess spirituality using a list of items or indicators, sometimes generating a 'score'. An interesting qualitative study which sought to test indicators of spiritual integrity and spiritual distress through hospital patients' self-narratives found that the long list of items could be boiled down to one significant expression in each case (Narayanasamy, 2004). Spiritual distress appeared, at core, to be indicated by people complaining that they are no longer 'themselves' and therefore 'at a loss' to understand their situation or know how to proceed – which echoes the existentialist definitions we discussed earlier. Spiritual integrity, on the other hand, was indicated by people sufficiently sure, and comfortable with, who they are, to be able to help others.

Example 1 – Spiritual distress

Melinda was a lone parent whose only child, Emily, had died on the operating table whilst undergoing an appendectomy. Initially she was obsessed with wanting answers about the medical complications, but gradually her search assumed a more existential character. She desperately wanted to 'know' what had happened to her daughter after death, but angrily dismissed the approaches from the hospital chaplain and began attending séances which she felt offered more certain promises. Nothing, however, seemed to relieve her deep pain, which she expressed simply and directly in its totality: 'I'm hurting because I've lost my child'. Although offered support from a range of professionals, including the hospital social worker, she indicated that her deepest needs were avoided by others: 'There's very few shared my pain, very few' (quoted in Lloyd, 1995, p. 23).

Example 2 – Spiritual integrity

Maureen was widowed in her early thirties and brought up her six children alone, without much money and with very little family support as her own mother was in poor health. Yet Maureen was known in her local community as someone you could always go to if you needed help, or simply cheering up. Maureen's attitude to the difficulties that she has faced in her own life is that, 'bad things happen to make way for the good', and she sums up her philosophy of life as, 'It's our faith to survive anything. Whether it be in God or whoever, you've got to have faith.... I appreciate life no matter how low the quality... and if you can be happy, that's what life is all about' (quoted in Lloyd, 1996, p. 305).

Exploring spiritual narrative

This next approach uses self-narrative as the assessment tool. The work of US scholars is in the forefront of developing spirituality assessment models specific to social work which take a biographical approach. David Hodge provides a review of a number of qualitative assessment approaches, which have tended to be favoured by social work in its engagement with spirituality. Hodge argues that qualitative approaches are better suited to assessing spirituality than quantitative because they are 'holistic, open-ended, individualistic, ideographic and process oriented' (Hodge, 2001, p. 204). All have in common the assumption of some kind of spiritual development over the life-course, but are presented as a continuum with increasing levels of theoretical construction. At one end Hodge locates approaches which take a spiritual history in such a way as to elicit the service user's own spiritual narrative, that is, using open-ended questions which invite the service user to tell their own story. At the other end of the continuum, Hodge places approaches which he describes as 'stage theories', that is, they interpret the service user's story according to a sequence of predetermined and universally applied stages of spiritual development.

A qualitative research study conducted with 23 African American women provides an interesting example of how individuals construct and use their personal spiritual narratives. The interview participants, randomly sampled from a large survey study which looked at how African American women cope with adversity, were asked how, if at all, religion and spirituality helped. Seventy per cent identified religion and spirituality as forces which helped them confront and deal with reality, and they described a range of ways on which they drew on this resource (Mattis, 2002). Although this is only one study, the implications for social work, which continues to struggle with explanations of both problem and response which fall outside of its secular parameters, are clear. In the context of managing tough lives, their spirituality was key for these women. Thompson, in his discussion of loss as existential challenge, asserts that existentialism is essentially a philosophy of realism, that is, it provides a framework for understanding and dealing with life as it is (Thompson, 2007).

Spiritual histories may encompass formal religious traditions and key public events within these, such as baptism or bar mitzvah, as well as private 'events' and experiences such as conversion or 'peak' experiences of heightened spiritual awareness. At the least structured end of the continuum, however, it is left to the narrator to select those parts of the story which they choose to tell. Other forms of spiritual history-taking routinely ask for certain types of information – for example, family religious background, current religious position, including diversion from background or tradition, level of present involvement in spiritual practices, crises of faith and importance of faith or spirituality to everyday life including when facing difficulties. In such examples, the questions may be increasingly orientated towards a therapeutic purpose, such as pointing the individual towards their sources of strength and support, or they may organise the information gathering in such a way as to cause the individual to reflect on their own spiritual development and the meaning of spirituality in their life. Spiritual histories may use particular tools such as spiritual genograms and spiritual life-maps (Hodge, 2005a and 2005b), in which pictorial and diagrammatic representations are made of significant relationships and events in the individual's spiritual journey. This is an approach familiar to social work from biographical assessment, life-course work and family therapy, but applied to the spiritual domain. In fact, Tanyi, a Californian family nurse practitioner, points out that a major deficit in most spiritual assessment models (Hodge's work, 2000, is an exception) is that they are designed to be used only with individuals, where research shows that a family's spirituality and religious life may be important sources of strength and resilience and promote family cohesion when the system is under stress (Tanyi, 2006). Tanyi interprets spirituality as expressed 'vertically' via an individual's relationship with God or a Higher Power, and 'horizontally' via their relationships with others and the self. She suggests the use of genograms and ecomaps to discern a family's spiritual orientation and understand the significance of spirituality in its functioning. Although Tanyi's discussion is couched in positive terms, this model also has the potential to illuminate dysfunction, unmet need and spiritual pain arising from family conflict.

The stage models which Hodge evaluates are largely based on Fowler's notion that faith development progresses through seven stages linked to development of selfhood, such that mature faith belongs to the mature self. Fowler traces this development through the stages of human growth and development, from childhood to adulthood. However, the interesting thing in the light of our contemporary expressions of spirituality, which Fowler recognises in his later work (Fowler, 1987), is that faith development is not necessarily 'in synch' with other aspects of psychological and social development. For the purposes of this account we have unhitched Fowler's stages from chronological age. Fowler suggests that faith begins in infancy, in what he terms the 'pre-stage' of 'undifferentiated faith'. In the baby,

> the seeds of trust, courage, hope and love are fused in an undifferentiated way and contend with sensed threats of abandonment, inconsistencies and deprivations in an infant's environment...the quality of mutuality and the strength of trust,

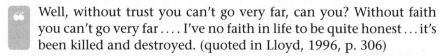

autonomy, hope and courage (or their opposites) developed in this phase underlie (or threaten to undermine) all that comes later in faith development. (Fowler, 1981, p. 121)

Compare this with one woman's characterisation of 'faith' in a research study conducted by one of us. This woman appeared to the author to be seriously disturbed by her profound and cumulative experiences of loss and abuse:

> Well, without trust you can't go very far, can you? Without faith you can't go very far.... I've no faith in life to be quite honest...it's been killed and destroyed. (quoted in Lloyd, 1996, p. 306)

Fowler represents Stage 1 of faith 'proper', as *Intuitive Projective Faith*. The individual's faith in this stage is influenced by that of those around them, and intuitive perception and imagination may take precedence over logical thinking. Fowler suggests that powerful images and feelings – positive or negative – may be acquired at this stage which at a later stage the individual may reflect upon and have to 'sort out' (p. 133). This process may begin in Stage 2 – *Mythic-Literal Faith* – in which deductive reasoning comes to the fore and the individual takes on the 'stories, beliefs and observances' of their particular faith community or orientation, with quite literal meanings attached. This is a 'more linear, narrative construction of coherence and meaning' (p. 149). However, there is little or no critical reflection on their faith. At this point it is worth noting, as indeed does Fowler, that internal contradictions may be what moves the individual on in their faith journey. Such a process is not without disquiet and may lead to the deep levels of spiritual need and spiritual pain which we looked at earlier in this chapter.

Fowler's Stage 3 – *Synthetic-Conventional Faith* – is where the individual's faith provides the basis for their wider cultural identity. It is a highly conformist stage in which the need to belong is a powerful reason for accepting rules imposed by religious leaders and patterns of behaviour prescribed by the religious community. Fowler does not distinguish this from the holding of personal belief, but it seems to us that there are strong parallels with Holloway's 'religion without religion' referred to in Chapter 2. What Fowler does point out, however, is how disturbing it may be to such faith adherents when the authorities argue among themselves, or some significant cultural shift takes place (such as the ordaining of gay clergy or the entering into peace talks in a religious conflict zone). Former regular church-goers or zealous followers may give up their religious faith and practices with all the attendant implications for their sense of self which this change in lifestyle and self-identification brings. If, however, the person survives such storms with some degree of 'faith', however defined, their journey is likely to take them into territory where they must work out for themselves the implications of a particular faith position and take responsibility for the struggles with dilemma and contradiction which are inevitably part of it. Fowler calls this *Individuative-Reflective Faith*, with the individual personally having to negotiate their inner and outer worlds. Throughout this book we talk quite a lot about the individual's 'world-view'. Fowler's model suggests that to arrive at such a philosophical stance, a considerable amount of faith journeying must have taken place.

However, in case we should think that we have *really* arrived, Fowler identifies two further stages which represent significant leaps onto higher but also more challenging planes. Stage 5, which he calls *Conjunctive Faith*, he describes as essentially concerned with ways of knowing (dialectical or dialogical) which sees relatedness rather than polarities. This is indeed a significant step to take, in terms of both our personal position and our perceptions as workers. It compels us to engage in dialogue with other positions and to grapple with complexity, seeing many sides of the issue simultaneously. It reaches behind the symbol to the deep understanding which it represents. It means that we can 'embrace paradox' (Lloyd, 1995) rather than always seeking to resolve it. It allows us to enter the darkness with the other person, knowing that without it, the liberating potential of light may never be experienced. But Fowler cautions, '(this stage) lives and acts between an untransformed world and a transforming vision' (p. 198). His sixth and final stage – *Universalizing Faith* – he terms a call to radical actualisation. Few people reach this stage, according to Fowler. They are those who have overcome the divisions and paradoxes by actualising universal and unconditional love and justice. Such persons 'have a special grace that makes them seem more lucid, more simple and yet somehow more fully human than the rest of us' (p. 201) at the same time having a selfless disregard for their own preservation and an unerring knack of disturbing complacency and limited vision in those around them.

It is important to remember that Fowler accepts that not everyone progresses through all stages, nor is this necessarily the goal; indeed, Fowler argues that faith communities need people at all stages of faith development. Moreover, sometimes it is necessary to return to earlier instinctive certainty, in order to nurture the soul battered by the horrors and contradictions which life can throw at us. It is important to remember this for ourselves as much as for the people we seek to get alongside. The purpose of the therapeutic spiritual assessment models, on the other hand, appears to be to determine the stage at which an individual is at, in order that they may be assisted to move towards the next stage, the implication being that not to do so is at best an impoverishment and at worst problematic.

An alternative reading of Fowler would suggest that each individual has faith or spiritual resources, regardless of their 'stage' of development. The objective of the therapeutic encounter is therefore to 'get in step with' the person in need, in order to help them to work out their own faith or spiritual resources (Lloyd, 1995). There is a long tradition in social work of 'starting where the client is' (Perlman, 1957). A biographical approach to spirituality assessment at its core seeks to enable the service user to get in touch with and develop their own spiritual resources through reflection on their personal journey.

Some of the most in-depth work on spirituality practice in social work has come from Edward Canda, who, with his colleague Leola Furman, characterises the spiritual dimension as being 'the heart of helping' (Canda and Furman, 1999). This approach takes as its starting point the essential wholeness and integrity of human beings, arrived at through a striving towards meaning and achieving of a sense of integration and integrity between different aspects of themselves. Thus Canda and Furman's model for spiritual assessment is through understanding spiritual development. The distinguishing feature of their developmental approach, however, is that they regard 'human' and 'spiritual' development as one and the same thing, the individual's spirituality 'emerging' over the life course:

> Spiritual development is not one aspect of life. Rather, spiritual development *is* everyday life. (Canda and Furman, 1999, p. 217)

From this prior assumption, therefore, Canda and Furman devote the majority of their text to refining understanding of diverse expressions of spiritual life and intervention 'techniques' which respect and work with these varying forms of spirituality. Their assessment model is a simple matrix for determining 'spiritual propensity', categorising an individual's spirituality as 'religious' or 'non-religious' and simultaneously 'extrinsic' and 'intrinsic'.

For Canda and Furman, the practice of the spiritually sensitive social worker is therefore 'transformative' and 'all forms and types of social work activities can be consistent with spiritually sensitive practice when they are conducted within a framework of spiritually sensitive values and contexts for helping' (p. 282). The only problem with this inclusive approach is when either the social worker or the service user rejects its definitional frame, arguing that they do engage with this dimension of human existence but would not see this as 'spiritual'. Some social workers who hold to a rationalist philosophy would insist that holistic practice is simply 'best practice' in line with social work's core values and principles (Holloway, 2007a).

The domain approach

A fourth approach is to understand the individual's life as a set of 'domains' – for example, physical, emotional, family and community.

This approach is familiar to social work in quality of life assessment (e.g. Oliver et al., 1997). Spirituality may be identified and explored as a separate domain, which may then be sub-divided into specific areas. Alternatively, spirituality may not be a domain in itself, but its impact within each domain considered as part of the assessment of needs and strengths. A good example of the domain approach is the Moral Authority, Vocational, Aesthetic, Social and Transcendent (Mor-VAST) model (Skalla and McCoy, 2006). The person's spirituality is mapped onto these five dimensions and the degree to which each is a strength or a need is assessed.

The *Moral Authority* dimension is concerned with moral duty but also with the right to make one's own decisions, which the authors argue is in itself a spiritual need. It is within this dimension, having established a sense of the right thing to do, that the individual must also gain permission to act on their moral instinct. Thus the Moral Authority dimension is concerned with the management of contradictory feelings such as guilt, remorse and resentment on the one hand, and forgiveness, compassion and self-righteousness on the other, which stem from the individual's overall moral sense of duty and obligation. The person who can negotiate this terrain has strengths in this area; others may exhibit considerable need and sometimes deep spiritual distress.

The *Vocational* dimension is concerned with sense of purpose. As such it is linked to moral duty and obligation in terms of the role(s) ascribed to or prescribed for oneself. Since it is one's place in life that is so frequently threatened or disrupted by problems such as illness, social or psychological trauma, social and interpersonal conflict, this dimension is particularly vulnerable to crisis, which to the authors is spiritual in that it occurs within the essence of the person. Equally, the person who retains an overall sense of purpose in life amid trouble, and the ability to continue to fulfil their fundamental obligations despite difficulties, displays considerable strength in the Vocational dimension.

The *Aesthetic* dimension encompasses the perception and expression of beauty and creativity. It is the dimension most commonly employed in nourishing the spirit and thus any diminishing of its resources or capacity to access such sources of spirituality may result in significant spiritual impoverishment and need. The lives of many users of social work services are characterised by poor physical surroundings, few social and community resources, material poverty and experiences of loss, abuse and other trauma. We might reasonably assume that significant spiritual impoverishment results. The strong adherence to their religious faith and practices which is seen, for example, among some immigrant and migrant communities may be their main source of spiritual replenishment. The desire to reconnect with nature through gardening and farm labouring, sometimes expressed by migrants from rural communities newly settled in American and European cities, may be another indication of this area of need.

The *Social* dimension is particularly relevant for social work since it deals with 'relatedness', in terms of family, friends and other significant social connections. Mental health problems, bereavement, the physical limitations of old age, drug and alcohol addictions, incarceration and removal to residential institutional care all threaten and disrupt social relations. Much of the business of social work is concerned with working to restore the social dimension for people experiencing problems of isolation, loneliness and alienation as a result. Skalla and McCoy (2006) emphasise that it is in social relations that the potential to experience 'unconditional acceptance, belonging, and connections to self, others, and the divine' (p. 749) occurs; literally translated from the Greek word *parea*, this dimension is experienced through 'the people who sit at your table and enrich your life' (p. 749). These social interactions may take place through rituals and practices, such as family gatherings, social clubs and, of course, organised religion.

The final dimension, the *Transcendent*, is the only overtly spiritual in this framework. It has to do with those experiences not directly accessible to the material senses and incorporates experiences of awe, awareness of the sacred and holy, and is common to both theistic and non-theistic religions. It involves the capacity to move outside of oneself and perceive something larger than oneself. The proponents of the Mor-VAST model link this to deep emotions, both positive and negative, such as trust, hope, peace, but also anger and despair.

The extent to which the Mor-VAST framework identifies needs and resources which are distinctly spiritual might be debatable and to some extent dependent upon one's philosophical assumptions. However, the areas which it covers are immediately recognisable to social work and yet often not engaged with via our standard assessment tools, at least not on the level envisaged here. An exception is Hodge's 'integrated framework' for spiritual assessment in social work practice (Hodge, 2001). Hodge proposes a framework which makes use of both self-narrative (albeit a guided narrative) and an interpretive framework exploring six psycho-social-moral domains: *affect, behaviour, cognition, communion, conscience* and *intuition*. The interpretative framework is intended to be used to flesh out the narrative and elicit spiritual strengths derived from the individual's world-view (inner and outer). This is in order to enhance existing coping strategies, but also replace counter-productive beliefs and behaviours driven by those beliefs, with productive ones. So (presumably) a person who believes their illness is a punishment from God might be encouraged instead to reflect on what their spiritual tradition has to say about suffering and its potential to deepen their understanding and spiritual life, while drawing on the resources of the tradition to sustain them.

stop and think

- Do any of these approaches fit comfortably with the assessments that you undertake routinely in your work?
- Do you address potential spiritual need at the moment?

Example – An alternative story

Leroy's foster parents agree with the social worker that he is more difficult to handle than Robbie, describing him as an 'angry little boy'. However, they point out that he likes to look at a family photo which the boys brought with them from home and asks about his mum, whereas Robbie doesn't seem to have any memory of her. The assessment undertaken on Leroy at this point identifies possible unmet religious and cultural needs. The children used to go to Sunday School in the Pentecostal Church that Sharon and occasionally their father, also attend, and the foster parents start to take Leroy to the Family Service at the Methodist chapel down the road. Leroy enjoys this for a few years but as he gets older he starts to object to going, complaining that he doesn't get on with 'all them white kids'. Over the next few years Leroy becomes progressively more challenging of his foster parents and their life-style, and once at High School he gets into a pattern of offending behaviour and glue-sniffing. Gradually the placement breaks down and Leroy becomes progressively more disaffected and acquires the reputation for being hard to place. By the time Leroy meets John, the student social worker, he appears to have no close relationships although he occasionally sees a couple of black lads who were in care with him at one point. All the social workers on the Leaving Care Unit find him hard to engage. John is the first black social worker Leroy has ever met, and he is curious about him – his family, interests and why he wants to be a social worker. He discovers that John likes Reggae music and spends quite a bit of his weekends in the company of friends from the Church he attends. John looks through the assessments on

Leroy's case file and thinks they are a bit one-dimensional, latterly almost entirely focused on his problematic behaviour. He decides to look with Leroy at the different domains in his life, to find out what things are important to him, what sort of life he wants to make for himself when he leaves care, rather than just focusing on the practical aspects of setting him up in his flat. Leroy says that more than anything else he wants to 'belong', and sometime to have his own family. He says that's the thing he remembers from Sunday School, that God is his Father – he likes that idea. He asks John whether he thinks Jesus was really black. Gradually, between them, John and Leroy construct a narrative which acknowledges Leroy's deep sense of rejection and hurt and unmet relationship needs, but which allows Leroy to reframe his story in a wider context of people who have cared about him, of his continuing cultural tradition and identity and of his own unique potential. Leroy asks John why he goes to Church and casually suggests that he might see if he can find any friends in the Church near his new flat, mentioning that he saw a group of black guys outside the last time they drove past.

Debates and dilemmas for social work

This chapter is deliberately titled spiritual 'need' rather than spiritual 'assessment'. For social work, there is a prior question before deciding on a model for spiritual assessment. That is *whether or not it is for social work to assess spiritual need*, even if we accept that it exists and is relevant to our interaction with the service user. The argument developing in this book is that all social workers should, at the very least, develop their personal 'spiritual awareness' so that they are sensitive to spiritual and religious need in the life of the service user. Research to date suggests that for the majority of social workers in the developed world (outside of the US), there needs to be considerable development of their 'spiritual literacy' if they are to reach even this first stage of awareness in their practice (e.g. Nash, 2002; Gilligan, 2003; Holloway, 2007a).

Should the 'spiritually aware' social worker take this any further, however? A useful illustration from another secular discipline, clinical psychology, is provided by Hathaway's description of his practice in a military mental health clinic. In one case, in which an African American woman presented with a depressive disorder arising from 'empty nest' syndrome, he reassured the client that it was appropriate for her to discuss spiritual issues that related to her depression, but at the same time clarified that he would be offering psychological not pastoral counselling. In another, in which the client perceived her problems of lack of social integration and marginalisation to arise from her pursuing of the Wiccan religion, he undertook a more detailed assessment of spiritual and religious functioning because this was central to her problems. In both cases, however, it was important that the significance of religion and spirituality for the service user was recognised and explicitly acknowledged.

Some social workers might feel uncomfortable if they do not share the spiritual or religious stand-point of the service user. Moore argues that

> In every case, the worker should be prepared to step back and examine the possibility of including spiritual resources from only one viewpoint – that of the client…. In every case, the worker should be prepared to validate the client's experience and to be supportive as the clients work things through for themselves. (Moore, 2003, p. 559)

This is perhaps too glibly stated. There are many situations in which social workers do not share the values of the service user and some in which we are bound to challenge their assertions and actions arising from, for example, prejudice. Why should religion and spiritual beliefs be exempt from this sort of challenge? Loewenberg (1998) provides a number of examples of problems arising from clash of values between the social worker and service user. For the moment we are focusing on the impact of this on assessment. First, it is clear that to make an accurate assessment the social worker must be able to disentangle those religious and spiritual practices which sit comfortably within a frame of reference shared by others, from those behaviours which are problematic. This requires both knowledge and sensitivity to the belief structure and content of the other person, even if, from the social worker's own point of view, it is perhaps bizarre behaviour. Second, the social worker must be prepared to utilise or facilitate religious ritual if it serves as a resource for the service user. Most especially, the social worker, whatever his or her personal views, should not undermine the faith of the other person. Loewenberg suggests that one way of ascertaining whether beliefs do in fact belong to a coherent and supportive faith, or are exacerbating or are part of the problem or disturbance, is to ascertain whether they are shared by others and whether or not other members of the group are in similar distress. Spiritual and religious experience is not always positive (Moore, 2003; Holloway, 2007b), and an accurate understanding of the problems and pain generated by the service user's spiritual experiences may lie at the heart of both accurate social work assessment and the potential for therapeutic intervention.

Satterly (2001) suggests that 'religious pain' is always connected to guilt and fear arising from the patient's religion (even, perhaps especially, when a lapsed believer). Satterly argues that since forgiveness and absolution may be found within the religious belief system, healing for religious pain may be easier to find than for more individualised spiritual pain. However, drawing on her 1991 study (Lloyd, 1996), Holloway suggests that internalised models of 'God' or an external force which represent a *punishing, unforgiving, disappointed* or *manipulative and controlling* being are highly problematic and damaging. Many of the intractable inter- and intra-personal problems which are so frequently embedded in the family problems with which social work deals have guilt at their centre. When this is linked to negative religious influences, the problem may be very resistant to resolution and the need for appropriate skilled help is indicated.

It is the relationship between these negative religious influences and mental health problems which continues to muddy the waters between religion and psychiatry. It is also the source of continuing tension for a mental health service users' movement which is increasingly calling for recognition of their spirituality as part of who they are, and a source of strength and healing, rather than part of their mental health problem (Coyte et al., 2007). As a feminist, Pirani (1988) is particularly concerned with the damage inflicted on women by 'spiritual politics' (illustrating her analysis by reference to the historical treatment of witches as a problematising and demonising of women's inherent spirituality) and affirms the healing and redemptive power to be found within women themselves at individual and group levels. Hathaway, a clinical psychologist, points out that 'not all religiousness present during psychosis is unhealthy', but, equally, 'some non-psychotic spirituality may appear quite bizarre to others' (Hathaway, 2006, p. 254).

We shall return to these complex areas when we look at spiritual care in Chapter 5.

Conclusion

This chapter has explored spiritual need and spiritual pain and their significance for social work practice. Perhaps because social work is in the main a problem-focused activity and social work assessment is designed to understand those problems or needs in all their dimensions, we have leaned towards the 'darker' side of spirituality. We should not forget, however, that one compelling reason for the social worker to include some consideration of spirituality in their assessment is that the service user's spiritual resources may be a major source of strength and resilience for that person. Social work is increasingly recognising the value of identifying and working from strengths rather than its habitual tendency to focus on problems and deficits, and to ignore the spiritual dimension may be to deny a significant sustaining and problem-solving resource. Our next chapter focuses on a topic frequently on the lips of social workers – quality of life – and looks at spirituality as a vital component in both assessment and experience. We have looked at a number of approaches to spiritual assessment and we will take further these discussions when we look at spiritual care in Chapter 5. Assessment and intervention are not the distinct processes which they sometimes appear, albeit they involve different tasks. A sensitively undertaken holistic assessment is itself a therapeutic process in which the spirituality of the worker is as important as that of the service user. We shall return to the question of the worker's own spirituality in Chapter 7.

taking it further

- Hodge, D. (2001) 'Spiritual assessment: A review of major qualitative methods and a new framework for assessing spirituality', *Social Work*, 49, 27–38.
- Kellehear, A. (2000) 'Spirituality and palliative Care: A model of needs', *Palliative Medicine*, 14, 149–155.
- King-Spooner, S. and Newnes, C. (eds) (2001) *Spirituality and Psychotherapy* (Ross-on-Wye: PCCS Books).
- Moore, R. (2003) 'Spiritual assessment', *Social Work*, 48: 4, 558–561.
- Ross, L. (1997) 'Elderly patients' perceptions of their spiritual needs and care: A pilot study', *Journal of Advanced Nursing*, 26, 710–715.

4 Spirituality and the quality of life

Introduction

Our discussion of the 'darkness' has necessarily taken us into the back-waters of human despair, where the water flows sluggishly if at all, and where all manner of detritus gathers unchecked. We can become 'rudder-less', lose momentum and become caught up with the sometimes swirling eddies that take us nowhere but leave us even more bewildered and lack-ing in direction. We yearn for fresh streams of clear running water, which gurgle and laugh and exhilarate; and when we see others paddling pur-posefully by, we are consumed with jealousy, envy, regret and remorse. It takes us by surprise, therefore, when someone chooses to paddle their canoe into our murky space, and offers as a fellow traveller to help lead us out. Human existence is a complex tapestry of dark and light, battleship greys and multicoloured rainbows. Or if we wish to stay with our watery imagery, the river of life will have its fast and slow sections: moments when we glide along effortlessly and enjoy the view, and moments when we are plunged into the rapids, or find ourselves marooned and stuck on a sandbank. At times we may even capsize; our travelling companions may lose their nerve or their strength; or we may lose them overboard and have to continue to paddle on alone. And we never know what is round the next bend, and whether there really is an ocean beckoning us at the river's end, or a yawning chasm of empty nothingness.

To begin a chapter in this way with such graphic imagery may seem strange at first: it does not have a very academic 'feel' to it for a scholarly reflection on social work. And yet it raises for all of us the important ques-tion of how we begin to give voice to the deeper aspects of our living and loving, our struggling and our dying. One contemporary way of express-ing this is to talk about 'quality of life'. The imagery which we have used, however, is at odds with much of the contemporary language of social work, where 'quality markers' and 'performance indicators' imply that the service user's quality of life is something that can be objectively measured and determined by the quality of service provision. This approach to 'service quality' developed as a preoccupation with easily quantifiable outputs. In part this is because the emergence of 'quality talk' in social work has gone hand-in-hand with changes in service provision driven by an approach to 'quality assurance' borrowed from the world of business and commerce (Cassam and Gupta, 1992; James et al., 1992; Adams, 1998). There is a tendency to assume that *service quality* equates with individual *quality of life*, whereas the fundamental point made by service users is that quality services do not of themselves necessarily achieve quality of life for those service users (Priestly, 2000). In fact, Beresford et al. (2000) argue that service users' concerns about the quality of people's lives are fundamentally different in terms of 'objectives, philosophy, concerns, forms and process' (p. 193) from the service quality preoccupations of agencies. Priestly points out that services which empower people to improve their own quality of life may have intrinsic value, even if this cannot be demonstrated through a measurable quality outcome (Priestly, 2000).

As if this were not complicated enough, there is also the danger that caring professionals may regard 'quality of life' as something that we are the experts at assessing on other people's behalf, and that our assessments are paramount. All of this begs a number of key questions, particularly when we are considering the relationship between spirituality and quality of life and the significance afforded to spirituality in the perceptions of service providers:

- what do we mean by quality of life?
- who determines what it is?
- whose definitions have greatest influence?
- can there be 'quality' moments in the 'dark times'?

These are not obscurantist philosophical quibbles. The answers that we give to them pervade the day-to-day practice of medical, health and social care professionals, faith community leaders and the great army of carers upon whom daily so many people in need depend. Issues around euthanasia and abortion; around child protection and vulnerable adults; around care for people with dementia, and those (both young and old) who are approaching the end of their life; around those experiencing various forms of mental distress or physical incapacity: for everyone involved in such situations and many more, the issues concerning the quality of their life – and also, we would argue, their spirituality – are absolutely central.

The questions underlying these issues challenge each and every one of us as human beings. To a greater or lesser degree, we all can give some responses to the question about what sort of quality of life we do, or do not, enjoy. We can identify the themes that interweave in our answer, themes which may include our health; sense of meaning and purpose; our relationships; music; what sort of accommodation we have; the quality of our educational and employment opportunities; our chosen world-view and how that sustains us; and so on. Quality of life issues, although extremely relevant to the assessments we make with our servicer users, are first and foremost issues to do with our shared humanity. So before we begin to explore the notion of quality of life for service users, we need to recognise what this means for us. We are, after all, human beings first, and social workers second.

There is a danger in these discussions of talking about social work practice as if it were a uni-facetted phenomenon, and of service users as a homogenous group. Every practitioner knows that the opposite is the case. The social work task will vary according to the needs and circumstances of the people involved. Although the value-base and the adherence to the appropriate professional Code of Conduct remain constant, the style of work will vary enormously. How we work with people experiencing severe dementia; those seeking to adopt a baby; young people caught up in the criminal justice system; disabled people struggling with unfair disadvantage; families 'trying to make ends meet'; people in residential homes losing their hold on independence; and those in the grips of substance abuse are but a few of the many differing scenarios that social workers deal with day in and day out. It is crucial that we use our understanding of the differences between each of us – as both service users and social workers – to broaden and refine our definitions and approaches to quality of life. It is to some of these different perspectives that we now turn.

Perspectives on quality of life

Although it may appear that the notion of quality of life has only recently burst upon the scene, it has in effect been a 'leitmotif' throughout history. The actual phrase may not always have been used, but the realities to which it points have certainly featured in all major cultural, religious and philosophical discourses. What constitutes a good life, for example, was a theme running through the Platonic Dialogues with the Greek philosopher, Socrates; but it may also be seen as a key theme and question that has underpinned the writings of Marx, Compte, Durkheim, Feuerbach, Weber, J.S. Mill and many others (Beckford, 1989). They have all explored fundamental questions about the nature and purpose of human life, what it means to live together and how all of this sheds light on the idea of the quality of life, even if that exact phrase is not used.

Religion and quality of life

In religious contexts the Judeo-Christian tradition lays considerable emphasis upon the concept of 'shalom' or wholeness, whereby human fulfilment and 'life in all its fullness' find expression in a relationship with the Divine Being. Within these traditions God/Adonai is the One who creates, and who also offers a loving friendship with those who respond. This leads to a whole set of healed relationships that people then develop with each other, and to a commitment to care for the fragile planet that has been entrusted to them and to all humanity. In these religious traditions, as well as in Islam, the whole nature of what constitutes quality of life is framed within the relationship to the One called Adonai/God/Allah. Indeed, within these traditions, life is understood as being incomplete, fragmented even, if this relationship with the Divine Other is not fully acknowledged and responded to, both individually and collectively. Moreover, it is this relationship that makes us fully human as the Creator intended.

Human beings fall short, of course – the word 'sin' is often used to express this notion in both religious and secular contexts – but the acknowledgement of it, leading to a request for and an acceptance of forgiveness, enables people to move step by step towards a fuller and richer quality of life. That being said, within these traditions it is also openly recognised that the journey is far from easy, and that continuous progress is not guaranteed. Ultimately this goal of completeness will only be achieved in the 'afterlife' where the relationship with the Divine Other can be fully achieved.

There are important implications of this approach for our understanding of what constitutes quality of life. Many religious traditions uphold the service to and care for others as being a religious duty. It is an obligation that stems from the relationship they enjoy with the Creator, a relationship that has profound implications for how they view the world and their immediate and global neighbours. There is a sense that individual happiness and contentment cannot be understood in purely individualistic terms: deeper fulfilment comes when they align themselves with a greater and higher purpose that puts the welfare of others first, so that the quest for social justice (however it is conceptualised) becomes an important benchmark for measuring the quality of their lives.

Secularism and quality of life

This is not an approach that is restricted to the religious domain. The concept of 'life in all its fullness' begins to resonate with us whether or not we hold a religious world-view. There seems to be within each of us a deep longing and need for 'something more' that will lift us beyond the mundane humdrum ordinariness of everyday life to a higher plateau of experience, at least from time to time.

Within our social work practice we see this need and longing being expressed in a variety of ways. It helps to explain a lot of sexual behaviour as well as much of what we call the 'offending behaviour' of young people who crave the buzz and excitement of challenging authority; it underpins much of the 'drug culture' which offers a chemical journey to moments of ecstasy, or at least provides a temporary release from the monochrome dullness of living. It helps us understand the attraction and emotionally satisfying 'pull' of religious faith, or of giving oneself to serve a greater cause. It also reflects something of the satisfying urge that social workers and other helping professionals (and indeed volunteers) experience in their work when they feel they are making a difference to other people's lives, the sense of satisfaction they gain from working with people and seeing them begin to flourish and develop. Colleagues with a secular world-view are just as likely to attest to such experiences as those who espouse a religious faith.

Similar views may also find expression in the world of art, sport and theatre, where a sense of giving to others, or of helping others release and express their talents, produces a similar 'glow of satisfaction'. For all the negative press they often receive, many people in the political life of a nation, at local or national level, will still say that what gives them greatest satisfaction as politicians is a sense of being able to make a difference to help improve the lives of ordinary people, and at times to make a modest contribution through legislation to help safeguard the planet. In other words, their contribution to the quality of life of others (or the common good) is an important benchmark of their own personal and professional satisfaction.

Within the work place the importance of this sense of well-being and satisfaction is being increasingly recognised. In a seminal UK study, Holbeche and Springett (2004) found that 70 per cent of the employees in their survey reported that they wanted to find *more* meaning in their workplace. They suggest, in the words of John Seely Brown, that

> when it comes to attracting, keeping and making teams out of talented people, money alone won't do it. Talented people want to be part of something they can believe in, something that confers meaning on their work and their lives.

There are profound issues to do with the quality of life raised here. If people find their work unsatisfying, lacking in meaning and purpose, and if

> the very activity which people expect to bring fulfilment and a sense of meaning and purpose to their lives fails them so abysmally, is it any wonder that the lurch into hedonistic pastimes or numbing anomie becomes the hallmark of people's weekend? (Moss, 2004)

Our discussion thus far has suggested that for many people issues around the quality of their life are located in a range of intangible factors such as: caring for others; feeling that one's life has meaning and purpose; being involved in serving a greater cause with or without a religious dimension to it; and finding meaning and satisfaction in work. Stimulating and challenging though this approach may be in helping us see the social dimensions to the concept of quality of life, there are some important 'caveats'. The implications, for example, are apparent: if work is not satisfying, or simply not available; if our personal circumstances force us into a period of inactivity or introspective self-centredness through illness or a disabling condition; if the themes we suggested in the introduction to this chapter simply do not apply, then such social definitions or indicators of our quality of life are bound to feel excluding and inadequate. Such considerations force us back to the underlying questions posed by the quality of life debate, and to the challenges to social work practice that they represent. How do we assess quality of life for ourselves and for others, especially when some of the more obvious social opportunities for enriching our lives are denied us? Is there (in existential terms) an 'essence' within each of us that not only guarantees our uniqueness, our intrinsic value and our individuality, but also lifts us from merely existing to some enhanced level of quality of life, even if some of the more common indicators are absent? These are questions that are easier to pose than to answer, except to reaffirm social work's core value-base about the unique individuality of each and every person who deserves to be treated with dignity and respect. In that sense there is a quality of life that we can certainly reflect back to, and perhaps even *give* to, other people simply by how we treat them.

One classic example of this is taken from the days of apartheid in South Africa. Archbishop Desmond Tutu records in his autobiography that one day when he was very young he was walking with his mother through their black township and noticed a white priest coming towards them. This priest, Father Trevor Huddleston, passed them by, but as he did so he raised his hat to offer his respects to Desmond's mother. Tutu later reflected on this profound moment where he suddenly realised that by this simple action his mother had been given back the dignity and respect which the apartheid system had ripped from her. As his biographer notes,

> Desmond was overwhelmed; he simply couldn't believe it – a white man raising his hat to a simple, black labouring woman. (De Boulay, 1988, p. 26)

Another example, but from the same country, can be found in Nelson Mandela's refusal on his release from prison to pour vitriolic scorn and abuse upon his white oppressors who had stolen so many years from him by incarcerating him for his political beliefs. He demonstrated a value-base of dignity and respect, and a commitment to reconciliation that, even without words being spoken, bestowed a quality of life upon those with whom he was called to work for the greater good of his nation. So, too, in our social work practice we sometimes forget how powerful our actions can be, and how we can confirm and enhance the quality of life and essential dignity of those with whom we work simply by 'living out' our values. Not only is this acknowledgement of the value of each person at the heart of social work, it is also fundamental to recognising what it means to be human and to be in relationship to others.

Example

Toni was delighted at the age of 22 to find employment at last having been unemployed since leaving the care of the local authority. She had developed what her estranged parents called a 'chaotic lifestyle' since being given a local authority flat, and for a while she wandered through life aimlessly, used drugs and alcohol inappropriately and entered several unsuccessful relationships. One day she happened to bump into her former social worker who had worked with her in the care home. He seemed genuinely delighted to see her, asked how she was and asked if there was anything he could do to help and support her. When she sheepishly said she still didn't have a job he immediately told her he knew of some vacancies in a local supermarket and would give her a reference. When to her delight and amazement she got the job she wrote in her diary that the *one social worker who had believed in her and encouraged her had made all the difference.*

The two sides of quality

We have already explored in this book how moments of darkness and despair are just as potent in our quest for meaning and purpose as moments of joy and ecstasy in how we understand our quality of life, and how we make sense of what happens to us. Theologians and philosophers have struggled with what is often called the 'problem of evil' – but for many people there is just as much a struggle with the 'problem and phenomenon of good'. Somehow we need to make sense of both, in whatever chosen world-view we inhabit, with its 'explanatory paradigm of humanity'. For both are inextricably intertwined, as the popular poet Gibran (1980) puts it,

> Your joy is your sorrow unmasked.
> The self-same well from which your laughter rises was oftentimes filled with your tears.
> The deeper that sorrow carves into your being, the more joy you can contain.
> When you are sorrowful look again in your heart, and you shall see that in truth you are weeping for that which has been your delight. (p. 36)

All such moments belong to our spirituality, whether this has a religious or a secular framework. Indeed, as we argued in Chapter 2, our spirituality and the world-view it represents need to take into account both light and dark sides of what it means to be human (as well as all the grey areas in-between) if it is to be emotionally, let alone intellectually, satisfying.

This is an important point to make. There is perhaps a temptation to put false boundaries around the topic, and to assume that it is only the good, positive and cheerful aspects of living that are entitled to be considered under this theme; or that we only discuss this concept when things are going well. And yet the existence of 'evil' and what is sometimes referred to as the 'problem of suffering' are etched into the very fabric of what it means to be human. The parameters around our quality of life are as much determined by such issues as they are by the experience of joy, beauty, wonder and mystery. How we try to understand suffering is one of the great challenges to our humanity and to our idea of quality of life. Speaking from the depths of his concentration camp experience, Viktor Frankl claimed that 'Man [sic] is not destroyed by suffering. He is destroyed by suffering without meaning' (cited in Nolan, 2006). This is clearly an issue that each of us needs to grapple with, and to explore the extent to which it finds a place within the explanatory world-view upon which we have chosen to base our lives, be that religious or secular.

The suggestion, however, that suffering is somehow intrinsically good for us and character-building (Ming-Shium, 2006) needs to be handled with considerable sensitivity, especially from a religious perspective. That the Divine Being would consciously and deliberately inflict suffering upon an innocent, or even upon a not-so-innocent, individual or group of people raises profound moral as well as theological questions and objections. If however we are in the territory of unintended consequences whereby terrible things happen to people who then have to choose how to respond, then the discussion has a different 'feel' to it. We can rise to challenges, or 'go under'; we can refuse to become embittered, or become 'blame champions'; we can reach out to others sacrificially, or turn inwards into ourselves. Our response will determine the extent to which negative experiences, even great suffering, will strengthen our resilience and enrich our quality of life, or detract from it. From a faith perspective (depending of course upon which particular religious world-view we choose), the issue will then be the extent to which such situations enhance our responsiveness to the Divine Other, and the extent to which we feel we are working towards a better life for ourselves and for others (for a Buddhist reflection on this theme, see Thurman, 2005). This also reflects one of the benchmarks of an authentic spirituality that will be discussed further in Chapter 7. Whether from a religious or from a secular perspective, care for others, especially in times of crisis, suffering or great need, is one of the hallmarks of humanity and of spirituality, and therefore constitutes an important feature of our quality of life.

Example

Tom, aged 73, retired early from work 12 years ago after having the first of a series of strokes. He and his wife, Miriam, aged 69, have no children and have lived a fairly self-contained life as a couple, looking forward to their retirement when they had planned to settle in Spain. Tom is now quite disabled and his illness has put paid to those plans. Initially they made the best of things, hoping that rehabilitation therapies would enable Tom to recover his speech and the use of his arm. However, improvement has been minimal and gradually the stress started to show. Tom is embittered and angry, and takes it out on Miriam, and she, in turn, feels resentful of the limitations Tom's condition places on their lifestyle. Miriam is fit and active and does not find the physical care too much of a burden, but she craves other company and struggles to make sense of what has happened to them. It does not seem fair, as they were good people, perhaps a bit selfish she now concedes, but never did anyone any harm. Miriam does have one friend, Lilian, who calls in now and again. Lilian has rheumatoid arthritis and is sometimes unable to get out of the house, but she stays remarkably cheerful and always does Miriam good when she visits. Miriam cannot understand why Lilian is as she is. Her husband left her for another woman when her illness was first diagnosed and she struggles financially. Lilian admits that she has not always coped so well; she stopped going to church for 2 years when she was first divorced, but got back into it eventually because, as she strongly maintains, her faith makes her 'who she is'.

stop and think

- Is it appropriate for social workers to encourage service users to undertake some activity for the benefit of others in order to enhance their quality of life?

Happiness

In our discussion so far no specific mention has yet been made of one aspect of the quality of life which many would deem to be central, namely, happiness. It is indeed a core theme that runs through religious and secular traditions, and the question of what makes us happy can both exhilarate and haunt us. The search for happiness was recognised by the Greek philosopher Aristotle to be a core human activity, and ever since it has been a question that has dangled temptingly and appetisingly at the forefront of the human mind. Some would claim that it is achievable by direct means; others would argue that it is (and can only be) a by-product of other activity. In recent years a rigorous scientific approach has been brought to bear upon this apparently un-rigorous and somewhat illusive subject. Davidson (2001), for example, who has studied the link between prefrontal lobe activity and deep 'trance like' meditation, argues that happiness is a physical state of the brain that can be specifically and directly induced. By contrast, Csikszentmihalyi (1991) has conducted large-scale studies to show that happiness occurs when a person is completely engaged in a creative activity. All of this has led Wallis (2005) to talk about the 'new science of happiness'.

The scientific approaches to happiness have some important things to say to us, although the various approaches are not necessarily mutually exclusive. The work undertaken by Masters and Johnson (1996) and others about the nature of sexual pleasuring, for example, demonstrated some of the physiological aspects to arousal and full enjoyment; but everyone who has experienced such climactic moments will know that there can be much more to it in terms of what it means emotionally and spiritually to the people involved. Although these further dimensions do not invalidate the physiological phenomena that scientists investigate to help us understand how the body works, they do remind us that there are further dimensions to human experience – such as what certain actions *mean* to those involved – that lie outside scientific measurement. In a similar way, studies about the response of the brain to the enjoyment of music or beauty, or the challenge of living adventurously 'on the edge', do not diminish the human appreciation of these activities. They may help to explain them but they do not 'explain them away', any more than they dissipate moments of awe, mystery and wonder.

Further work being undertaken in this broad area includes exploring the potential link between happiness and religion that is being researched by a network of scholars and researchers in Manchester, UK, through the William Temple Foundation. The importance of Csikszentmihalyi's work, however, is its emphasis upon the 'ways in which people who are engaged in self-controlled, goal-related, meaningful actions may more easily attain happiness' (Paquette, 2006). This clearly makes helpful links with the discussion at the beginning of this chapter. If we are to give due weight to Csikszentmihalyi's work, then it would suggest that in social work practice there needs to be an appreciation of the positive emotional benefits of feeling that one is doing something worthwhile and contributing in some ways to the benefit and well-being of others, however difficult one's own immediate circumstances may appear to be.

Although this is not the place for an in-depth evaluation of various scientific approaches, it is perhaps worth pausing for a moment to reflect on the extent to which happiness features in everyday social work practice. This question could apply equally to social workers themselves and the extent to which they feel happy in their work, let alone whether they feel any happiness personally; the question can also equally apply to those with whom they work. To what extent does the presence of service users' happiness feature in the assessments made by social workers? Does it contribute to the ways in which work is undertaken with them? These are not unimportant questions, because the extent to which anyone does or does not feel happy will colour to a significant extent their outlook upon life and their attitude towards tasks in hand. Deeply unhappy people-workers are more likely to experience burn-out and therefore fail to deliver a high-quality, compassionate and dynamic service to others. Deeply unhappy service users are less likely to respond creatively to help and support, and will feel less able to draw upon their strengths and resilience. Happiness is not the only consideration, of course, but it is a significant quality of life issue that deeply impacts upon everyone, whether they are on the giving or receiving end of help.

Hope

One further dimension to this discussion which deserves brief attention is the theme of hope. The idea or concept of hope is a powerful component to our spirituality and world-view, whether or not we adopt a religious or secular approach. The election of Barack Obama as President of the USA was significant because it somehow symbolically both expressed and met the hopes of many ordinary Americans whose colour, race and background had previously been systematically marginalised. The full power of their hopes was only realised when a black-African President took the oath and entered the Oval Office. The fervour of their celebrations from election night onwards indicated the depth of their previous hurt and the height of their hope.

Within social work practice we often find the word 'hopeless' slipping unguardedly from our lips when describing a person or situation we are struggling to deal with. Sometimes we hear the people we work with using the same word to describe how they feel. Kelly (2004) offers a comment from a nursing perspective that can ring equally true in social work practice:

> Although hope has long been recognised as a significant factor in patient recovery and survival, the phenomenon receives little attention until the patient becomes hopeless. (p. 167)

The importance of hope – both at an individual and at a wider level – cannot be over-estimated. It is a crucial ingredient to our quality of life, whether we hold religious or secular beliefs. It shapes who we are and how we would like to be: it also defines to some extent the limitations we have imposed upon ourselves, or which society has drawn around us. The powerful nature of oppression and inequality, for example, fundamentally determines the quality of life for so many people, whether this is through the 'postcode lottery' within heath care, or the many ways in which discrimination and oppression undermine and restrict the life chances of various groups and individuals (Thompson, 2006, 2007b). Social work practice, with its mandate to challenge discrimination and oppression, is (or should be) an agent of hope; its commitment to social justice is a channel of hope to people who feel marginalised and without hope. This is an activity that both expresses our spirituality (Moss, 2005) and contributes significantly to people's quality of life and their hopes for a better future. We shall pick up this discussion again when we look at spiritual care in the next chapter.

Quality of life, health and well-being

Having emphasised these aspects, however, we need to move towards some more specific indicators of quality of life. The World Health Organisation (WHO) has undertaken a significant amount of work in this area particularly in the past two decades, developing a model and an instrument of measurement, The World Health Organisation Quality of Life Assessment (WHOQOL) (WHO, 1995, 1997, 1998). Six domains of quality of life are suggested:

1. physical health
2. psychological well-being
3. level of independence
4. social relationships
5. environment
6. spirituality/religion/personal beliefs

From a social work perspective, the first five of these domains will be extremely familiar, even if the full implications of environmental perspectives have not been fully explored, as we shall argue in chapters 7 and 8. These five themes have featured in core social work curricula for many years. In our comprehensive assessments, each of these features will be given due weight and consideration, whether or not we cluster them under a quality of life banner. We have also recognised that although it helps to separate out the various strains and domains in order to give them due emphasis and consideration, they actually interweave and interconnect in a complex relationship, where the influence of each aspect will vary from individual to individual.

As far as the sixth domain is concerned, however, the picture is somewhat different. Until relatively recently social workers have been reluctant to explore religious and spiritual aspects to an individual's life when completing their assessments or when working with individuals and their families. If they have not completely ignored this dimension, they have either adopted a 'tick box' approach without exploring how this domain really impacts upon a person's life and being, or they have pathologised it and regarded it as somehow being part of the problem. There has also been a genuine perplexity about how to respond appropriately and professionally to spiritual and religious issues, particularly if the social worker is finding this to be bewildering and challenging territory on a personal level.

It is helpful therefore to explore in more detail how the WHO approaches and tries to unpack these complex issues, themes and topics. Teichmann et al. (2006), for example, discuss the World Health Organisation's Quality of Life Assessment (WHOQOL-100) spirituality domain, using language that is very much in tune with the discussions in this book. They argue that 'spirituality is a broader concept that captures an individual's sense of peace, purpose and connection to others, as well as beliefs about the meaning of life.' They continue:

 We define spiritual needs as the need of the person to have a system of beliefs and values ... Spiritual needs, if satisfied, help a person to cope with difficulties in his or her life and provide more generally to the person a sense of well-being. For many people religion, personal beliefs and spirituality are a source of comfort, well-being, security, meaning, sense of belonging, purpose and strength (WHO, 1995). (Teichmann et al., 2006, p. 149)

This immediately resonates with a social work approach, and helps us understand how we might begin to grapple with these themes. The WHOQOL-100 suggests four questions that can help us begin to explore this domain:

1) [to what extent] do your personal beliefs give meaning to your life?
2) To what extent do you feel your life to be meaningful?
3) To what extent do your personal beliefs give you the strength to face difficulties?
4) To what extent do your personal beliefs help you to understand difficulties in life? (cited in Teichmann et al., p. 148).

These 'open' questions serve two important purposes. First of all, they help to demystify spirituality and its relationship to quality of life issues. You can almost hear a sigh of relief as practitioners realise that this is familiar territory after all, and not a set of some arcane mysteries into which they dare not trespass. Secondly, they provide some very accessible jargon-free 'tools', which fit well with the generic approach to the assessment of spiritual need which we identified in the previous chapter, as equally relevant to those who have a religious faith as to those who hold secular beliefs.

It is worth pausing at this point to recognise that other professions have been grappling with these issues, and have added to the list of useful open questions that facilitate discussion. One key example comes from the field of mental health, where Dr Andrew Powell helped to establish the UK Special Interest Group in Spirituality within the Royal College of Psychiatrists (Special Interest Group; Powell, 2003). Powell (2007) observes that

In mental health care treatment is largely pragmatic, based on the prevailing bio-psycho-social model of our times. It is a good working model yet spirituality, the highest function of the imaginal mind, has got left out. This is something of an irony since psyche means spirit or soul . . . so we need to develop a bio-psycho-socio-spiritual model of health care. (pp. 170–171)

In a DVD produced by Croydon Mind titled, 'Hard to Believe', Powell offers some further suggestions about ways in which these issues can be explored, if appropriate. These include,

■ What impact, if any, did religious beliefs have upon you when you were young?
■ How does your personal, spiritual or religious belief system affect your attitude towards treatment and taking medication?

- Do you believe in some kind of higher power that is controlling your life?
- Do you pray at all? If so, what does this mean to you?

Again, these are accessible questions that, with very little adaptation, could be used within social work practice to help explore a person's spirituality and this quality of life domain.

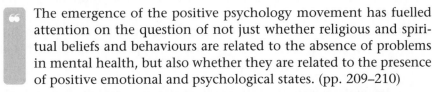

stop and think

- In what ways should social workers consider 'quality of life' issues in their assessments and intervention plans?

A strengths perspective and resilience

Two other recent developments deserve attention at this point: first, the contribution that positive psychology has made to the debate and, secondly, the evaluative studies that have been undertaken into the contribution that spirituality in general, and religion in particular, can make to health, well-being and the quality of life.

Positive psychology has begun to make a significant contribution to our understanding of quality of life issues. Watts et al. (2006), for example, argue that positive psychology is building a bridge between psychology and religion, and they draw attention to the work they are doing at Cambridge into the topics of forgiveness, hope and gratitude. Joseph et al. (2006) suggest that

> The emergence of the positive psychology movement has fuelled attention on the question of not just whether religious and spiritual beliefs and behaviours are related to the absence of problems in mental health, but also whether they are related to the presence of positive emotional and psychological states. (pp. 209–210)

The contribution of positive psychology is particularly relevant here for social work practice which is increasingly recognising the themes of resilience and a strengths perspective (Saleeby, 2008). One of the key contributors to this field of study is Martin Seligman (1990) whose contribution to our understanding of learned helplessness is well-known and appreciated within social work. This approach emphasised the contribution that settings and environments can have upon individual behaviour. In brief, if you place someone in a particular context (e.g. a residential home) where everything significant is done *for* them, then they quickly lose their capacity to cope, to look after themselves, to take the initiative and to be creative and independent. Ultimately it can undermine their zest for life and even life itself. His purpose in stressing the dangers of learned helplessness was not only to highlight its difficulties and dangers inherent in much residential care but also to emphasise the benefits of the opposite position. This has come to be known as positive psychology.

Seligman's position on positive psychology is captured well by Paquette who describes it as

> Cultivating personality strengths and honing an optimistic approach to life rather than cataloguing human frailty and disease. Seligman maintains that the way to find more happiness is to first recognise our natural skills, what he calls 'signature strengths'...Cultivating qualities such as valor, originality, perseverance, authenticity, or intimacy can help an individual buffer the mind against the inevitable things that will go wrong. (Paquette, 2006, p. 2)

We are talking here about another major theme that features in our understanding of spirituality, namely, resilience. Whenever someone faces a major crisis in their lives, how they tackle it and the impact it has upon how they move into the future are features of the world-view they have chosen, and the extent to which it sustains them in their moment of need. A world-view that is able to offer some sense of meaning and understanding for what has happened, and to place it in a wider and coherent context, is an important contributory factor to their resilience and ability to deal with what has happened. We would argue that this falls within the domain of our spirituality, and that resilience is also spiritual strength. We will explore this concept of resilience in more detail in Chapter 5.

There are also clear parallels here with the discussion about Spiritual Intelligence propounded by Zohar and Marshall (1999) (see Moss, 2007a, chapter 11). In terms of the contribution of positive psychology to the underpinning knowledge for social work practice, the benefits are considerable, as Hirtz (1999) explains:

> Psychology is not just the study of weakness and damage; it is also the study of strength and virtue. Treatment is not just fixing what is broken, it is nurturing what is best within ourselves. (p. 22)

Positive psychology is thus casting a spotlight upon an area of our lives that is often overlooked by social workers. Inevitably, when people come to us in moments of crisis, difficulty or despair, the focus is on the immediacy of their need and what steps can be taken to alleviate it. A similar scenario is played out within acute health and medical services, when sick patients are given immediate treatment to help them overcome the medical crisis that has afflicted them. Success is achieved when the person 'pulls through' the crisis and regains some sense of equilibrium. They are out of the danger zone, and better able to cope with whatever life subsequently brings. At this point the professional helpers may well withdraw, feeling that their job has been well done. But this is only half the story, albeit a crucial half especially when life itself may be at risk.

This may best be illustrated perhaps in the field of mental health. People who experience severe mental distress will need psychiatric help and support that may well include appropriate medication to help restore chemical brain imbalance, as well as a range of 'talking therapies'. A hallmark of success in such situations will be the moment when the person begins once again to feel in charge of his or her life, and to be able to face the future less fearfully, and (perhaps) with a reduced reliance upon medication or therapy. But this is not the same as feeling 'on top of things', or experiencing a zest for life or the exhilaration at facing and overcoming life's challenges. In terms of the journey of recovery, the person may have been rescued from plunging over the steep rapids, but there is still the challenge of paddling back out into the main stream and deciding in which direction to travel. Paquette (2006) expresses this well when she observes that

> Mental health is oftentimes seen as a lack of pathology which is a neutral position, as opposed to a positive position denoting the addition of qualities that can serve as buffers when the person is compromised with a disorder, stress or temporary maladjustment...Mental health should be more than the absence of mental illness. It should be something that nourishes the human mind and spirit. (p. 2)

Example

Kevin is an 18-year-old young man who has just received a diagnosis of schizophrenia. In the preceding weeks his sense of personal disintegration had been escalating, much to the consternation of his family and his own sense of bewilderment and confusion. He no longer knew which voices he could trust. It came as a great relief, therefore, when he began to receive, and to respond to, psychiatric help and medication. The 'old' Kevin returned. However, to his dismay he finds that his life opportunities have become limited by his diagnosis. He does not know what to do, he finds it difficult to get employment and he begins to drift through life. Without anything much to live for, he fears that all hope is beginning to fade for ever.

As we have noted, social workers are used to dealing with people in crisis, and helping them re-occupy the somewhat 'neutral' territory where the crisis has been resolved, even if only temporarily, and they can 'get on with the rest of their lives'. As social workers we may sometimes feel that our job finishes at this point: after all, who are we to get involved in these deeper discussions about how a person wishes to conduct the rest of their lives? And yet for some people the temporary place of safety gained with our help when they have been pulled back from some crisis or disaster is itself scary as they recognise the risks of the crisis returning. For them this 'place of safety' also brings with it the challenge of facing some life-changing decisions if they wish to avoid returning to the lifestyles that had precipitated the crisis in the first place. The whole 'change agenda' which characterises so much of social work practice, therefore, takes us implicitly, if not always explicitly, into this 'value-added' territory of 'quality of life' and spirituality.

The relationship between spirituality and health

A key question arising from these discussions of the relationship between spirituality and quality of life is the relationship between a person's spirituality (and also religiosity) and their health. At first glance, this may appear to be a particularly challenging topic especially in the context of western emphases upon evidence-based practice. If spirituality is difficult to define, then it is even more difficult to 'measure' and evaluate; therefore, it is well-nigh impossible to quantify its impact upon a person's health, or upon their journey to recovery from illness. At least, so it would seem.

Before tackling this question 'head on' it is worth noting that this is a particularly western 'difficulty'. In other cultures no such dilemma arises. In many Chinese, Aboriginal and African cultures, for example, religious and spiritual beliefs play a key role in how illness or disease is understood and 'treated'. The ways in which the impact of 'black witchcraft' or the practice of voodoo can negatively affect people's health and wellbeing are also well-known. But even in western cultures there is evidence that the issue is not as 'cut and dried' as we might think. Many people, for example, read their horoscopes in newspapers and magazines, and believe to some extent at least that the stars control their destiny. Some go to have their fortunes told on a regular basis and will not take any major life-changing decisions without such consultations. For some people, a belief in good luck and bad luck appears to sit comfortably alongside their more conventional Christian beliefs (Francis, 2006). The use of complementary therapies has now become much more mainstream and is accepted by many medical practitioners as having legitimacy. The 'placebo effect' has been a well-known phenomenon in medical research studies for generations. The phenomenon of the 'broken heart' may be difficult to prove scientifically, but there are many examples of people who lose the will to live because they feel that life is no longer worth living following the death of a loved one.

All of these are different examples of the ways in which people's beliefs and world-views can have a powerful impact upon their health and quality of life, for good or ill. Factors that foster or diminish people's resilience are just as likely to be spiritual, religious or emotional. What people believe, therefore, has a huge significance upon their health, well-being and their quality of life. So, in spite of the hesitations from evidence-based practice that it is almost impossible to measure or evaluate the impact of spirituality and religious beliefs upon health and well-being, there are many studies that have attempted to undertake precisely that task. These studies are often more medically based than having a social work perspective, but nevertheless they have some important messages for social work to take on board.

It is perhaps easier to begin with a religious perspective, partly because more studies have been undertaken from this point of view, and partly because for social workers it is the area of religion that seems to have caused most professional discomfort and suspicion. If evidence emerges, for example, that a religious faith is a positive factor influencing good health and a good quality of life, then this would be an important consideration to incorporate into a social worker's reflective practice when working with individuals or families for whom this is really important. If it could be shown that a religious faith was a significant part of a creative solution, rather than always being assumed to be part of the problem, or to be ignored as not being very relevant, and if it could be seen as a potential strength rather than as a perceived weakness, then this would fundamentally affect the ways in which people-workers in general should approach their work.

Koenig et al.'s (2001) seminal work pulled together and critiqued 1200 separate studies that explored the interaction of religion and health, leading one of the reviewers to comment on the dust jacket of the book that

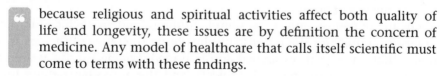

because religious and spiritual activities affect both quality of life and longevity, these issues are by definition the concern of medicine. Any model of healthcare that calls itself scientific must come to terms with these findings.

This comment places the ball firmly in the court of traditional scientific medicine by stating that the case has now been made in these studies for the positive impact of religious and spiritual beliefs upon health and the quality of life. In other words, evidence-based practice *must* now take these issues seriously.

Clearly such massive claims need to be carefully examined, which is part of the *raison d'etre* of Koenig's work. In his introduction he readily acknowledges the 'precarious and turbulent 8000-year relationship among religion science and medicine'. (For a fascinating 8000-year 'timeline' review of the relationship between science, medicine and religious thought and belief, see his chapter 2). Nevertheless, he also seeks to bring a scientific approach to this important quality of life area of study. He recognises and catalogues many of the negative ways in which religious thought and belief have undermined health and well-being, including such topics as the burning of witches, the profound misunderstanding of the nature of mental illness and various aspects of abuse conducted under the name of religion. But the bulk of his book is given over to an evaluation of a wide range of scientific studies that show a positive correlation between religious faith and well-being.

Some key findings are summarised below:

- Religiousness is associated with less coronary artery disease, hypertension, stroke, immune system dysfunction, cancer and lower overall mortality, as well as fewer negative health behaviours such as smoking, drug and alcohol abuse and risky sexual behaviours.
- Involvement in religious community is consistently related to lower mortality and longer survival.
- Many people use religious or spiritual beliefs and practices to help cope with cancer, and there is some evidence that those who use religion as a coping resource adapt better, experience less anxiety and are more hopeful.
- Religious involvement also appears to be an important beneficial influence on the risk of myocardial infarction, mortality from coronary artery disease (CAD) and survival following coronary artery bypass graft surgery.
- The majority of studies show a positive correlation between religious involvement and well-being, happiness and life satisfaction; hope and optimism; purpose and meaning in life; higher self-esteem; adaptation to bereavement; lower rates of depression and faster recovery from depression; lower rates of suicide; less anxiety; lower rates of alcohol and drug use or abuse.

These are, of course, only a few sample findings, and are included in our discussion purely for the purpose of illustrating the range of themes and topics that have been researched and critiqued. Koenig is fully aware of the limitations of the research projects, and the areas that require further investigation. Although not limited to the USA – research projects from other continents are included – there is nevertheless a high preponderance of US-based studies, the findings and implications of which are not necessarily automatically transferable to other cultures or settings. King et al. (2006) found, for example, in their EMPIRIC study of six ethnic populations in England (Irish, Caribbean, Indian, Pakistani, Bangladeshi and White [n = 4281]) that there was no difference in the prevalence of common mental disorders between people who were religious and those who were not. But they also found that people who held a spiritual life view *without* any religious practice were more likely to have a common mental disorder than people who held a religious life view. This would suggest perhaps that a vague, 'ungrounded' sense of spirituality has less therapeutic impact than a religious faith that is rooted in a defined tradition and has a community support system to hand in times of need.

Such findings remind us that we must always view research findings cautiously, and not try to make them carry more weight or expectation than they deserve. Tempting though it is, we must let the research speak for itself, within its stated limitations, and not use the findings inappropriately to bolster a particular world-view or ideology. Nevertheless, even with these important 'caveats', the findings from Koenig's review are significant in that they demonstrate that religious and spiritual beliefs and practices can have positive health-enhancing benefits across a wide range of conditions, and that they are an important aspect of the quality of life discussion.

Conclusion

This chapter has explored a number of themes bound up with the notion of 'quality of life'. A common theme running through every situation we work with is the question of the quality of life that people either currently enjoy, or to which they aspire, or which perhaps they feel they have lost, temporarily or permanently, or which we wish to help them achieve. Quality services are concerned with improving the quality of life of those who need and use them. Quality of life issues can only be addressed by seeking to understand the whole context and responding appropriately (holistically) to the totality of the way in which problems and needs are experienced. Approaches which place quality of life concepts at the centre of service quality measurement tend to apply the 'life domains' approach (Oliver et al., 1997). Even so, despite the domains identified by the WHO discussed in this chapter, quality of life measures employed by social work rarely encompass a spiritual domain. Yet as we tease out what 'quality' means to each individual, we will be exploring their spirituality: how they view the world and what has happened to them; how they see their future and their contribution to it; what makes them 'tick' and makes life worthwhile. *Their* attitude towards their quality of life will significantly impact upon how they choose to work with us; and *our* attitude towards their quality of life, how we explore it with them and how open we are to religious and spiritual dimensions where appropriate will determine how comfortable they are about exploring such issues with us.

The growing convergence of quality concepts is moving us in the direction of what Adams (1998) terms 'quality maximisation'. It is these themes which provide the platforms from which to develop and anchor an understanding of spiritual care which can sit comfortably (by which we mean it has a 'good fit') in mainstream social work practice. Far from being a marginalised activity, spiritual care when viewed in this way belongs to the core social work task. Adams explains it thus:

> One way forward for progressive practice is by means of a fully theorised, social, holistic, *transcendent* politics of ablement... in other words, a holistic, democratised and empowered approach to maximising quality. (Adams, 1998, p. 195) (our italics)

We shall consider the potential within spiritual care for transformation and transcendence in Chapter 5. There is a profound depth to each and every human being that in itself radiates a quality of life, dignity and respect that is also reflected in the value-base of social work practice. People's value and dignity lie as much in who they are as in what they can or cannot do or achieve. Furthermore, that quality of life can be affirmed or denied by how we treat people in our social work practice. We argue, therefore, that the concept of quality of life is a central theme for social work education and practice, however difficult it may be to define or explore. Like spirituality, it is a 'gateway' word. As part of a bundle of concepts that help us understand ourselves and our spirituality, quality of life is a pointer to each person's essential value and uniqueness as human beings. That is both the challenge and the opportunity that social workers tackle each day in their professional practice.

taking it further

- Joseph, S., Linley, P.A. and Maltby, J. (2006) 'Positive psychology, religion and spirituality', *Mental Health, Religion and Culture*, 9: 3, 209–212.
- King, M., Weich, S., Nazroo, J. and Blizard, B. (2006) 'Religion, mental health and ethnicity. EMPIRIC – A national survey of England', *Journal of Mental Health*, 15: 2, 153–162.
- Koenig, H., McCullough, M. and Larson, D. (2001) *Handbook of Religion and Health* (Oxford: Oxford University Press).
- Paquette, M. (2006) 'The science of happiness', *Perspectives in Psychiatric Care*, 42: 1, February.
- Powell, A. (2003) *Psychiatry and Spirituality: The Forgotten Dimension* (Brighton: Pavilion/NIMHE).

- Seligman, M (1990) *Learned Optimism: How to Change Your Mind and Your Life* (New York, NY: Vintage Books).
- World Health Organisation (WHO) (1997) *WHOQOL, Measuring Quality of Life* (Geneva: Switzerland).
- Zohar, D. and Marshall, I. (1999) *SQ: Connecting with Our Spiritual Intelligence* (London: Bloomsbury).

5 Spiritual care

Introduction

In Chapter 3, we explored the concepts of spiritual need and spiritual pain and identified some of the situations in social work practice where both might be evident, and sometimes, even, be the root of the problem. We then looked at how a spiritual dimension might be incorporated into social work assessments. This chapter will engage with the tricky question of what, as a secular caring profession, we *do* about that? Some people, encountering a chapter titled '*Spiritual Care*', might immediately assume this has nothing to do with social work, not least because for a 'caring profession' social work often seems to pay little attention to its caring role, preferring the term 'intervention'. Furthermore, many of the recipients of 'care' dislike the term, preferring to be seen as 'users' of a service. Nevertheless, none of us can manage our daily lives wholly without services and support, and interacting with people who 'care about us' is an important element of our sense of well-being.

Thus social work's difficulty with the notion of offering spiritual care is not solely because it is uncomfortable with the religious and spiritual connotations, but in part because such a caring role implies a type of close personal engagement which does not belong to much, if any, of contemporary social work practice. In those settings in which the caring role is recognised to have a legitimate place – for example, a residential therapeutic setting – this is accepted because the recipient of the care belongs to a dependent category such as a child, and much energy is invested in making sure that professional boundaries are maintained. Nursing has no such problems with the notion of care, as the copious nursing literature on spiritual care demonstrates, but nursing is a 'hands on' activity which more easily transfers the concept of care across physical, emotional and, in principle at least, spiritual domains.

By contrast, social work has barely addressed the notion of spiritual care and its potential role in its relationships with service users. Most of its writing on spirituality focuses on defining and recognising spiritual need and concerns itself with the problem of social work's reluctance to engage with this area. Only in the US is there a well-developed social work literature on spiritual care, and here writers prefer the term 'spiritual interventions'. This fits with the model of social work as a process which first undertakes an assessment and then plans and intervenes on the basis of that assessment. This approach to spirituality sits less comfortably within social work practice outside of the US. In the highly secularised professional cultures of the UK, Northern Europe, Australia and New Zealand there is a suspicion that for social work to 'intervene' in the spiritual lives of service users is a step too far, even for those social workers who are sympathetic to the notion of spirituality as part of being human. By contrast, in countries of southern Europe where many social work services are provided through faith-based organisations, spiritual care may be seen as simply an embedded part of their culture. Social workers in the Global South and those working within First Nation communities, meanwhile, may not see the need to distinguish spiritual care from any other intervention, since 'secular' and 'religious' are not distinguished as in the Anglo-Saxon cultures of the world. These different approaches to spirituality and hence to spiritual care will be explored in Chapter 8.

Our main task in this chapter, therefore, is to make connections between the spirituality discourse and predominant discourses in contemporary social work (Holloway, 2007a) in order to build onto core themes and key approaches in contemporary social work an inclusive model of practice which allows *each social work practitioner to engage with spiritual need in a manner and at a level with which s/he is comfortable.* Understood in this way, social work intervention includes recognising and acknowledging the spiritual needs of service users, even if further assessment and intervention are left to someone else, or, indeed, are not required; the therapeutic potential of simple recognition of a person's spirituality should not be underestimated.

We shall look first at two themes which feature across the international spectrum of social work intervention – empowerment and partnership – and consider their connections with spirituality. From this foundation, we shall explore concepts from spirituality which are less familiar to social work but which, as we shall demonstrate, have direct relevance to mainstream social work practice: transcendence, transformation, wholeness and hope. We shall then return to two interventions which have come to the fore recently in social work practice, particularly in specialist practice settings – resilience building and narrative approaches to meaning-making – to make further connections between contemporary social work practice and spirituality. Finally, we shall weave all this together into a model which presents the social worker as a 'fellow traveller' on the service user's spiritual journey.

Empowering spirituality

Social work defines itself as an empowering activity. A fundamental value in social work is to align oneself with those who are disempowered, marginalised, discriminated against and oppressed. A deep-seated sense of powerlessness is frequently seen to lie behind attitudes and behaviours ranging from the most disruptive to the most withdrawn or depressed. When social workers talk of 'empowering' the service user they usually mean lending their strength and utilising their power to assist the service user in challenging their disempowered state and overturning their powerlessness. However, as disabled activists have pointed out, empowerment cannot be 'given' – it must be grasped (Swain et al., 1993). Genuine empowerment therefore implies facilitating the service user's own developmental journey. When the notion of empowerment is applied to the spiritual journey, the service user is encouraged to get in touch with and nurture their own spiritual resources, as well as to find new resources and learn to draw on these, so that they are strengthened as a person and better equipped to deal with their situation. The following references to personal faith resources illustrate the very different levels at which this may operate, yet still be identified as significant:

'When you've been brought up with it you don't have to reach out – it's always there';

'I believe in Jesus but it isn't very deep . . . if you've got something like that I think it helps you and keeps you going';

'My faith's been tremendous . . . fight, I've got such fight and strength in me'. (quoted in Lloyd, 1996, pp. 299–300)

Social workers all too frequently limit their concept of empowerment to helping the service user achieve control over their current problem. The implications of this *inner* strengthening go way beyond such a limited vision related to the immediate external context.

stop and think

■ What do you really mean when you talk about empowering the service user?

Partnership and spiritual care

A second theme which is fundamental to contemporary social work practice is to work in partnership with the service user. This is underpinned by a theoretical perspective and ideological position which sees the service user as the 'expert' on their own situation. Sometimes such a position is used to deny that the social worker has any professional expertise and to rely solely on the service user's articulation of both problem and solution. However, this is a misconception of both the responsibility and potential of working in partnership. Genuine partnership requires that both parties contribute their own expertise at the same time as they respect and utilise that of the other person. Such a relationship is non-hierarchical but allows that one person may have more to offer in a particular aspect than another.

A partnership approach which is underpinned by spiritual awareness and sensitivity as well as respect for the other person's perception and experience of spirituality is another core approach which fits well with the offering of spiritual care. It is most effective when it is coupled with an approach from pastoral theology known as the 'wounded healer' (Nouwen, 1972; Campbell, 1981). The wounded healer is able to heal *because of* his or her own wounds. In other words, we occupy the same ground. From a psycho-social or political-economic perspective, the social worker rarely occupies the same ground as the service user, even if at one time we may have done so. But as another human being, we are grounded in the same existential dilemma. The spiritual journeys of the social worker and service user will more than likely not have progressed to the same point nor have taken the same route, but we are on the same voyage of birth, life and death. To work in partnership with the other person as they navigate their spiritual journey, complete with obstacles, is a humbling experience and removes any dichotomy between 'helper' and 'helped'. As one chaplain put it: 'I would challenge the assumption about "help". They often help us' (Lloyd, 1995, p. 23).

stop and think

■ What wounds do you carry with you?
■ How do they help you to help someone else?

Fowler's model for spiritual development (see discussion in Chapter 3) is also helpful here. Fowler asserts that each stage has value and integrity in itself, and not everyone will proceed through all stages. Moreover, Fowler's argument is that our shared spirituality in community is enriched by interactions between people at different stages of spiritual development.

Example

Susan and Joe have four children. Their third child, Joanna, has learning disability and their oldest boy, David, has recently developed diabetes. Susan and Joe are both teachers, but the stresses and strains of their family life gradually led Susan to give up work. This has allowed her more time to concentrate on Joanna's educational needs, but financially things are a bit tough. The family attends their local Baptist church and have some good friends there, but Susan sometimes feels that their friends don't have a clue really what her life is like – if they did, they wouldn't moan about their relatively minor problems. She still finds herself thinking 'Why us?' about Joanna's disability. One evening after venting her feelings about a particularly difficult day to Joe, she goes upstairs to settle Joanna in bed. Joanna thanks God in her bed-time prayers for her family and friends and gives her mum an extra big kiss. Susan suddenly realizes that she has what so many people do not have – a loving, caring family and community, from which she derives her strength and spiritual bonds. Joanna's implicit trust opens up for Susan a new perception of her quality of life and she is overwhelmed with thankfulness for Joanna's life.

Transcendence

Despite these assertions of natural meeting points between spiritual care and some core skills and approaches in social work, it is important to acknowledge where the two may diverge. Spiritual care is distinguished by its reliance on particular concepts which cannot necessarily be applied to all social work intervention. The charge that almost anything can be deemed 'spiritual' if one is sympathetic to the idea of a spiritual realm, and that this wholesale inclusiveness renders the notion of 'spiritual care' meaningless (Paley, 2008), is a serious one.

In his very helpful paper on spiritual need, Kellehear (2000) identifies the concept of transcendence as key to determining whether or not a need may be defined as 'spiritual' or is simply, for example, psychological or social. Transcendence is also, for Kellehear, the starting point for spiritual care:

'Good spiritual care' may mean ... understanding that the meaning of wellness ... is dependent upon the successful ability of all of us to transcend the ordinariness of everyday life. (p. 154)

This 'ordinariness' may be problematic, painful or limiting, even, perhaps, oppressive. Such situations are the stuff of social work intervention and are reflected in its key tasks of problem-solving, therapeutic intervention and empowerment. The implications of effective spiritual care are that, even where the source of the problem, pain or oppression cannot itself be removed, the service user is able to *transcend* the situation such that it no longer has a problematic, painful or oppressive impact. There are, of course, links with psychological interventions such as cognitive re-framing, in which the person is helped to see and understand situations and events differently so that the 'message' they take from them is changed in positive and life-enhancing directions. These approaches fall into the bracket of 'spiritual' care or intervention when transcendence is achieved through discovering, building and drawing on *spiritual* resources, both internal and external.

Transcending or challenging oppression?

Kellehear identifies a sense of purpose, hope, meaning and affirmation, mutuality, connectedness and social presence as the building blocks to 'situational transcendence' (Kellehear, 2000, p. 151). At its heart, he identifies 'making sense of' or 'making the most of' circumstances of hardship or suffering. There is something of a danger, when we are talking about spirituality and religion, that a valid criticism of religion as projection, escapism or a stupefying force may apply if we understand transcendence as 'making the best of' difficult circumstances. Does this undermine the whole notion of spirituality as a quest for meaning and purpose which lends value to life and is personally liberating? Another perspective on this is the argument which claims that projection *creates* meaning and that as creators, human agency exerts power over our environment (Chopra, 2006).

This is a central issue for social work and spirituality and we need to explore and consider it. In social work we frequently deal with situations which *should* be challenged, not by-passed or even leap-frogged over. Liberation Theology, applied to the context of social work practice, offers a helpful bridge between challenging and transcending. Liberation Theology has at its heart the notion that spiritual liberation is achieved through *changing* the conditions of everyday life. The ability to *transcend* everyday life carries with it the implication that in so doing one is no longer trapped by its material conditions. This may result in the strength to change or overturn those conditions, or it may result in their *no longer having power over one's sense of self*. Sometimes this may be as simple as learning to let go of things which are not really important, a re-ordering of priorities ('no-one ever says on their death-bed, "I wish I had spent more time at the office"'). In extreme circumstances it may be life-saving and health-preserving as Viktor Frankl discovered in the concentration camp (Frankl, 2000). Most of the situations in which social work service users find themselves fall somewhere in between. One interpretation of the maxim 'The truth shall make you free' (St John's Gospel, ch 8 v 32) is that 'the truth' is discovering and connecting with one's spiritual essence and maintaining one's spiritual integrity, and therein lies liberation.

Transformation

A second key concept is that of transformation. Central to Canda and Furman's argument that spiritual interventions are at the heart of social work practice is their characterisation of social work as potentially a *transformative process*. Canda and Furman take as their starting point that social workers see themselves as agents for change. From a theoretical perspective, this derives from systems theory, which conceptualises the experience of the individual or family as determined by the functioning of a number of overlapping social systems (such as home, school, work and community) in which problems or movement in one system will have knock-on effects in another (Pincus and Minahan, 1973). The task of the social worker, as the 'change agent', is to intervene in these dynamics so as to prevent or halt negative effects including, at worst, disastrous 'domino-falling' consequences, promoting instead problem-solving and change-enhancing approaches. When the social worker as change agent engages in 'spiritually sensitive practice', this process

> ...includes but is more than problem solving. It includes but is more than promoting coping, adapting, or recovery...spiritually sensitive practice identifies people's talents, skills, capacities, and resources and mobilises them in the service of both their immediate goals and their highest aspirations and potentials. (Canda and Furman, 1999, p. 252)

Henery has argued that the problem with much of the contemporary spirituality discourse among the helping professions is that it portrays spirituality as just another health-promoting life-style option (Henery, 2003). The above description could be read as depicting spirituality and spiritual practice as a sub-discipline of ego psychology and cognitive therapy. However, Canda and Furman go on to say,

> When change is transformational, it moves people forward on their spiritual paths. (p. 252)

We shall turn shortly to consider what such change might look like and how it might be promoted in the interactions between social workers and service users, but for the time being it is worth reminding ourselves of Fowlers 'take' on the process of spiritual development (Fowler, 1987). Fowler characterises spiritual development not as a process of self affirmation but as a coming to terms with paradox, establishing a dialogue with polarities, and grounded in the 'other'. Thus the basis for one's identity is the transforming of the self through struggle with contradiction and challenge to one's comfortable sense of self.

Wholeness

Social work, in common with other 'helping professions', may talk of 'holistic practice' but rarely addresses the question of wholeness. In fact, what social work usually means by holistic practice is a 'whole person approach' to assessments, by which it means covering all areas of the person's life. In current UK government policy, this has transmuted into 'person-centred practice' (e.g. Department of Health, 2005). But a focus limited to assessment and an understanding of holistic as person-centred suggest an approach which falls some way short of achieving 'wholeness'. If we consider social work as an activity which privileges the uniqueness of each person and family in their particular situation, but understands that situation as shaped by social, economic, political and philosophical contexts, then the aspiration of wholeness embraces far more.

We need to take a systems theory approach so that we see wholeness as embracing wholeness in persons, in systems (social systems such as the family, community and organisation, as well as political and economic systems) and also in the interactions between them. A holistic approach to individuals and families which continuously shapes itself in response to prevailing social and policy dynamics is the only way for social work to hold onto its core professional and ethical identity in the managerial and market-driven climate of contemporary health and social care (Lloyd, 2000). One of the features of this culture is the breaking down of everything into small units for monitoring and evaluation. In contrast to such a 'unit' approach, both Adams (1998) and Hudson (2000) call for 'whole systems' change in order to effect 'whole person' health and quality of life (Hudson, 2000). Thus a holistic approach to the assessment and meeting of the needs of individuals requires an integrated focus on the social structures which shape their lives and the mechanisms which impact upon their experiences of services. One of the arguments for social work to take spirituality seriously is that it operates at the levels of personal, social and political concerns. Nash (2002) argues that a spiritual perspective facilitates social work breaking out of the perennial dilemma of taking a social constructionist view of the world, but finding itself actually intervening at the level of the individual, with problems firmly located at the individual's doorstep. We shall look at the community dimensions of spirituality in the next chapter. A whole person approach implies not so much a comprehensive assessment of all areas of their life as a response to their whole experience. We may indeed arrive at this response through a focus on different facets but the whole must always be appreciated as more than the sum of the parts. Moreover, wholeness is not the same as either 'wholesome' or 'perfection':

> ... wholeness for large numbers of people may actually mean managing to hold all the messy bits together whilst frequently raging and maybe resolving some of the issues some of the time. These people experience doubts and fears, as the different parts jostle together in the process of integration. (Lloyd, 1995, p. 25)

Transcendence, transformation and wholeness may at first sight appear to be beyond the reach of most of us except in those rare moments which lift us beyond the routine and the mundane, let alone those service users whose daily lives are so frequently experiences of oppression, hardship, pain and trauma. However, if we are able to see their potential in the minutiae of daily life, as well as at extreme moments, the 'fit' with what social workers do is not so far off. Every social worker will resonate with the knowledge that sometimes all we can do is provide support which helps to 'maintain the spirit', but that this can enable the other person to endure and survive – sometimes, quite literally (Lloyd, 2002). This, surely, is transcendence. Social workers will also recognise that a changed perception of a problematic situation or relationship can be the key to problem-solving and open the way to enhanced quality of life. When we are instrumental in bringing this about, our intervention is transformative. Social workers also know that when the 'final straw' causes a tenuously balanced situation to break down, often with spiralling disastrous consequences for the service user and those around her/him, what has happened is that the 'whole' has disintegrated. Restoring wholeness may be a long process, and may involve discovering a new whole and centre, but it is ultimately the only way to recovery. When we are privileged to be part of this rebuilding, our practice is healing because it 'makes whole' again. This older woman draws on her spiritual maturity to acknowledge what 'real life' wholeness is all about:

> when you get older you understand better ... I've just had to make a whole of all the bits and pieces. (Lloyd, 1996, p. 304)

The importance of hope

One strategy which social work has largely evaded but which service users constantly refer to is the employment of hope. Why are social workers cautious about nurturing and engendering hope? As with so much else in the field of spirituality, much of the problem lies in the way in which hope is conceptualised. Social workers are trained to help people see their problems realistically and to engage in realistic strategies for dealing with them. Any form of thinking which relies on 'wishing' the problem away is seen as refusal to face up to it. The gambler whose response to acute financial problems is to put another bet on the 'hot tip' horse is seen as failing to accept responsibility for his/her own problem. Putting personal disasters down to 'bad luck' and, conversely, putting their 'faith' in superstitious behaviours or 'bargaining' with some super-being are seen as unhelpful and irrational responses which undermine genuine coping behaviours. But are such behaviours really what hope is about? And do they have anything to do with 'hope' as a spiritual resource?

There is some evidence that people mix superstition, religious and 'everyday' versions of hope interchangeably. For example, one of the authors found in her research that the words 'hope', 'faith' and 'trust' were used by different people in different ways, sometimes to represent a religious belief and sometimes a generalised sense about life:

'(Religion) is just another form of hope isn't it? That's what it is'.

'I trust in Him above'.

'A lot of people accept it as fate. Well, I don't think of it as fate'.

'Well, without trust you can't go very far, can you? Without faith you

Embedded in all these conversations is the idea that we need something to hold onto which enables us to endure, survive and perhaps transcend. The medical profession has been more inclined to recognise this than has social work. Culliford, a consultant psychiatrist, says,

> I have found the question, 'what keeps you going?' (sometimes phrased as, 'what sustains you when things start getting you down?')...goes directly to the heart of the matter. People draw strength and sustenance from the spiritual realm. (Culliford, 2004)

Where social workers worry about giving 'false hope' – for example, allowing parents to think that they will get their children back when the social worker knows that this is highly unlikely – medical professionals have taken the view that *it is precisely when the situation appears hopeless* that it is essential to nurture hope within the person. This question has been most especially addressed in palliative care, where the maintenance of hope has always been part of the hospice vision. Twycross addresses this in the context of suffering, quoting Frankl: 'Man is not destroyed by suffering, he is destroyed by suffering without meaning' (Twycross, 2007). Another way into this is Rumbold's continuum of helplessness and hope (Rumbold, 1986). Both concepts – the notion of finding meaning and of overcoming helplessness – move us in the direction of affirmation of the essential person. Rumbold describes this as a process in which 'mature hope' struggles with reality but maintains trust; it can live with confusion and doubt, and it is focused around establishing meaning. Twycross quotes a husband speaking of his wife's terminal illness: 'Nothing that creates such tenderness can be all waste.' It is in such meanings that hope for tomorrow can be found.

Understood in this way, 'mature hope' can be engendered even in the person whose actions have apparently destroyed all that made for meaning in their life. Spiritually informed empowerment practice is not afraid to nurture hope. Houghton (2007) suggests that many ordinary people who have survived difficult, sometimes dreadful, events and circumstances feel they have done so *precisely because* they have not given up 'hope':

> Hope is their word and they interpret it very personally, not as some depersonalized reference to goals or expectations. For them hope is not about naïve or excessive optimism. It is not solely about achievement. It is about not losing sight of the goodness of life even when it is not visible. (Jevne, 2005, p. 267)

Other writers suggest that people who have hope believe that positive outcomes are always possible and it is this which creates new energies and rekindles the spirit after traumatic events and in the midst of hardship (Akinsola, 2001; Houghton, 2007). The alternative, it is suggested, is to be confirmed as a victim rather than a survivor (Radcliffe, 2005).

In an interesting study of mental health social work practice in Australia, Darlington and Bland (1999) found that both the social workers and the service users recognised the importance of the development and maintenance of hope in their relationship. It was a key strategy employed by the social workers, operating in much the same way as task-centred casework with elements of crisis intervention. That is,

- the approach is centred on the service user's own frame of reference and dependent upon a genuine encounter in which the service user feels valued and respected;
- it involves ascertaining their hopes and working with them towards realising some of them;
- it focuses on strengths rather than weaknesses;
- it acknowledges small positive steps;
- it helps to identify and draw on resources employed in the past;
- it maintains hope in the service user and their future.

One of us has referred to this form of support as 'maintaining the spirit' (Lloyd, 2002). Unfortunately, so much of what social workers have to do runs the risk of *extinguishing* the spirit – persuading the older person that they are putting themselves at serious risk by continuing to live on their own because they cannot take care of themselves; telling the child or young person that their mother does not want them home again; having to make people face the consequences of abusive, destructive and criminal behaviour, particularly when these consequences are the loss of relationships on which they depended. The challenge for social workers is to deal with such issues with people in such a way as to nurture their ability to transform the bleakness of the present into hope for the future, engendering the energy for fresh beginnings.

stop and think

- What are some of the most hopeless situations you have had to work with?
- Were there potential sources of hope which you employed, or could have employed in your interactions with these service users?

Houghton discusses social workers' employment of the 'recovery vision' when working with people with depression, which 'includes the hope that the individual can build a life worth living' (Houghton, 2007, p. 2). In her research, she found that 'losing hope' was strongly related to the onset of depression, and recovery from the depressive episode involved reconnecting with the mechanisms for engendering hope. In line with Rumbold's continuum of helplessness and hope, Houghton's participants gave accounts of spiralling 'backwards and forwards' towards hope. Crucial in this process was a relationship with a professional which was in itself 'hopeful' – that is, the professional gave of themselves to the service user because s/he valued the other person and engendered in the service user their own belief that s/he would come out the other side. Houghton argues that the social worker must not close off any dimension which is giving hope to the service user; rather, the social worker should enable the service user to explore their own conceptions of hope. The implications of exploring the spiritual dimension and its potential as a resource, rather than being seen as the problem, which mental health service users so frequently complain is their experience (Coyte et al., 2007), are clear.

Building resilience

Linked to this notion of hope is another idea which is gaining increasing currency in social work practice. The concept of resilience has become increasingly important in our work with children and young people, and the fostering of resilience seen as part of the duty of care for children subject to state interventions. There is a burgeoning literature on this general theme (Rutter, 1985, 1999; Dugan and Coles, 1989; Garmezy, 1991; Fonagy et al., 1994; Kirby and Fraser, 1997; Seligman, 1998; Daniel et al., 1999; Fraser et al., 1999; Gilligan, 1999, 2001, 2004; Early and Glenmaye, 2000; Rayner and Montague, 2000; Greene, 2002; Newman et al., 2004; Ungar, 2006). The question that this concept of resilience seeks to address is how the impact of negative events upon a child can, for some but clearly not for all, lead to positive outcomes and a successful recovery from traumatic experiences. As Ungar (2006) observes, this is a complex issue where resilience, as a concept, can include a 'constellation of circumstances' that contribute to a child growing up successfully; to a child's capacity to handle stressful and challenging situations well; and to the capacity to recover from adversity. Factors influencing successful outcomes include (inter alia) personal traits and capacity; positive and supportive networks and relationships; and the opportunity to develop problem-solving and emotional coping skills. There are also, as Ungar notes, societal and structural influences upon a child and a family that strongly influence the capacity to cope with adversity.

Williams (2007) coins the term 'bouncebackability' to capture the essence of what resilience is all about. Williams outlines six domains of resilience that are internationally recognised markers that help protect children and develop their emotional capacity to cope with setbacks. These include,

- *Talents and Interests* – feelings of success from talents, interests and aptitudes; encouragement for their development;
- *Positive Values* – empathy, helpfulness and caring towards others;
- *Education* – curiosity about the environment and support for cognitive development;
- *Social Competences* – self-efficacy, autonomy and self-control;
- *Secure Base* – strong attachments;
- *Friendships* – strong relationships, the ability to make and keep friends.

Important though these themes are for strong emotional development and for coping with future adversity, it is crucial to acknowledge, however, that resilience is not some kind of panacea that makes everything better. Far from it. As Newman points out,

> It's about recognising that damaged children may never fully recover, and that our task is equipping them with whatever emotional and technical skills they need *in order to survive*. (our emphasis) (Newman, in Williams, 2007)

It is clear therefore that the concept of resilience rightly belongs centre-stage in all our work not only with children and young people, but with everyone, no matter what age they are.

For our discussion in this chapter, therefore, the work and research undertaken with children and young people around this theme of resilience will be used as a springboard for a wider debate. Important though resilience is for children and young people, it is not age-specific. As we have suggested in previous chapters, there are powerfully searching and disconcerting questions that burrow deep into us during times of crisis. We can all be tested, sometimes well beyond our capacity to cope, and our response to such experiences tells us a great deal about ourselves, our strengths and our resilience. The factors that influence our response will be as many and varied as those identified for children and young people, probably more so. We are likely to ask such challenging questions in the midst of grief and loss such as 'why?' 'why did this happen to me/him/her/them?'; 'why does God allow such things to happen?'; and 'how can human beings behave in such a way to each other?'

These profoundly challenging responses take us to the heart of who we are and how we understand ourselves and our place in the world. Moreover, they also take us to the very foundations of our understanding about the world, and our place within it. For this reason, if for none other, we are in the territory of our spirituality, whether or not it has a religious dimension to it. For, as we have argued earlier in this book, an important aspect of our spirituality is how we see the world – in other words, our world-view. We would argue that one of the contributions that our spirituality potentially can make is to enhance and deepen our resilience in the face of adversity. Murray Lloyd goes so far as to say that ' "spiritual nurturing" means the same as "resilience promotion" '(Lloyd, 2005).

It is of course only a potential: there is nothing automatic about it. A faith that has withstood many challenges previously may crumble at the next; someone whose world-view has previously seemed adequate and fit for purpose may radically change it in the light of a major catastrophe – a change that could as easily be towards a religious faith as away from it. The point being made here is that our spirituality – that which gives us a sense of meaning and purpose and a particular world-view – can play a significant role in developing our resilience and enhancing our strengths and capacity to deal with adversity.

Example

Corinne had been brought up in a faith community when young, but had always struggled with the idea of a loving God and how to reconcile this belief to some of the things that she saw happening in the world, and in her work as a social worker.

After one particularly distressing case of abuse, she suddenly realised that her internal struggle was proving counter-productive to her well-becoming and her capacity to cope. Suddenly she realised that if she gave up trying to 'bring God into her world-view' she could simply get on with life as she found it and deal with things at a human level. This insight seemed to release her from a burden she was carrying, and she found that her capacity to cope, and her resilience, was greatly enhanced. The curious thing was that in letting go of the religious beliefs imposed on her as a child, Corinne discovered her own innate spirituality, embedded in her appreciation of humanity.

Meaning-making and spiritual narratives

There is probably not a definition of spirituality in contemporary discourse which does not include within it the *search for meaning*. Surprisingly little of the discussion of spiritual care, however, focuses on the process of meaning-making. One of the main proponents of meaning-making as a therapeutic approach is Neimeyer's application to the field of loss (Neimeyer, 2001). Neimeyer uses the term 'meaning reconstruction' to describe the process by which individuals reconstruct their personal narrative after the disruption to that 'script' caused by a significant bereavement or other loss. Dying and bereavement are without doubt situations of existential challenge in which the need to find meaning is particularly strong. However, there are other points in the construction of one's spiritual narrative and biography where the spiritual quest is essentially a quest to make sense of past, present and future.

The use of biography and self-narrative which we looked at in Chapter 3 was concerned primarily with conducting a spiritual assessment. Social work has developed biographical models of assessment into therapeutic interventions which weave together life course models and concepts of narrative. The two most developed are the use of life-story work with children and young people and also learning-disabled adults and the use of reminiscence therapy in work with older people. The therapeutic purpose of life-story work is, in the main, to facilitate the re-working of painful events or unresolved losses and the relationship issues bound up in them, so as to achieve a healthier resolution and enable the individual to disengage from the 'emotional baggage' which is hindering their present functioning and future progress. The main therapeutic purpose of reminiscence work with older people, however, is positive reinforcement. The underlying idea here is that returning in memory to a time of life about which recall remains sharp is both enjoyable and beneficial in terms of present functioning. However, it is also acknowledged that there are aspects of each process in both types of therapy. Some experts on reminiscence therapy also warn that reminiscence is a largely negative process for some older people, who feel bitter about a past which they cannot change and may feel themselves to have little capacity to influence the remainder of life.

Parton argues that many service users feel powerless in the face of the construction of their personal narrative by professionals and service providers, and that the empowering social worker should assist with the process of service users 'reclaiming' their own narrative (Parton and O'Byrne, 2000). This is particularly applicable to the process of making sense of one's personal spiritual biography since it is in constructing the narrative around the history that the sense-making may take place. This may include 'laying to rest' painful memories and aspects but also discovering joys, strength and fulfilment which have been submerged or hitherto unappreciated. Both transcendence and transformation are highly relevant to this process of reclaiming the narrative and reconstructing meaning. Moreover, meaning-making, in its bringing together of past, present and future, makes an important contribution to the establishment of spiritual identity. Gilbert has referred to personal identity in the spiritual realm as a 'travelling identity' (Gilbert, 2007). In other words, spiritual development takes place on a journey, with the spiritual core carried forward from one step to the next.

The Fellow Traveller model

Even where social work has shown itself able to recognise spiritual need, there is, for the most part, confusion, ambivalence and helplessness when it comes to how to address such need (Holloway, 2007a). Moreover, many social workers feel out of their comfort zone when it comes to spirituality and religion, particularly if the suggestion is that they should actively offer spiritual care or spiritual interventions. In this chapter so far, we have tried to show how spiritual care might be built onto some core approaches and interventions in social work. There remains the question of *how to start* – for those desirous of including spirituality in their approach – and *what to do about spiritual need* for the social worker who might recognise the significance of spirituality in the life of the service user but feels unable or unwilling to engage with this area themselves.

If we conceive of the spiritual life as a journey, there is another tried and tested approach in social work which might help. When social work first established itself as a professional activity, it centred its interventions around the *casework relationship* (e.g. Biestek, 1961; Hollis, 1964). It was through the development of a professional relationship over time (initially long-term but the 1970s saw the emergence of 'brief casework' models) that the helping intervention took place. More recently, social work has struggled with the impact of a global trend towards managerialism, more concerned with service delivery performance targets and outcomes than the preserving of that relationship between the social worker and the service user. The fact that this trend has created so much 'angst' among social workers is indicative of how important that professional relationship is to the activity of social work. One important maxim from those early caseworkers which has not been supplanted by any assessment model since, was to *start where the person is*. From that point, things can move on, sometimes in a pre-planned programme of intervention, sometimes in a more open-ended way, subject to periodically 'taking stock', re-assessing the problem(s) and maybe jointly setting a different course. All of this implies a type of 'journey' – indeed language such as 'milestones' and 'end-points' is frequently used in planning documentation.

The model presented here is that of the 'fellow traveller', which allows the social worker to go with the service user on their spiritual journey for as far as they feel comfortable and competent to assist. The model is one of travelling alongside, rather than carrying a passenger, although it recognises that the person in need of help may stumble, lose direction or wish to give up at difficult points in the journey. That said, it is also a reciprocal model in which the traveller may either bring a particular vista to the attention of the other or suggest a direction which strengthens the relationship or proves beneficial to either person. It allows for others to join the travelling party, for a time or to take on the role of ongoing companion. Finally, although the route of the spiritual journey may coincide with other journeys for part of the way and may set the overall direction for a time, it does not preclude another focus assuming equal or greater priority for the social work intervention.

Example

Bernadette is a 20-year-old single mother of Jodi, aged 3 years. Until recently, Sean, Bernadette's boyfriend, had been living with them. However, Sean left when Bernadette disclosed to him that she was sexually abused by her oldest brother (Sean's friend) for several years, until she became pregnant with Jodi. Sean became verbally abusive and physically violent at this stage, shouting that Bernadette was a 'slag' and Jodi was obviously 'not normal'. Alongside her feelings of rejection and the trauma of the abuse, past and present, Bernadette is consumed with guilt and the feeling that God is punishing her. Bernadette's family are Catholic, and the first occasion on which her brother abused her was during the party celebrating her first communion. She felt dirty and was stuck with the conviction that her sin was too great to confess. Over her teenage years she developed a drug and alcohol dependency and was constantly told by everyone that she was a 'bad girl'. However, when Jodi was born, she was determined to be a good mother and 'redeem' herself. Until this point she has remained drug-free and generally started to feel quite good about herself. But Sean's accusations have brought all the bad feelings back. Besides, she has a suspicion that he is right about Jodi. Her development is slow and sometimes her behaviour is very difficult. The health visitor is sending Jodi for assessment at the Child Development Unit. Bernadette thinks that God must be punishing her and that she can never be 'saved' from her past. When one of her old friends offers her drugs she sinks quickly back into the old patterns of behaviour.

Bernadette turns up at the Child Development Unit with Jodie, who is withdrawn and showing signs of physical neglect. Bernadette herself is in an intoxicated state. The social worker, Marie, is asked to undertake a full risk assessment. As Bernadette pours out her story, Marie, herself from a Catholic background, recognises her deep spiritual pain. However, she feels there is no alternative in the short-term but to place Jodie in foster care. At the present time Bernadette appears to alternate between indifference to and hatred of Jodie. Marie suspects that the restoring of their parent-child relationship may be possible only through addressing the spiritual need and spiritual pain tied up with Bernadette's core sense of self.

The Fellow Traveller model is conceptualised as having four intervention stages: *joining, listening, understanding* and *interpreting* (Figure 5.1).

1. *Joining*

Every social worker should be able to engage in spiritual care at this point. What this means is that they are sufficiently spiritually aware to

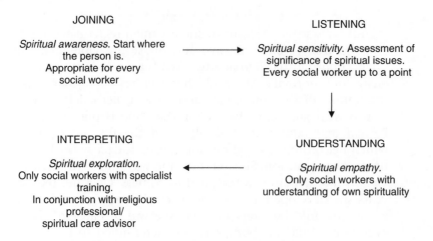

Figure 5.1 **The Fellow Traveller model for spiritual care**

recognise the spirituality of the service user and to identify those people for whom spiritual concerns are important. This may be either because spiritual issues are part of their problem or because their spirituality is an important resource which contributes to their overall well-being, or, quite commonly, because the spiritual dimension is *both* problematic and potentially life-enhancing or preserving for this person. Already we are beginning to move into a terrain which may be difficult for some social workers. Nevertheless, we would argue that 'starting where the service user is' requires that *every* social worker engages with the spiritual issues sufficient to acknowledge their significance and to recognise the way in which the spiritual dimension is affecting the service user at this point. This moves us into the next stage.

2. *Listening*

The ability to listen with an attuned ear is an essential component of the core set of skills which social workers transfer across settings, user groups and types of intervention. At the first level, the social worker should be able to 'hear' what the service user is saying and pick up the clues as to what they mean as well as what they are not saying. This may be the expression of unmet spiritual needs, signs of spiritual distress or simply a failure to access those spiritual resources (external or internal) which have sustained them in the past. In order to determine whether these factors are coming into play, the social worker must pursue the 'spiritual conversation' beyond the initial recognition of the service user's spirituality which 'joining' implies. This is sometimes referred to as 'active listening' and it enables a preliminary assessment of the nature and significance of the spiritual issues to be made. At this point one of four courses of action may ensue:

- The social worker may decide that the spiritual issues are closely bound up with other aspects of the case but realises that they are getting out of their depth or not comfortable with the spiritual dimension. Therefore they set up some joint work with another member of the team, possibly another member of the multidisciplinary team.
- The social worker may assess that the spiritual issues are the priority and, with the agreement of the service user, refer them to a religious professional.
- The social worker may assess the spiritual issues as important but not the main focus. S/he decides to keep the case, but with support from a religious professional or spiritual care advisor on the spiritual aspects. This may also be the most appropriate way of proceeding in instances where the spiritual issues are relatively important but the service user does not wish to discuss their spiritual needs with anyone else – for whatever reason, including that they may have no defined religious belief or may be suffering a crisis of faith in which they are rejecting the 'help' which they perceive might be offered by a religious professional:

 It seemed to be a pointless job...you just wanted to shout at him for believing in God. (bereaved mother referring to the hospital chaplain, quoted in Lloyd, 1997, p. 187)

- Both the social worker and the service user may feel comfortable with the spiritual engagement and it moves into a deeper level.

The extent to which the social worker engages with the spiritual dimension at the listening stage will depend on their personal empathy with spirituality, combined with their level of knowledge and training in this field. It is at this stage that some social workers will cease to travel alongside the service user. They may continue to work with the person in other dimensions of their life, but they have reached the edge of their capacity to work with the spiritual dimension. The service user should not be cast adrift, however, if they continue to exhibit spiritual need. Rather, other support should be offered.

3. *Understanding*

It is probably not possible for any social worker to proceed to this stage without having, or having had in the past, an active spiritual life. This is not necessarily through committed adherence to a particular religious faith, but the worker does need to have a strong awareness of their own spiritual identity and journey. This is because it is essential that they are able to understand and convey empathy with the kind of issues and dilemmas that may be raised for the service user as well as the high spots of spiritual experience and understanding of how spiritual resources might be utilised. It is important to recognise that the social worker does not turn into a kind of 'secular chaplain' at this point, but instead, that the core social work skills and approaches are applied to assist in exploring spiritual issues and resources for the service user and their interaction with other aspects of their life. Empowerment, partnership and building resilience are all employed but with the social worker drawing on their *spiritual* understanding and applied to the spiritual dimension in a genuinely holistic model of practice. Jointly holding onto the concept of wholeness (as we explored earlier) is central to the interaction between the social worker and the service user and frames the intervention objectives and plans.

4. *Interpreting*

Sometimes there is a need to go still further into the spiritual issues. To use the journeying metaphor, the traveller may enter a dark valley or rocky or hazardous terrain in which s/he is reliant on the knowledge, experience and expertise of the guide. A crucial tool here is the use of meaning-making as discussed earlier. It is at this stage that the concepts of transcendence and transformation may be employed within those core social work approaches already identified. Also crucial is the employment of hope: the guide knows that this section of the journey, although arduous and perhaps long, has an end. Equally, the guide knows that there may be damage inflicted on the way and access to healing resources is essential. Importantly, the guide knows this because s/he is a 'wounded healer' who makes her/himself vulnerable through choosing to travel with the other person (Lloyd, 1995; Thorne, 2007).

There may be few situations in which it is appropriate for the social worker to take on this role and task. Equally, there may be few social workers who are able and willing to share the service user's spiritual journey this far. Most social workers would probably consider it more appropriate to suggest a religious or spiritual care advisor. However, there are a number of caveats to this. First, to have reached this point of disclosure about spiritual issues with a secular professional such as a social worker, the service user will have invested considerable trust in that professional and their willingness to respect their spirituality. Lloyd quotes one of her respondent's views on the hazards of raising spiritual issues with social workers:

> You can't share it with everybody because some people would think you had gone over the edge or something...they've got to understand the spiritual dimension. (Lloyd, 1997, p. 187)

The mental health service users' movement likewise continues to cite examples of the risks of talking about spiritual and religious issues with professionals (e.g. Nicholls, 2007). Given this background context, the social worker's withdrawal would need to be handled with great care, and the better option might be for the social worker to work alongside a specialist in spiritual care. Second, there are some situations, such as palliative care, where the social worker may not be able to avoid the service user's spiritual distress and there is little choice at a particular point in time but to engage with it or ignore it. Sister Frances Dominica of Helen House Children's Hospice in Oxford refers to this as 'going deeply into the moment', and talks of 'time as depth not length'. This is not to suggest that the social worker should try to be someone s/he is not or do something with which s/he is not comfortable – intervention can only be effective if it is authentic. Nor does it preclude the possibility of introducing a specialist in spiritual care alongside.

In our final practice illustration we shall return to Leroy, considering the spiritual journey which he takes to arrive at the point where we left him in Chapter 3.

Example – Leroy's journey

Joining

The first time John meets Leroy he is sullen and uncommunicative. Although John's own background is very different from Leroy's, he is reminded of himself at a difficult period in his teens when he rejected everything his middle class parents stood for. He felt alienated from the culture of his grammar school and took to hanging about with some lads in the town centre who were into petty crime. John acknowledges that but for the shock of a Police caution and his parents spending time and emotional energy in exploring with him their shared black identity, he might have gone seriously off the rails at this time. Looking at Leroy's case file, John guesses that he has a lot of other issues to do with his sense of self to deal with as well. John agrees with his supervisor that he will spend time just 'getting alongside' Leroy as well as helping with the practical aspects of moving into his flat.

John is able to empathise with Leroy because he acknowledges that he is a 'wounded healer'.

Listening

Leroy doesn't know whether to trust this new social worker but he is curious about him. How come he, Leroy, is where he is in life and this other young black guy is going to be a social worker? He seems to be more interested in finding out what Leroy thinks about stuff than in buying bedding and furniture and he hasn't lectured him about staying out of trouble. Still, Leroy has to admit that they've bought some pretty cool stuff for the flat! In truth, Leroy is a bit scared about leaving care and it's bringing back all that stuff about his family. He tells John that it's bound to go wrong because everything does for him, probably because he's basically a bad person. John wants to know where Leroy got that idea from and Leroy tells him that his sister Sharon always said he'd got the devil in him, whereas Robbie was a child of God. Leroy thinks she was just making excuses for the fact that she didn't want to look after both of them, but still, it hurt. Anyway, Leroy thinks it might be true. He never seemed to be able to stop screwing up in his various foster homes, even when he quite liked it there.

John is puzzled by this way of looking at religion and the world. He sees from Leroy's file that the family attended the Pentecostal Church. He's beginning to sense a lot of pain coming through from Leroy and thinks he might be getting out of his depth with the religious stuff. He's worried about talking to his supervisor about it because he doesn't think she's very sympathetic to religion and he's afraid she might suggest that Leroy should go for psychiatric assessment. He decides to talk first to his vicar in general terms about these sorts of beliefs.

Understanding

Leroy is a bit worried that he might have said too much. John didn't seem to understand what he was saying about the devil, and his experience of social workers is that they tend to see him as a problem. John did, however, say that his religious experiences can't have been all bad – he seemed to enjoy Sunday School for a time at the first foster home. That's when Leroy remembered that what he really liked was the idea of

God as his father – that had helped him sometimes when he felt very rejected by everyone around him. John meanwhile learns from his vicar that certain evangelical groups do personify the devil and some maintain beliefs in demon possession and will pray for the affected individual to be 'delivered'. So Leroy is actually reflecting what might have been said to him or at least beliefs which might have been common in the church which his family attended, rather than experiencing some personal delusion. Feeling more confident of his ground now, John discusses this issue with his supervisor. They agree that it's not hard to see how Leroy has very low self-esteem and his problematic behaviours could well be a product of self-fulfilling prophecy combined with getting in the wrong company and so on. The supervisor suggests that John looks at narrative theory as a possible approach to working with Leroy, but is insistent that if Leroy needs in-depth counselling he should be referred to the psychological services. In part this is because John's placement will soon be over, and the case will be closed by the Leaving Care team at about the same time if all goes to plan and Leroy is settled into his flat. They agree that John should use the remaining time to focus on the positive things in Leroy's life which he can build on (he has, for example, recently started a job at a local garage where he is getting training as a mechanic) as well as encouraging Leroy to seek out other supports, including, if John thinks it appropriate, contact with a local church. Leroy gives John the clue here by casually mentioning that he had seen some black guys outside the church just down the road from his flat and he thought he might give it a try one day.

John is very concerned to continue to engage with Leroy as a whole person and therefore continues to show interest in all areas of his life. He thinks that although some of Leroy's more complex psychological, and, as he now believes, also spiritual, problems may be beyond what they can work on together, one thing he can do is to nurture Leroy's sense of wholeness. He has, after all, shown considerable resilience throughout his life and has many positive qualities which have been remarked on before. For his part, Leroy is relieved that John continues to treat him as normal and trusts him with more disclosures about how he feels deep within himself at some of his worst times. To his surprise, through sharing this with someone else he also identifies some of his inner strengths and realises that his spirituality is an important part of who he is.

Interpreting

Leroy moves into his flat and shortly after John finishes his placement and says his goodbyes. Leroy is feeling optimistic about life at this point, and, although grateful to John for his help, is not too bothered about him going. However, shortly after, the garage where he works closes down without warning as far as Leroy is concerned. Without seeing people at work every day he starts to feel very lonely, and he can no longer manage his money. He calls in at his last hostel but John has already left and no one else seems very interested in him, telling him that his case is now closed. He remembers that John had encouraged him to try that church down the road and wanders in one Sunday morning. However, there just seem to be a lot of young families and he doesn't see any of the young black guys that he had seen outside a few months ago. Although he is invited to stay for coffee, he feels like a fish out of water and leaves quickly after the service. He starts to feel the old despair creeping in and returns to what he knows – hanging about on street corners and talking to other lads doing the same. It isn't long before he is back in the old pattern of stealing to buy food and drugs, even though he is disgusted with himself for relapsing because he had been clean for some time. He wonders what John would think of him now, thinking that his life going downhill again just confirms that he is fundamentally no good. Eventually, Leroy finds himself up in Court for burglary and is remanded in custody.

Peter, the prison chaplain, is asked to see Leroy as the prison officers are worried that he might be suicidal; apparently he has said he would like to talk to a pastor. Peter finds that although Leroy says he thinks his life has been a waste of time so far, he has not given up altogether. However, he wants to know whether Peter thinks his sister was right and he is really bad through and through. Peter begins to explore with Leroy what he himself thinks and why. Very gently, Peter offers Leroy a different view of God and human nature and they begin to 'co-construct' a different narrative for Leroy's life. Peter knows that work is done when Leroy volunteers that he has turned a corner, that regardless of what sentence he receives from the Court, he sees the world and himself with fresh eyes. He has positive plans for life outside should he receive a community sentence, but equally, should he receive a prison sentence, he intends to use the time to read and reflect, to write to his family, explaining that he understands now the difficulties that they all faced, as well as pursuing his education and vocational skills. Leroy comments that suddenly it all seems to be coming together and says he feels 'transformed', and Peter marvels that such a troubled young man has managed to transcend his hurtful past.

Conclusion

This chapter has explored how spiritual care might be offered as an embedded aspect of mainstream social work practice, growing out of those core approaches and skills which social workers employ routinely. We have seen how such an approach to spiritual care is rooted in the casework method developed as social work established itself as a secular profession yet also resonates with key contemporary interventions. The argument has been put forward that if social work as a professional activity is to be truly responsive to the service user need, and is to rise to the challenge of anti-discriminatory practice, every social worker should be prepared to go some way along the road of spiritually sensitive practice. Nevertheless, there will be huge variation in the extent to which an individual social worker is both willing and able to offer spiritual care.

What this chapter has *not* done is to suggest a set of spiritual interventions which employ spiritual practices common to faith communities, such as praying with and for another, or which are based on theological precept or religious rite, such as 'forgiveness techniques' (Canda and Furman, 1999). This is a significant break with the social work spiritual practice developed in the US. It is our view that social work remains a secular activity, even when delivered by faith organisations, and the place for such distinctly spiritual or religious practices is not within the social work encounter but within the private or community spiritual life. The task of the social worker in offering spiritual care is more about facilitating spiritual understanding and connection with helpful spiritual resources than about engaging directly in spiritual activity. Nevertheless, the spiritually sensitive interaction between the social worker and the service user might itself be spiritually empowering and a significant resource from which the service user may derive strength and resilience.

One reason for eschewing direct spiritual or religious practices is that any such practices are located within a particular religious or cultural tradition, whereas social work practice should endeavour to be both multicultural and transcultural. We shall look further in Chapter 8 at how the practice of social work which draws on cultural and spiritual traditions other than those of the Anglo-Saxon and developed world can open up our understanding of spirituality and our vision of spiritual care. One critical difference is the emphasis placed on individual autonomy as opposed to community responsibility, and the one-to-one engagement favoured by western models of social work. Although our focus in this chapter has been on the spiritual care of the individual, we have repeatedly looked to wider sources of support. Chapter 6 looks at the context and contribution of the multidisciplinary team.

taking it further

- Canda, E. and Furman, L. (1999) *Spiritual Diversity in Social Work Practice: The Heart of Helping* (New York: The Free Press).
- Coyte, M.E., Gilbert, P. and Nicholls, V. (2007) *Spirituality, Values and Mental Health: Jewels for the Journey* (London: Jessica Kingsley).
- Darlington, Y. and Bland, R. (1999) 'Strategies for encouraging and maintaining hope among people living with a serious mental illness', *Australian Social Work*, 52: 3, 17–23.
- Greene, R. (ed.) (2002) *Resiliency: An Integrated Approach to Practice, Policy and Research* (Washington, DC: NASW Press).
- Mathews, I. (2009) *Social Work and Spirituality* (Exeter: Learning Matters).

6

chapter

Spiritual care in the multidisciplinary team

Introduction

So far in this book we have been exploring spirituality, spiritual need and spiritual care largely from the perspective of the individual (albeit the individual in community) and in terms of the one-to-one encounter between the social worker and the service user. However, as the 'Fellow Traveller' model indicates, there may be several travellers for part or perhaps all of the journey. Such a model is very familiar to social work. Social work has increasingly found itself looking to combine its expertise with that of other members of the multidisciplinary team to provide a more effective response. Moreover, in the UK, where statutory work is the primary shaper of social work practice, interprofessional and multi-agency working is increasingly a government requirement. In this chapter we shall trace the development of the concept and practice of multidisciplinary working and consider how this applies to spiritual care.

Spiritual care does not carry with it the same statutory imperatives as many other social work roles and tasks, but it did feature in one of the earliest examples of the multidisciplinary team – the hospice model as established by Cicely Saunders (Saunders, 1990). We shall look at the example of the palliative care team as one of two extended case studies which will form a substantial section of this chapter. The other example is taken from an area of practice which has more recently become the focus of the multidisciplinary team – youth offending teams built around the model of Restorative Justice.

Finally, this chapter will also consider the personal spirituality and spiritual needs of the individual social worker and of colleagues. A growing literature on reflective/reflexive practice over the past decade has highlighted the importance of each worker understanding the personal characteristics which they bring to the professional intervention and their relationship with the service user's unique make-up and situation. These two sides of the coin have reciprocal impact on the worker–user interaction, both generally and in the specific 'caring moment'. It is in social work training that the foundations for reflective/reflexive practice must be laid down, and therefore we shall also consider the spirituality and spiritual needs of social work students and the impact of group and classroom dynamics. Some students grapple with a perceived conflict between their personal belief system and contemporary social work values. Others, coming from a culture which does not distinguish between secular and religious, experience profound dissonance with the neglect of spirituality and assumptions of secularity embedded in social work education in the Anglo-Saxon western tradition.

Spirituality is of particular relevance to the dynamics of the multidisciplinary team, where it may be that one member needs the support of another in order to sustain their contribution at times of significant personal need. Research into stress and burn-out has indicated the importance of the team providing mutual support. This is acknowledged to be crucial when working within situations of severe trauma and existential challenge, where spiritual needs commonly come to the fore.

Background to interprofessional working

The current emphasis on interprofessional and multi-agency working has been building in the UK since the mid-1970s, when a series of Government consultative documents, guidance and directives aimed at promoting collaborative arrangements between Health Authorities and Local Authority Social Service Departments was issued. The concentration during this period was on joint planning and joint finance, since the division between health and social care created through legislation in the early 1970s resulted almost immediately in disputes about responsibilities (particularly budgetary) and problems in coordinating services to the individual. It was these two aspects – better use of public money and more tailored, efficient individual care packages – which were foremost in the drivers for the reform of community care in the 1980s. The 1989 White Paper, *Caring for People*, devoted chapter 6 to 'Collaborative Working', in recognition of the fact that the reforms would not work without strategies for effective working together.

Right from the outset, however, the focus was on achieving cost-effective, streamlined outcomes, and away from the machinery of process. Service outcomes are measured, not the inputs of different professionals. This has particular implications for spiritual care, where 'outcomes' are notoriously difficult to identify and certainly to measure (Holloway, 2007). This context for health-care provision through the 1990s may conceivably have influenced the popularity of standardised measures of spirituality among health care professionals who also increasingly found themselves charged with the responsibility to meet the 'spiritual needs' of patients alongside all other aspects of care. Throughout the 1990s the importance of the health and social care interface was increasingly recognised, not just in terms of services for adults with long-term conditions – frail older people, people with mental health problems, physically disabled and learning-disabled people – but also for the care and protection of vulnerable groups of all ages. Thus the twin concepts of risk and safeguarding were added as a second major driver shaping models of interprofessional working. This has widened the network of professionals considerably, most notably in respect of education professionals and police and Criminal Justice agencies. What hope does spiritual care have of retaining a voice when squeezed between such powerful imperatives? We shall return to this question in the case studies.

Although the specific context in which interprofessional working has developed in the UK is particular to the policy and statutory requirements placed on UK social work, the broader context of changing demographic patterns and a distinct shift in the culture of human services is common across the world. The global context demonstrates that this theme of interprofessional working to deliver care which is more person-centred, flexible to the needs of the individual and which balances respect for different cultural patterns and empowerment of individual choice, with the need to manage risk and protect the vulnerable, is shared across the world (Holloway and Lymbery, 2007). Viewed globally, with the huge variations in that intricate meshing of individual, family, local community and wider society which different cultures demonstrate, the significance of understanding religion and spirituality in achieving these goals of interprofessional working begins to emerge. We shall explore this particular aspect further in the final chapter. Yet we can also see its significance in the case studies, set as they are in the multicultural contexts of contemporary social work practice.

What is multidisciplinary working?

The current interest in multidisciplinary working stems largely from the results of public enquiries when things go wrong, where, repeatedly, the failure of agencies to work together is cited as one of the main reasons for tragic outcomes. We have to return to work which is now a decade or so old to find detailed consideration of what it is that constitutes multidisciplinary working, where and how does it flourish and what are the obstacles and inhibiting factors.

One of the issues in achieving better understanding between professionals and agencies is that terms are used interchangeably and it may be that we start from the false premise that we are all talking about the same thing. Leathard's analysis of the language used is helpful here in that she points out that some terms deal with a professional concept, some are describing a work process and a third category is concerned with the relationships and working arrangements between agencies (see Leathard, 1994, p. 5, table 1.1). So, for example, *joint working* describes the process of working together, but unless it is genuinely *interprofessional* – that is working at the interface between one or more professions, based on shared concepts, values, assumptions and sometimes shared roles and tasks – it may be more accurate to say that joint working describes a number of professionals working simultaneously on the same case where the *working arrangements* between their agencies are the main vehicle for coordination and collaboration. Biggs (1997) further explicates this by defining *interprofessional* as the relations between different professionals, whether they be based in different agencies or within multidisciplinary teams; *interagency collaboration* as the relations between different organisations or agencies; and *multidisciplinary working* as the working arrangements, whether that be in multidisciplinary teams, networks or interest groups. Biggs goes on to point out that there are also subtle but significant differences in the meanings attached to what it is we say we *do* together. *Collaboration* implies working together to achieve what no single professional or agency can achieve on its own; *cooperation* contains positive connotations of each agency or professional adjusting their own practice for the common good; and *coordination* implies taking account of each other's activities and agendas to address a shared task.

Let us pause for a moment to consider the implications of this discussion for spiritual care. In the first place, the only person who is automatically deemed to have responsibility for spiritual care is the chaplain or minister of religion from the person's community. The only setting in which chaplains or ministers are formally part of a multidisciplinary team is within the hospice, and possibly the hospital (more so in the US than, for example, in the UK). In other institutional settings, such as the prison, university or school, the chaplain may be formally appointed to the institution and have regular access to other professionals in that setting; but they will often be based outside in the community and potentially could do their job without any actual *joint working* with other professionals. Equally, those other professionals – teachers, social workers and prison officers – may pay scant attention to the chaplain or regard his/her job as limited to a number of routinely undertaken tasks (such as leading services or combined worship). This was not quite what we had in mind when we referred in Chapter 5 to the resources of the multidisciplinary team in providing spiritual care. Nor does it do justice to the potential contained within Biggs' definitions of collaboration, cooperation or, indeed, coordination, as discussed above. To take this further, we need to look at the organisational structures through which multidisciplinary working may operate.

Organisational structures

Ovretveit (1997) suggests that interprofessional working takes place across a spectrum of arrangements, ranging from loose networks to integrated interprofessional teams. Interprofessional teams may either operate according to collective responsibility – that is, the case is held by the team – or may operate as a team of coordinated professionals where one person may hold responsibility while others contribute to the intervention. A formal network, on the other hand, operates around a focal structure, such as a monthly meeting of agency and professional representatives, while each single professional and agency carries on its business separately. A loose network will typically operate within a particular geographical area and may rely on a patchwork of collaborative arrangements, including 'ad hoc' meetings as the need arises, not necessarily involving all members of the network on any one occasion. Any of these arrangements may be supported by posts specifically set up to facilitate multidisciplinary working. For example, social workers may be attached to schools or GP (family doctor) surgeries; liaison workers (who might be from any profession) may have designated responsibility for maintaining the contacts between an institutional setting and specific agencies or groups of professionals within the community (such as between a hospital team and a community child development clinic).

Let us apply these arrangements to a range of multidisciplinary teams in which social workers are employed, to see how spiritual care might commonly be 'covered'.

- We can see that a hospice team is commonly an example of the fully integrated team holding collective responsibility, in which the chaplain or spiritual care advisor is a recognised team member. The extent to which spiritual care is left to the chaplain or seen as a team responsibility with the chaplain making her/his particular contribution will depend on the interests, experience and skills of the other team members.
- A child development unit also provides an example of an integrated multidisciplinary team, but is unlikely, unless in a faith organisation, to include a chaplain. Despite increasing attention being paid to the religious needs of the child (Horwath and Lees, 2008), the extent to which the child's spirituality will be taken into account in any assessment or intervention plan is questionable and probably reliant on the predisposition of individual workers.

- A community mental health team is more likely to operate as a team of coordinated professionals, usually based in the same place, in which one person will carry lead responsibility. It is not usual for a religious professional to be a member of such a team, although if religious or spiritual issues are significant (often seen as part of the person's mental health problem, such as delusions with a strong religious theme) a rapport may be built up with a community pastor. In some mental health teams, however, spiritual assessment may routinely form part of their initial assessment.
- A person with learning disability living in supported housing is likely to be supported by a key worker within a formal network made up of health and social care professionals within a single agency or specific joint provision. Spiritual care may be included in their personal care plan, but it is unlikely to be offered directly by the key worker or other member of the network, although they may facilitate it. For example, it may be identified at assessment that observation of their religion is an essential need for the service user and the key worker may arrange for a member of that religious community to accompany the service user to religious services. Under such arrangements, it is most likely that if a particular spiritual need or crisis arose, the key worker would contact the 'friend' or minister.
- At the furthest end of Ovretveit's spectrum, a person with serious alcohol dependency may well be known to a wide range of health, Criminal Justice and social work agencies, any one of which may carry formal responsibility for the 'case' depending on the most recent events, but this would be operating as a loose individualised network, dependent for coordination upon the initiatives of individual workers. It might include a church which runs a social action programme and it is highly likely that the health and social care professionals would assume that any spiritual needs were being taken care of by the church.

So the extent to which spirituality and spiritual needs are routinely addressed will vary tremendously, and for the most part, the social worker is likely to assume that it is not their responsibility.

Interprofessional issues

All this is well and good, provided we assume that people's spiritual needs arise in neat compartments of their lives. Not even the tightly knit multi-disciplinary team can offer spiritual care as part of their integrated mission unless the professionals themselves are willing and able to work together in relation to the spiritual dimension. Our Fellow Traveller model pre-supposes that all the 'team' will engage with spirituality at some level, even if it is simply to determine whether or not spiritual need is present and its significance for the service user.

Biggs suggests that for professionals to work together successfully in the contemporary world of health and social care four things are fundamental. First, each professional must recognise the specialist expertise of each other. This has to do with their core identity and therefore the particular contribution which each can make, and it is as important that we recognise this in ourselves as that we acknowledge it in others. Clearly there is overlap, and problems occur when a particular profession loses direction or confidence, or feels that its core identity is under threat from external factors. Sometimes, this results in 'territorial wars' as one group is perceived to be encroaching on the work of another.

It might be thought that when it comes to spiritual care there is clear recognition that this belongs to the chaplain or other religious professional. Although this is self-evidently true, it is rather more complicated in practice, partly because contemporary definitions of spirituality have distanced spirituality from religion, and also because chaplains working in secular settings have increasingly seen themselves as offering general listening and counselling and certainly not perceived their role to be that of the evangelist or to force religion onto people (Billings, 1992; Lloyd, 1995). Lloyd argues that chaplains should see their role as 'distinctive yet integrated' (Lloyd, 1995), pointing out that one major contribution that the chaplain can make on the multidisciplinary team is in challenging the dominant ethos of effectiveness measurement, underpinned by positivist assumptions about 'what works'. Pastoral care is familiar with the notion that staying with the questions is as important as finding answers, and this insight from spiritual care has considerable applicability in the dilemmas and paradoxes of contemporary health and social care. On the flip side of the coin, however, Paley (2009) argues that nurses in the US, and potentially in the UK, are accruing to themselves the remit of spiritual care and functioning as 'nurse chaplains', bypassing the chaplain on the team. Social work, as we have already seen, is unlikely to follow this path, but it has a long way to go in working out both its own contribution to spiritual care and its relationship with other professionals, particularly religious professionals and spiritual care advisors. One model which has been suggested is that social work should adopt the idea of 'spiritual champions', which is becoming increasingly popular in health services (Whiting, 2009). In this model one member of the team particularly 'looks out for' the spiritual needs of the service user population, ensuring attention is paid to recording their spiritual and religious preferences (including those of atheists) and to facilitating and protecting 'sacred spaces' as well as spiritual practices. The Mayday Healthcare NHS Trust reports that 96 per cent of their patients had their spiritual needs recorded after the introduction of spiritual champions, compared to 18 per cent before (www.mayday hospital.org.uk).

The reason for social work to make progress on this lies in Biggs' second fundamental criterion for successful interprofessional working: that all members of the team must recognise that the tasks facing health and social care services are too complex to be undertaken by one single profession, and the required as well as the best outcomes can only be achieved through a combination of different inputs. The powerful voice of mental health service users who articulate that spirituality, spiritual need and spiritual pain constitute an essential dynamic in their wellness and well-being provides one clear argument that should persuade professionals to include spirituality in their 'working together'. We have looked at many other illustrations in this book. The current emphasis on person-centred practice should lead social work to the position that if something is important for this service user, it should be included in their care plan. But how do we know if spirituality is important unless we find some way with which we are comfortable of asking and assessing that?

stop and think

- In your experience of working in teams, is there any formal way of including spiritual needs in multidisciplinary assessments?
- Does it happen in practice?

Third, Biggs suggests that in interprofessional working, each separate profession, including its management and administration, must recognise a shared primary goal. Fourth, this primary goal must be grounded in meaningful user participation throughout all processes and levels. If we are required to distil our many separate objectives into one 'primary' goal which runs across health and social care, this surely has to be the *enhanced well-being* of the service user. This may be achieved through addressing their physical, emotional, social or spiritual needs, separately or together, and it will need to take account of vulnerabilities and rights. The unique balance of those for each service user will determine the particular roles and tasks of any one professional and the priority given at any one point in time. We can only reach this working agreement through listening to the service user's own narrative, and this may well include their spirituality – why should it not? It is our own biases, stereotypical assumptions, mistrust of or lack of respect for the unfamiliar or culturally alien, and our inability or unpreparedness to work flexibly across boundaries which might prevent us from recognising spiritual need and spiritual care within the whole picture. These are the same problems which are said to be the continuing obstacles to successful interprofessional working, whatever policy initiatives or joint structures are put in place!

We shall turn now to examining how the multidisciplinary team works in two areas of practice which have at their heart concepts which are core to spirituality and spiritual care. First, palliative care, with its origins in the hospice, has from those earliest beginnings recognised the importance of the multidisciplinary team, where different professionals not only offer their distinctive contributions but also combine their expertise in a team approach. Second, Restorative Justice, one of the most recent practice developments, is an approach which is spreading through Criminal Justice agencies, police and penal institutions and social care agencies. Agencies and professionals which espouse restorative approaches are working from a common value-base, with a shared primary objective which requires the voluntary participation of both the offender and the victim, and it is this framework which gives direction and purpose to their arrangements and mechanisms for working together. That both areas of practice are complex and require multi-agency resources and interprofessional expertise to achieve the best outcome is unquestionable. Spiritual care has always been an accepted part of palliative care and for some at least, it is equally embedded in Restorative Justice. These two areas of practice may seem to be worlds apart and for social work, to represent opposing axes in their remit – the age-old dilemma of care or control. However, both are centrally concerned with suffering and healing.

Palliative care

The philosophy of palliative care is integrally bound up with a holistic approach, which neither prioritises one area of the patient's need or pain over another nor automatically privileges the role of any one profession over another. In practice, since the objective of palliative care is the comfort and dignity of the dying person up until their death ('care not cure'), the relief of physical symptoms so as to achieve a peaceful death is of prime concern. This means that medical practitioners and nurses are the first line of care, increasingly supported by physiotherapists who have introduced rehabilitation techniques into palliative care for the further relief of symptoms and to help the dying person achieve greater control over their life. Despite the understandable focus on physical problems, however, there is widespread recognition in palliative care that social, emotional and spiritual issues can exacerbate physical problems and interfere with their treatment and management. Thus social workers and chaplains are regarded as essential members of the team, which often includes occupational, art and complementary therapists.

However, Reese and Sontag (2001) argue that social workers continue to feel that there is a lack of understanding of their role, a failure to use social work to its potential and competition between social workers, nurses and chaplains over psychosocial and spiritual care. The authors suggest 'solutions' which reiterate those principles for successful inter-professional working which we have already examined in the general context: respect for each other's expertise and understanding our different value positions but bringing these together in the shared goal of the best interests of the service user. Likewise, chaplains complain that their role is frequently seen by other members of the team as limited to ' "hand holders" or last minute performers of religious rites' (McClung et al., 2006, p. 149).

Saunders' original vision of hospice care included attending to spiritual pain, and recent definitions of and standards for palliative care include spiritual care as essential to good palliative care and the responsibility of every member of the team (Puchalski et al., 2006). The question of how and by whom spiritual care is offered is, however, rather more complex and likely to vary according to the members of the team, the patient and the specific care context. One study found palliative care workers feeling daunted by the expectation that all members of the team should provide spiritual care and also fearful that such an approach can be an imposition and overwhelming for the patient. For some workers, however, their work *is* their spiritual vocation and therefore spiritual care is implicit in all they do (Sinclair et al., 2006). For others, it is an explicit aspect involving particular tasks such as spiritual history taking, where more specific or complicated spiritual needs should be referred to the chaplain (McClung et al., 2006; Puchalski et al., 2006).

Case study

Tim had developed a brain tumour at the age of 30. He was referred to Ella (an art therapist at the hospice) by the psychiatrist following a period as a psychiatric in-patient being treated for severe depression. Tim's wife, Claire, was receiving cognitive behavioural therapy from the clinical psychologist but Tim himself had become completely withdrawn when the tumour was diagnosed and it was felt he might benefit from non-verbal therapy. The psychiatric episode appeared to have been triggered by existential despair – Tim had been brought up to believe that if he worked hard, the rewards would follow, and now he felt both cheated and a failure. Tim was quite resistant initially to engaging with the therapy and avoided the topic of illness altogether in the limited conversations which he had with people, including his wife.

Tim's speech was by now quite badly affected, but he managed to get across to Ella that he was afraid of failing the task. When he did start to draw (after about a month), he became very anxious but continued nevertheless. At times he was both angry and frustrated. Ella sees her role as being available to the patient, as a resource or companion on their therapeutic journey. With Tim, she tried to create a calm accepting environment in which his drawings could be lodged.

In Tim's notes it was recorded that he was a Catholic, but he had angrily declined the ministrations of the priest when in hospital. However, one day, a few weeks before his death, he drew a picture of a man struggling to climb the steps of a church whose door was closed with a large key protruding. Tim presented this picture to Ella, watching for her reaction. Ella guessed that Tim was experiencing barriers in his spiritual life and asked him whether he was able to draw on the resources of his faith. When Tim shook his head, she asked whether he would like the priest from the Church which he used to attend to visit him. Tim nodded and smiled. Over the ensuing weeks in which Tim received Holy Communion each week, his drawings became more peaceful.

Tim had initially been rejecting of Claire, wanting to cut himself off from his family. Tim and Claire have a 1-year-old daughter, Bethany. Ella had asked the social worker to talk to Claire, thinking that, although she was receiving psychological treatment for her own depression, she might benefit from the social worker's family perspective. Claire is pleased to talk to the social worker (Sheila) and shares her terrible sense of loss of Tim as a parent for their only child. She understands why seeing her and Bethany might be too painful for Tim, but at the same time, she worries about how she is going to give Bethany any sense of her father if she cannot create a memory box which includes a photo of the three of them together. She also wants to have Bethany christened before Tim dies. Claire is not a Catholic but they had agreed that their children would be christened as Catholics. However, Tim's diagnosis shortly after Bethany was born had pushed that event onto the back-burner. Somehow she feels that if she could only get Tim to agree to Bethany being christened now, it would create a spiritual bond between them that might help to heal the wounds and make up for the lack of verbal communication.

The social worker doesn't know what to do about this issue. It is not something she has come across before. She talks to Ella about it and discovers that Tim's drawing has led to his re-establishing his own spiritual practices. Ella suggests that she should ask Tim whether he would like to do a drawing for Claire and Bethany. Tim shakes his head but blurts out 'see', pointing to his eyes. Gradually Tim starts to spend time with Claire, and a bit later, with Bethany. They organise Bethany's christening together at the hospice, taken by Tim's parish priest, with close family and several members of the hospice team attending. It was an occasion which seemed to bring them all together as a 'family'. The professional team shared with each other how it had seemed to be an occasion of reconciliation which had helped each of them to deal with their own difficulties in this case. At the same time it was a celebration of a new life, and representation of hope both now and for the future. These were themes which Tim and Claire carried through into planning for the funeral.

Shortly after the christening, although his art therapy sessions had ceased, Tim did one more drawing which he presented to Ella two days before he died for her to keep (his previous drawings had been discarded). Ella believes that Tim had finally found a new way of valuing his life.

Restorative Justice

Restorative Justice provides an illuminating case study not only of how the themes of this book interweave, but also of how a holistic understanding of spirituality, as proposed in this book, provides an 'ultimate framework' for this area of work. From time immemorial, societies have had to grapple with the challenges of what in current parlance is now called 'anti-social behaviour'. There have always been individuals and groups of people who have challenged and 'transgressed' the particular set of norms that are deemed to be necessary for community coherence and well-being. Criminal Justice systems have therefore been established to deal with such behaviours, with the dual purpose of protecting a community from such destructive excesses, ultimately by removing the offender's liberty, and of deterring and ideally transforming the offender's behaviour into a more positive and creative lifestyle. Traditionally – in the UK at least – this involved a separation of the offender from the victim and the direct consequences of the offending behaviour. The judicial process 'took over', determined the outcome by imposing a particular 'sentence' and where necessary placed the offender under the supervision of designated professionals. Throughout the process the focus was upon the individual whose behaviour caused such offence.

The desire to understand the causes and contributory factors leading to various types of anti-social behaviour continued to intrigue students of criminology and those involved in Criminal Justice systems. Criminal Justice and Youth Justice professionals have been charged with the responsibility of presenting reports to the court that seek to place the offender and the offence 'in context' to enable the court to balance its dual role of protecting society and punishing the offender when passing sentence. Although there has been some understanding of the 'ripple effect' of anti-social behaviour and its impact upon the community, it has only been relatively recently in the UK that these concerns have moved centre-stage with various 'victim support' schemes being introduced, and the development of Restorative Justice (United Nations Commission, 2002; Home Office, 2003, 2004).

Restorative Justice, Liebmann (2007) argues, helps to

 restore people after harm has been caused, whether in a family, school, community, criminal justice or prison context... restorative justice is now a global movement. (p. 17)

This approach clearly applies to a wide range of situations where people are hurt, damaged or victimised by the behaviour of others. For the purpose of our discussion, however, we will continue to focus upon aspects of Criminal Justice, in which Liebmann outlines some of the basic principles. These include,

- *Offenders taking responsibility for what they have done.* Taking responsibility means saying, 'Yes, I did it and I take responsibility for the harm I caused'. It is the starting point for restorative justice.
- *There is a dialogue to achieve understanding.* Some offenders do not understand how they have harmed their victims. It is only when they hear from the victim that they realise the upset they have caused.
- *There is an attempt to put right the harm done.* Sometimes an apology is enough, but often more is needed as there may be practical issues to put right.
- *Offenders look at how to avoid future offending.* When they realise the harm they have done many offenders wish to avoid repeating it... the strong point of restorative justice... is that it provides the offender with the motivation to build a different kind of life.
- *The community helps to reintegrate both victim and offender*... victims too need re-integrating into the community – they often feel alienated and cut off as a result of crime (p. 27).

These fundamental principles of Restorative Justice are powerful illustrations of a question we will consider in greater depth in the final chapters of this book: *how can we live well in this place?* It is no longer the offender and the victim being seen in isolation: it has now become a community issue that raises the future focus of 'how can we move on into the future creatively and positively, and avoid getting stuck and entrapped by what has happened?'. Meaning, purpose and interconnectedness – themes identified with an understanding of spirituality – are clearly of central importance. Some of the language of Restorative Justice – reconciliation, guilt and forgiveness, for example – has strong religious overtones not least because there is within many religions a strong impetus to work hard to heal fractured relationships at both individual and wider levels. But in secular terms they are equally powerful concepts, which is why we argue for an understanding of spirituality that has both secular and religious frameworks within which these terms powerfully belong.

A striking example of this was The Forgiveness Project (1993) in London which highlighted the ways in which forgiveness is an important dynamic in the healing process. Tim Newell, former Governor of Grendon Underwood Prison, commented on the project:

> It's interesting to see that people recognise how essential forgiveness is to recovery. The main dynamic which stops victims, offenders and their communities of care from moving on after the trauma of crime is the inability to forgive the person responsible for the crime. This identifies forever the person with the deed and can freeze relationships and life stories for ever. (cited in Moss, 2005, p. 58)

In Restorative Justice, forgiveness is an activity that respects other people as being intrinsically worthy as individuals; it is costly to request and costly to grant; it is not 'going soft' but is the opportunity for a courageous new start (Moss, 2005). Of fundamental importance to the process of moving forward is the mutual commitment of everyone caught up in the 'hurt', to forgive, and to put an end to the anti-social behaviour. DiBlasio (1993) argues that

> Forgiveness is conceptually defined as letting go of the need for vengeance and releasing associated negative feelings such as bitterness and resentment. (p. 304)

Ellis (2000) takes this further by linking it into the theme of social justice by commenting that

> Forgiveness is only possible when the violence stops. It is in the ending of injustice and the journey towards a mutual and just future that forgiveness becomes revolutionary. (p. 276)

stop and think

- How comfortable are you with the notion of forgiveness in social work practice?
- Does it raise any particular dilemmas for you?

In the next chapter we shall consider environmental perspectives which help us understand not only the impact of the environment upon people and their behaviour but also the impact they in turn have upon the environment. 'Concrete jungles' which undermine our interconnectedness; environmental pollution that affects our health and well-being; and cut-throat entrepreneurship that tramples upon and disregards the value of people and communities have a powerful impact upon people and their behaviour, their ability to live well in their various 'places' and the quality of life they experience. While none of these aspects removes the individual's responsibility and accountability for anti-social behaviour, they do provide a rich interactive framework of meaning and interpretation that we dare not ignore. Spirituality, with its complex but important layers of meaning as outlined in this book, provides an 'ultimate framework' for understanding Restorative Justice that links together personal, cultural, societal, environmental and spiritual perspectives.

Case study

Jason was a 15-year-old young man who was very unhappy and troubled at school and was facing the prospect of leaving with very few academic qualifications and with little idea about what he wanted to do with his life. He was bored at school, but although he was looking forward to leaving, he was also afraid that he might not be able to cope or find a job. His parents were active members of the British National Party and frequently railed against the members of the local community from minority ethnic groups who (they said) were taking local jobs from British workers and making it difficult for young people like Jason to make their way into the world of work.

One evening Jason had been out drinking with a couple of friends, and on their way home they saw two Asian elders cautiously making their way along the street. Jason suddenly remembered everything his parents had been saying about the Asian community, and within seconds he led an attack against this couple, knocking them to the ground. He and his friends seized the woman's handbag and wrenched the man's wallet from him. After kicking them both, Jason and his friends ran off. Jason was unaware that the whole attack was captured on a CCTV camera, and prosecution inevitably followed. As part of the sentence of the court he was strongly encouraged to attend a meeting with the two people upon whom he had led the attack. He felt very upset and worried by the prospect, but after several meetings with the social worker allocated to him by the court spent discussing the offence and the ways in which his parents' views had influenced his own behaviour, he reluctantly agreed.

At the meeting the two Asian elders spoke softly about how frightened they had been by the attack; how they no longer felt able to go out in the evening; and that on the day of the attack they had missed their bus and had been walking home from helping out with a youth club in a deprived area of the city, where they were part of a team of people who provided refreshments and general support. Apparently they were 'honorary grandparents' to this youth club and all the young people enjoyed talking with them.

Jason had already begun to realise that his parents' values and attitudes were wrong, and that he and his friends had really hurt two good people who were trying hard to make a difference to young people like Jason who were struggling to make their way in life. He mumbled *sorry* to them, but wanted to get away from this painful encounter as quickly as possible. To his amazement, the woman then invited him to come along to the youth club to see it for himself. She reassured him that they would make sure he was welcomed, and promised that they would not say that Jason was the young man who had attacked them. After discussing it with the social worker who offered to take him along to the first meeting, Jason agreed.

Several months later, Jason was a regular member of the club and had begun to play a leading role. He made good use of the car mechanics club and was later offered some work experience at a local garage. His 'world view' and, indeed, his world had been transformed.

Spirituality and ourselves

Implicit in all that has gone before in this chapter is the recognition that a vital part of interprofessional working is concern for each other and recognition of our own needs, strengths and resources. No discussion of 'working together' would be complete without considering ourselves as individuals within that team context – as social work practitioners, students and educators – our individual needs and the mutual support we provide for each other. The claim we make in our professional value-base about the individual worth and dignity of each and every person with whom we are called to work applies just as much to us. We are not automata, mechanistically dispensing the benefits of our social work expertise: we are real flesh and blood, with feelings and emotions, hopes and fears, joys and hurts. However much we are called to keep a professional 'distance' between us and those with whom we work in order to focus upon *their* needs, not ours, we are still vibrant, even spiritual, human beings. The interpersonal team dynamic is as important in the spiritual domain as in any other. If we are not sufficiently in touch with our own inner core to help us understand and express what we do in our professional as well as our personal lives, we are significantly diminished. If in our practice we do not recognise, respect and respond to the spirituality of our colleague, then we not only do them an injustice, we diminish them too.

Reflective practice and spirituality

How we put this profound understanding into practice is a feature of two concepts very familiar to all social workers: reflective practice and reflexivity. These concepts are particularly important because they act as constant reminders to us to avoid mechanistic approaches in our work; to respect and value the unique individuality of the people we work with; and to be ever aware of the impact we have upon the 'helping' process. The contribution of Schon (1983) is widely acknowledged in this area. He was keen to help 'people workers' understand the rich complexity of their work and to move away from a rigid approach full of 'right answers' in which 'theory' was applied to 'practice' in an almost formulaic way. Schon by contrast talked about the 'swampy lowlands' of practice where things are far from 'cut and dried' and require instead a measure of professional artistry to ensure that the complexity of people's lives is taken seriously in our assessments and interventions. Thompson and Thompson (2008) capture this well when they suggest that

> ... we cannot expect professional knowledge to provide 'off-the-peg' solutions, like garments in a clothes shop. Rather, it is a matter of the knowledge base serving as a resource (a set of insights and understandings) that needs to be adapted to suit the circumstances. In other words, the reflective practitioner acts like a skilled tailor, using the knowledge base of his or her profession as the cloth with which to cut appropriate solutions to fit the requirements of the specific practice situation. (p. 15)

The language and imagery of artistry may not immediately sit comfortably with those for whom the stern demands of evidence-based practice weigh heavily. And yet social workers will instinctively recognise that such an approach lies at the heart of their practice and their value-base. In fact it expresses much of what we have been arguing for in this book about an understanding of spirituality within social work practice.

Schon drew a distinction between reflection-on-action and reflection-in-action. Both are important for social work practice. The former refers to the thoughtful standing back after we have completed a particular task to see if we have responded appropriately. We need also to check that we have not missed anything important or overlooked aspects of legislation or policy guidelines that were relevant to the person we were working with. In some ways it is a professional audit of our behaviour, as we assess what we did well and what we might have done differently. In this respect supervision is a crucial tool to help us develop our reflective practice skills as we review the work we have done. It is also similar, as Thompson and Thompson suggest, to reflection-for-action as we plan carefully for what we need to do (p. 16).

Reflection-in-action by contrast is the immediacy of the moment in our practice when everything is very real; when our nerve ends jangle and we have that heightened sense of awareness when the adrenalin pumps round and we have to react quickly and authentically in order to respond to the person we are working with. We are required to be very 'self-aware', especially about the impact we have upon the other person and how our values, opinions and behaviour can significantly affect the outcome of our intervention. We may need to respond to 'high or low' emotional reactions, both in the service user and in ourselves; we may feel challenged, disturbed even, as service users raise questions implicitly or explicitly about how they can or cannot make sense of what has happened to them, for example. Throughout the process, however, we need to be deeply attuned to how we are feeling and the impact this has upon the other person. This is a different aspect of being thoughtful and reflective, which has led to the popularity of the term 'reflexivity' to express this quality of self-awareness. Although some would see clear distinctions between the two terms reflective and reflexive (e.g. Rolfe et al., 2001), we prefer to see them as being closely linked in an interactive relationship, emphasising the intellectual/thoughtful and the emotional/spiritual dimensions of a working relationship.

The implications for social work education and training may be considered at a personal/individual level and also in a much wider context. As individuals, whether in training or in practice, we need to be fully aware of our spirituality, and that of the people with whom we work, as we have argued consistently throughout this book. In current trends in social work education, however, at least in the UK, this is somewhat difficult to achieve. In other parts of the world, as we have shown in this book, some social work curricula are attempting to include spirituality as a core theme. In the UK, by contrast, perhaps because of the assumed linkages with religion, there is much more caution, with the resultant lack of attention being paid to either religious or secular aspects of this theme. Social work programmes sometimes report that an individual student who has strong religious convictions has had to be counselled carefully in order to ensure that professional values are recognised, respected and practised. That this is a wholly appropriate response is in no doubt: what seems to be lacking, however, is a requirement by the General Social Care Council in the UK for a systematic exploration in social work curricula of individual faith, belief and world-views, and how these impact upon professional and personal values.

This is not to suggest that important work in this area is not being undertaken by social work educators. We are all under a professional obligation to ensure that social work students develop the skills and values that are at the root of social work practice. Spirituality seems only to appear explicitly on the curriculum, however, if it happens to interest a particular member of staff who is keen to explore it with their students. Even more rare is an exploration of these issues between academic colleagues, or with practice educators, upon whom a heavy burden of responsibility lies when they are supervising the students' practice learning. While we are not advocating a return to the 1960s enthusiasm for encounter groups as a means to sharpen students' self-awareness, we are suggesting that social work programmes need to look closely at how they work with students and help them on their individual journey, including, where appropriate, their spiritual journey.

stop and think

- How easy is/was it to talk about religion and spirituality on your social work training programme?
- As a practice educator, do I see it as part of my remit to address these issues with students?

The wider context of spirituality involves exposing students to the challenges and opportunities of what David Ford (2004), as we noted earlier in the book, calls our 'complexly religious and secular' society. Social work curricula have traditionally been very strong in their commitment to helping students understand the various cultural and structural dimensions to their social work practice. Thompson's (2006) PCS analysis of oppression and discrimination, for example, challenges any understanding of practice that is narrowly individualistic. The commitment to anti-discriminatory practice, and to taking seriously the themes of anti-racist, anti-sexist practice, alongside understanding Marxist and feminist critiques, for example, are all mainstream components of a contemporary social work curriculum. We are arguing that spirituality also has a rightful place in this endeavour, in order to ensure that religious perspectives are appropriately considered and critiqued and that secular and environmental dimensions are also included. Social work education has a commitment to ensure that students feel prepared not only to own their 'spiritual place' within this complex society but also to be able and comfortable to practise professionally in communities where faith communities are often flourishing and provide major contributions in social capital. We would argue therefore that social work students must accept the challenge of expanding their reflective learning to look into their own spiritual core.

Spiritual needs and spiritual care within the team

Perhaps because the work is so emotionally demanding, it is in the palliative care team that most attention has been given to the spiritual needs and resources of the professionals themselves, and their 'duty of care' for each other. However, research is only just beginning to uncover the complexities of this process.

A Canadian study which looked at how palliative care nurses coped with the stress of continually facing death in their work identified that they avoided burn-out if they were able to help dying people find meaning, and they were able to 'get alongside' the dying person and bereaved relatives only if they themselves could engage in personal meaning-making. Those nurses who did this most successfully were those who scored highest on what the authors termed 'spiritual quality of life' (Desbiens and Fillion, 2007). However, a Belgian study which explored spiritual and religious needs and pain among multidisciplinary health care workers found significant disparities between perceptions of their own and each other's needs. Professional groups which were seen by others to be least likely to experience spiritual distress (e.g. medical practitioners and clergy) in fact reported much higher levels of spiritual need. Most disturbing was that, regardless of the fact that there was a general affirmation of the importance of self-awareness and the ability to communicate personal needs to colleagues if one is to be able to address the spiritual needs of patients, these false assumptions about each other's needs appeared to be getting in the way of colleagues offering support to each other (Cornette, 2005). The true position is likely to be somewhere in between these polarised assumptions, with all types of staff struggling with spiritual darkness as much as light, experiencing stress and tensions within themselves and with each other, but nevertheless conscious of their mutual 'connectedness' (Sinclair et al., 2006).

Another significant contribution which is relevant for the contexts of social work practice has recently been made by two studies, one conducted in the UK and the other in the US, which examine the importance of understanding spirituality in police work (Smith and Charles, 2009). The authors highlight the territory of much police work as being

> very demanding and threatening, repeatedly dealing with death, serious injury, horrific crime scenes..., the need to be constantly on the alert,...being ostracised by communities, friends and family. All take their toll on police officers: their health, fitness and well-being. (p. 1)

These are issues which resonate with much of contemporary social work practice. It is significant therefore that these studies purport to show how spirituality as a concept illuminates the predicament faced by many police officers and how a spiritual dimension may assist with the development of effective coping strategies. Smith and Charles further believe that there is a spiritual component to much of the work undertaken and the issues being faced:

> The reality of facing death and human destructiveness on a daily basis...at a fundamental level these challenges have a spiritual component to them, [that] is often unrecognised by the police service. (p. 1)

> ... It is not just a question of whether an officer has the right uniform or if the officer's boots are shined. It is clearly just as important to ask whether the human inside the uniform has a connection, compassion, an inner strength to meet human destruction and suffering and to see his or her way to the other side, and to remain whole in the process. (p. 16)

Smith and Charles are in no doubt that spirituality needs to be taken seriously by policing organisations not only for the welfare and quality of life for their officers, but in order to deal with the profound issues that have to be tackled head-on day by day. For social work, we might say that it is not just a question of meeting performance targets and tightening safeguarding procedures but of social workers and service users managing to meet each other as whole persons in the midst of suffering, chaos and destruction.

Conclusion

It is this ability to establish and maintain meaningful connections with each other that brings together all that we know about successful working together and spiritual care. To return to the notion that each profession should be 'distinctive yet integrated' (Lloyd, 1995, p. 27), we must ask the question, *what is that distinctive contribution of social work and can it enhance the understanding and practice of spiritual care as it currently operates in health and social care services?* Hugman has suggested that a global definition of social work contains four elements: social change, (social) well-being, human rights and social justice (Hugman, 2007). Throughout this book we have shown how each of these elements connects with spirituality. The contemporary spirituality discourse is overwhelmingly concerned with the individual. For social work to put the social back into the spiritual is a contribution long overdue. Some of the ways in which we might do that are informed by an understanding of spirituality which challenges western models of both social work and spirituality. We shall explore some of these contributions from the international scene in the final chapter of this book.

The other challenge to social work is to make meaningful connections between the practice of working in partnership with service users and utilising the spiritual resources and expertise of other members of the team. If we might be forgiven for paraphrasing slightly Beresford and Trevillion's challenge for the successful delivery of integrated community care:

> Collaboration with service users and carers, and collaboration between different groups of practitioners, should not be treated as two separate issues, but as part of a single transformation of the

whole way in which we think.... This is the *spiritual* revolution for which we are still waiting (*our substitution*) (Beresford and Trevillion, 1995, p. 7).

taking it further

- Leathard, A. (1994) *Going Inter-professional* (London: Routledge).
- Orchard, H. (ed.) (2001) *Spirituality in Health Care Contexts* (London: Jessica Kingsley).
- Reese, D. and Sontag, M. (2001) 'Successful interprofessional collaboration on the Hospice Team', *Health and Social Work*, 26: 3, 167–175.
- Rumbold, B. (ed.) (2002) *Spirituality and Palliative Care* (Oxford: Oxford University Press).
- Sinclair, S., Raffin, S., Pereira, J. and Guebert, N. (2006) 'Collective soul: The spirituality of an interdisciplinary palliative care team', *Palliative and Supportive Care*, 4, 13–24.

7 Spirituality and community

chapter

Introduction

The extent to which spirituality has a community as well as an individual orientation has already been touched upon in earlier chapters. Time and time again we have recognised the importance of a social perspective to our discussion, not least when our quality of life, well-being, health and happiness are deeply influenced by our relationship with others, and in the ways in which we can often 'find' ourselves when we 'lose' ourselves in the care for others. We noted that in the post-modern era one of the attractions of the concept of spirituality is that it encourages individuals to explore their own interpretations of it, whether from a secular or a religious viewpoint. Each individual's spirituality is therefore a reflection of, and to some extent a working out of, the world-view that they have chosen, in order to give meaning and purpose to their lives. In this regard it does not matter whether or not this individual 'version' of spirituality 'chimes' with other people's: the acid test is whether it 'works' for the particular individual.

But none of us lives in isolation. Who we are, how we behave, how we treat other people and how other people treat us are equally power-ful aspects of being human. The challenges of how to enable people to live together creatively, peacefully and productively have been with us for ever, and lie at the heart of social policy and much political endeavour. As Crisp (2008) argues,

> At the very minimum it [i.e. spirituality] should at least nourish some human connections, if an expression of spirituality is to have any authenticity.

In this book we have been arguing for a broad-based understanding of spirituality that engages with our common humanity, refusing to limit the discussion to those whom Crisp (2008) describes as a 'sensitive elite with a desire for the sacred' (p. 365). Spirituality raises and seeks to engage with issues about our common humanity, and how we relate to our various environments. It is not a minority interest, or only the domain of particular groups. It is about the meaning(s) and purpose that we find in, as well ascribe to, our common humanity in its complex contexts. The community aspect to spirituality is thus an important dimension without which the spirituality discourse would be seriously limited, and reduced to an individualistic silo.

In case these observations appear remote from social work practice, it is worth reminding ourselves that social work also has its individual and community perspectives. Each individual social worker has the responsibility to develop his or her personal professional 'style' and approach in ways that encourage our personalities to shine through and enrich our practice. But there is also a shared common knowledge base, and a set of guiding principles and values that provide the framework for professional practice. If we ignore them or blatantly 'transgress', then we are held accountable to our various governing bodies, depending upon which country we work in. As a last resort our registration as social workers can be suspended or withdrawn on the grounds that dangerous practice puts vulnerable people at risk. Codes of Conduct and Statements of Ethics spell out what it means to belong to social work organisations, what standards of conduct can be expected of those who belong and what values and knowledge base underpin their practice. This is not meant to stifle debate or to clone a set of workers; but it does seek to answer a similar set of questions that are posed by contemporary spirituality: who are we; how do we behave towards others; what are our values; and what is the world-view that we seek to uphold?

It will be argued, rightly, that social work does not espouse, or uphold, one single world-view. It is, as we stated clearly in Chapter 5, a secular activity; but within the profession throughout the world there will be social workers who as individuals subscribe to religious and secular world-views. There are colleagues who espouse Marxist analyses and those who belong to a wide range of political parties or faith communities, or to none. But that is not the point being made here. Whatever world-view an individual may choose in order to provide meaning and purpose for his or her life, as a member of the social work profession there is a shared world-view that is at the heart of our enterprise. This shared world-view, which includes our values, underpins and guides our professional practice, and may be summed up in the following phrase: *celebrating diversity with social justice*. As a social work slogan, almost, it encapsulates the 'community dimension' of this chapter. We would also argue in passing that it serves as a benchmark and litmus test for all human behaviour, and therefore provides a relevant 'authenticity test' for our understanding of contemporary spirituality.

This chapter will therefore explore the community dimension of spirituality and social work: what this means and its implications for understanding both elements – spirituality and social work. This will take us into the realms of social justice, community development and the contributions of faith communities. Finally, we will consider our relationship as human beings with our environment – both natural and developed by human interventions – to introduce the ways in which contributions from an eco-perspective can enrich and deepen our understanding of spirituality.

Meaning-making in society

Societies create meaning and identity for themselves that distinctively mark them out from other societies or nations. Decisions are taken about societal structures, and how national resources are gathered and allocated for the common good and collective security. Organisations are created to deal with the darker sides of human behaviour and to respond to the needs of those who stumble or become marginalised. In effect, nations and societies grapple with the same sort of issues at the macro level as individuals do at the micro level: how to make sense of, and express, who they are, how they relate to others and the extent to which their chosen world-view sustains them in good times and bad. In other words, the very issues and themes which we were exploring around individual spirituality also ring true at the macro level.

This chapter is not the place for detailed global political analysis, but two examples of this wider context of spirituality may help to show how world-views may be challenged, modified or changed. The issue of nuclear capability has for many years pre-occupied the (so-called) super-powers, all of whom agreed that the possession of nuclear arms was an essential ingredient for their national identity and sovereignty. The world-view they had chosen as an expression of their national identity involved them having, and *in extremis* being willing to use, what are often referred to in the post-Saddam Hussein era as weapons of mass destruction (WMD). But as soon as other nations began to buy into this model of national pride and identity, and to develop a nuclear capability, a huge furore erupted, based upon the premise that only western powers could be trusted with such powerful and dangerous technology, and that developing nations should not trespass on this territory. But it is hardly surprising that with so many examples of WMD being used by major powers as expressions of their national pride and identity, other nations would also wish to express themselves, and give meaning to their nationhood, in similar ways. If there is 'one rule for the rich and another rule for the poor', then conflicting spiritualities and world-views are likely to prove politically toxic.

A further example can be found in the financial crisis that broke world-wide in 2008. This highlighted the essential world-view of contemporary capitalism: *in the dollar we trust*. The level of panic and fear that followed the banking collapse and the plummeting stock markets reminded us of the extent to which people's world-views, security, identity and essential well-being were inextricably intertwined with financial prosperity. Significantly, one of the questions these events raised was the extent to which this crisis contributed to a greater understanding of, and action towards alleviating, the debt crisis in the (so-called) third world where lives have been lived under the spectre of debt and poverty for generations. Here was an example of how the impact of a crisis upon our 'common humanity' was so often taken to mean the impact upon 'ordinary people in the rich west', not common humanity worldwide. But that the financial crisis also had a powerful impact upon the poorest of the poor globally there can be no doubt. In times of crisis, self-preservation kicks in – and that speaks volumes about the world-view we hold, and its underlying spirituality.

These are but two examples at the international level where differing nation-based world-views have been put under the spotlight, and where the range of questions posed by our discussion of spirituality have demanded an answer. They also highlight the importance of developing a community dimension to our theorising of spirituality. They illustrate the diversity in our understanding of 'community' as a concept: it can range from small local neighbourhoods to the international arena. As Coates et al. (2005) argue, we are seeking 'a new understanding of what it means to be human', because

> everything is *interdependent* and connected and, within an overarching and integrated whole, there are many overlapping and interlocking sub-systems, e.g. families, villages, cultures, economies and ecologies. While all living beings may be conceived as independent in particular contexts, they are also tied into many systems... To understand one part, you must understand how that part is connected to other parts. (p. 11)

At all these levels, therefore, the questions posed by the contemporary debate about spirituality are deeply relevant.

Celebrating diversity with social justice

We have already argued that spirituality, as a 'gateway word', invites us to explore key questions and issues about who we are, the meaning-making that we engage in and the nature of our relationships with others. The community aspects of this have already been lightly touched upon in the introduction to this chapter, but for the moment we will continue to focus on social work as a profession, and as a collection of professional bodies and workers worldwide. The linking of *celebrating diversity* with *social justice* we would argue encapsulates the heart and values of social work, and may indeed be seen as an expression of the profession's 'spirit'. It is a commitment to these linked themes and values that 'makes us tick'; it is the denial of them that stirs up in us not only our human compassion but also our indignation and anger; it is also the vision that sustains and nourishes us in challenging and difficult times.

The linkage is important. It would be perfectly feasible, for instance, to promulgate a celebration of diversity that has no moral basis, or no benchmarks by which to judge the outcomes of people's behaviour. Those who espouse a world-view that discriminates negatively against people of colour, for example, could claim that their position deserves to be equally celebrated as part of the rich tapestry of human opinion. In response, social work (and we are not alone in this) would assert its value-base and make a value judgement that would cause us fundamentally to disagree with such views. As a profession, therefore, we would argue for a benchmark that helps to evaluate such positions. It is for this reason that social work would want to link social justice with the celebration of diversity, *precisely because it provides an evaluative benchmark*. There are limits to the extent that diversity can be celebrated, and these limits are contained within the value-base of social work that eschews oppressive discriminatory behaviour and anything which diminishes and demeans another human being. So, for social work, we are bold to claim that an authentic spirituality acknowledges, and operationalises, both aspects of this statement. Furthermore, we would argue that any world-view that undermines either or both aspects represents an inauthentic spirituality. Such a position is unashamedly values-led and makes no claim for neutrality or even-handedness; it is nevertheless the core of our professional value-base, and is an important expression of the spirit of social work.

These commitments are enshrined in various professional statements. Hodge (2007) refers to the US National Association of Social Workers' declaration that 'Social justice is a central social work value' (NASW, 2000). The British Association of Social Workers' Code of Ethics (2002), having re-affirmed the fundamental value, dignity and worth of every human being, goes on to stress the importance of social justice, emphasising 'the fair and equitable distribution of resources to meet basic human needs', together with

> the pursuit of social justice [that] involves identifying, seeking to alleviate and advocating strategies for overcoming structural disadvantage. (3.2.1)

Furthermore, the definition of social work adopted by the International Federation of Social Workers and the International Association of Schools of Social Work includes the following statement:

> The social work profession promotes social change, problem-solving in human relationships and the empowerment and liberation of people to enhance well-being... principles of human rights and social justice are fundamental to social work. (1994)

The implications of these core values are considerable, and represent an ongoing challenge to all social work educators and practitioners. But for the purpose of this chapter they make abundantly clear the shared, corporate and community-based nature of social work. These values represent the heart, soul and spirit of who we are. Consedine (2002) makes the firm link with spirituality when he says:

> What makes for a holistic spirituality is the recognition that we are all interdependent, that we need to see the divine spark in one another and respect that, and that we need to specifically protect the most vulnerable, the poorest and the most powerless. (Consedine, 2002, p. 45)

stop and think

■ What does 'Celebrating diversity with social justice' mean for you in your work?

A human rights framework

It has to be agreed, nevertheless, that the term 'social justice' is in itself a 'gateway' word that can mean different things to different people. Some writers suggest that it is a highly contested construct (Boucher and Kelly, 1998; Hodge, 2007), especially in the post-modern era, where the rejection of meta-narratives might suggest that

> ...constructs that apply to all individuals, such as human rights, are no longer tenable. Conceptualisations of social justice are individual, local and particular – a multiplicity of justices exist as opposed to any single universal understanding of justice. (Sterba, 1999, p. 140)

Hodge also notes the views of Pateman (1998) that

> Human rights have been criticised as an expression of Western values, and implementing these values in Western and particularly non-Western cultures is, at best, a dubious enterprise and, at worst, an unethical implosion of culturally foreign values. (p. 140)

Important though these caveats are – and social work is particularly sensitive worldwide to the demands of culturally appropriate ways of working (Thompson, 2002; Canda and Furman, 2010) – there is a similar danger here to the one we noted with the concept of spirituality: that if it is broken down into an individualistic, micro-level phenomenon, without any commonly agreed benchmark for the evaluation of its impact, then it loses much of its power, especially at the meso and macro levels.

For this reason social work is generally determined to continue to locate its passion for social justice within a human rights framework (George, 1999). It recognises that some sort of universally agreed benchmark, such as the UN Declaration of Human Rights (1948), acts as a guardian framework within which to challenge oppressive behaviour. As Hodge argues,

> Human rights are commonly defined as those characteristics that are necessary for us to live as human beings...[they] flow from the fact that *all* (*our emphasis*) human beings have inherent dignity and worth...social justice is exhibited by working to ensure that human rights are respected [individually], nationally and internationally. (Hodge, 2007, p. 140)

It is worth noting here that religious freedom is specifically included within this framework. Article 2 prohibits religious discrimination, and Article 18 affirms individual rights to hold, practise and, indeed, change religious beliefs. Interpreted in its widest sense, this clearly includes the expressions of individual spirituality we have previously discussed.

The commitment of social work to celebrating diversity with social justice is therefore clearly aligned to the human rights 'agenda'. The centrality of anti-discriminatory practice (Dalrymple and Burke, 1995; Dominelli, 2002; Thompson, 2006; Moss, 2007b) in social work's core activities is a practical out-working of this central value and professional world-view (Moss and Thompson, 2007). Anti-discriminatory practice both recognises, and names, the damage that pervasive oppressive behaviour, systems and structures can cause to individuals and communities, and emphasises the importance of challenging such injustices, not only in individual social work practice, but in wider contexts.

One practical example of the working out of these overarching principles can be seen in community development models of social work practice.

Spirituality and community development

It is perhaps surprising that with this emphasis upon structural, societal and cultural dimensions to discrimination and oppression, and the often stated importance of social workers challenging injustice, the theme of community development does not feature very highly, if at all, in social work's curricula requirements. Certainly this is the case in the UK where the role of the community social worker seems in some areas at least to have almost disappeared from statutory social work. This is in spite of Bob Holman's (1983 and 1993) sustained and acclaimed work in this field, which we would argue fits very closely with the model of the fellow traveller we are exploring in this book. Holman chose not only to practise but also to live among some of the most socially deprived and marginalised communities in Glasgow, Scotland – a city deeply divided in socio-economic terms. Positive, creative community development work should be seen as a powerful counter-balance to the pathologising tendencies of some individualistic approaches to what used to be called 'casework'. If the 'problem' lies within structures rather than being an individual's 'fault', then clearly there is a role for social work to challenge such structural deficits, even if in the short term our responsibility to the individual in difficulty has more of a 'first-aid' feel to it, where we are tackling the symptoms of the crisis, rather than the cause.

An interesting example of this 'two-pronged' approach can be seen in the UK in the work of the independent organisation Citizens Advice (CA), which sees itself as having a dual role. Through its local bureaux CA gives advice, help and support to individuals who, for whatever reason, are struggling financially and unable to cope. But it also collates examples of social injustice and inequities that are uncovered 'in the system' through its social policy programme. It presents these from time to time to local, regional and national government agencies to argue and campaign for positive change.

Chile and Simpson (2004) highlight the importance of such an approach, and demonstrate the link with our discussion of contemporary spirituality, when they argue that

> the underpinning link between community development and spirituality is the connection of the individual to the collective, acknowledging that the well-being of the individual influences *and is influenced by* (our emphasis) the well-being of the community. (p. 319)

Such an approach resonates with the views held by many social workers who, in their work with service users, see on a daily basis the lived-out tension between individual responsibility and collective influences. The challenge to all of us as individuals is always to maximise our full potential, and to work to a strengths perspective which seeks to rise above adversity and (if at all possible) refuses to be submerged or overcome by its 'darkness'. But the challenge to the collective is just as powerful: government, at local, regional or national levels, has a deep responsibility not only to remove barriers and oppressive systems that damage individual and community well-being, but also to foster a spirit of creativity and encouragement that enables individuals and communities to thrive and flourish. It is this conviction that underpins Thompson's (2003 and 2006) personal-cultural-structural (PCS) analysis of discrimination, and leads Chile and Simpson (2004) to argue that

> community development focuses on the dynamics inherent in the interaction among community members who seek to deal with change in a deliberate and sustained attempt to strengthen the horizontal patterns of society... Community development has as its foundation an ideology that motivates people to link with each other. This ideology provides the context for questions that inform community development work. For example... what is wrong with inequity? why should we really care about the person next door, let alone someone on the other side of the world? (p. 321)

These authors suggest that it is through reflection upon such basic questions that individual and collective meaning and purpose are uncovered, and that the 'answers to such questions are often informed by our spiritual constructs' (p. 322). Furthermore, they suggest that

> the connection between spirituality and community development is the fire of social justice that brings about radical transformation of structures of society. (p. 322)

Here, from the parallel people-work discipline of community development, we find articulated something of the vision that influenced the development of social work as a profession, and still 'warms the heart' of many contemporary practitioners. The barriers remain, however. Many social workers will hesitate to 'bite the hand that feeds them', and will recognise that their organisational structures often prevent or undermine the range of structurally challenging activities that they would wish to practise as they work out their commitment to *celebrate diversity with social justice*. It remains true that to engage in such challenges requires courage and determination, and the support from managers and colleagues alike.

There are some interesting parallels here with the impact of communitarianism as propounded by Etzioni (1995), who argued for the role that a variety of community groups could play in facilitating social cohesion and community well-being. In some ways his work was in response to what he saw was an increasing fragmentation of community through a heightened individualism that (in the UK at least) many associate with the influence of Thatcherism. Etzioni's emphasis was upon a community-orientated strengths perspective, where organisations, groups and communities 'play to their strengths' and work to develop and enhance the communities to which they belong.

So far we have been discussing the issue of community from a secular organisational perspective, but there is another dimension that deserves to be explored. This involves the key role that faith communities currently play in community cohesion and well-being, something that the faith communities themselves have known for a long time but have felt has not been sufficiently acknowledged by society at large (Smith, 2001).

The contribution from faith communities

For many faith groups, the shared community aspect of spirituality is vital. They highlight the importance of shared gatherings for worship, mutual support and encouragement especially in times of crisis or difficulty, and for developing disciplined approaches to the study of holy books, to prayer and meditation. Some faith communities strongly emphasise the spiritual benefits from shared pilgrimages to special places, or meeting in small groups to discuss aspects of faith, belief and discipleship. From this perspective, faith and belief are as much a shared, corporate and inherited activity as they are individualistic approaches to these issues, not least because in times of difficulty it can be the faith which upholds and supports the individual rather than the individual who upholds the faith. It is worth reminding ourselves again of Fowler's model for spiritual development which we drew on in chapters 3 and 5. Fowler suggests that the spirituality of the community must be seen as a whole, mutually sustaining individuals at different points in their spiritual development.

A further dimension to the community aspect of spirituality lies in the area of doctrine and theology – or 'god-talk'. The importance and significance of these aspects may vary between faith communities; but one common element is that these represent an accumulated wisdom, often developed over many centuries, to help people in their own personal journey of faith and bewilderment, and to provide a fellow travelling companion, 'rough guide' or 'vademecum' to support and encourage them on their journey. It is true that in some faith communities the official teachings and pronouncements, including the holy books, are held in such high regard that they brook no challenge or disagreement. They are deemed to be infallible, and to contain the 'final word'. But more often in other faith communities they represent the ways in which those who have gone before have struggled and grappled with the deep mysteries of living. They capture the certainties and ambiguities that flow from the deep questions we have already begun to explore in the context of contemporary spirituality. These writers suggest world-views that have worked for them, and invite succeeding generations to test them afresh. Importantly, they map out their struggle with the darker sides of human existence, at both individual and community/national levels, and seek to hold in a creative tension the dilemmas and paradoxes of living in this complex world.

None of this releases anyone from their individual responsibility to grapple with such issues for themselves: to do so would be to diminish our humanity and our constant search for meaning. But from a faith community perspective, and from similar philosophical frameworks which accord no significance to religious perspectives, the message is the same. Previous generations have struggled with these deep questions and can offer insight and at times wisdom to help illuminate our own journey, our own search for meaning within a coherent world-view. Whether our spirituality is grounded within a secular or religious framework, the shared contributions from fellow travellers can become precious life-enhancing gifts that help us shape and refine – and at times re-define – the world-view we have chosen.

The challenge to injustice

As much as faith communities may support and encourage individuals in their personal journeys, there is also a strong element, certainly in the three monotheistic religions of Judaism, Christianity and Islam as well as in others such as Buddhism, of prophetic challenge to injustice. This involves a practical outworking of the concept of liberation theology which places the emancipatory liberation of the oppressed centre-stage in its thinking and praxis. This is expressed in the everyday language of parables and stories such as the Good Samaritan (The Christian Bible: Luke 10 vv 25–37) where it is the actions of a religious outcast (who meets the human needs of an individual who had been 'mugged') that were praised and commended, rather than the religious leaders of the day who 'passed by on the other side'. It is also found in the demands for social justice that pervade the Jewish/Christian texts and prophetic writings (e.g. Isaiah, Amos and Hosea), and in the Qur'an with its demands to 'establish justice' (chapter 2 v 110; 148; 177; 215). The challenge of Buddhist monks in 2008 against social injustice in Tibet is another powerful visual example of the working out of such commitments, based on the teachings of the Buddha that

> human rights and freedoms are integral to growth and self-realisation, and that social justice and full participation are essential to the organic interdependency of all beings. (Jones, 1993)

The deprivation of individuals leads to the impoverishment of the collective. (Chile and Simpson, 2004, p. 327)

This commitment is not limited to those who belong to faith communities. Indeed,

> The passion for justice which is an important dimension to spirituality, has taken root in the lives of many people who have no religious allegiance but whose commitment to the betterment of the social order burns as fiercely and brightly as anyone else's. (Moss, 2005, p. 63)

This striving for social justice, therefore, may be seen to be an essential ingredient of spirituality, whether from a secular or a religious perspective. Indeed it may even be argued that one of the indicators of a spiritual life, religious or secular, is the extent to which it stirs up within people a passion for social justice.

Faith communities as caring communities

Social work is very familiar indeed with the concept of care in the community which has been such a powerful driving influence for decades in how services should be conceptualised, legislated for and delivered. Caring for others is also a deep imperative at the heart of many faith groups who often seek to provide it 'without strings attached' (Nash and Stewart, 2002; Boddie and Cnaan, 2006; Coates et al., 2007; Pierson, 2008). Across the whole spectrum of need, faith communities are often in a strong position to offer help, encouragement and support whether this be to young parents or older people feeling isolated and neglected; to those who are homeless or misusing drugs or alcohol; to those who are long-term unemployed; or to families fleeing from domestic violence. These are but a few examples where practical help and support is often provided by faith communities working sometimes on their own initiative and sometimes in direct partnership with statutory agencies. In addition to this many faith groups also have an international perspective and actively support work to feed the hungry, to oppose oppressive regimes and to uphold human rights.

The point being emphasised in this section is that the imperative to care and to work for social justice which is at the heart of our social work commitment is also shared by many faith groups who may therefore rightly be regarded as common allies, even if their religious tenets of belief are not shared. The caring dimension, from either a secular or a religious perspective, is a shared, important dimension to our understanding of spirituality.

There is one further dimension to this discussion that has recently begun to gain in importance within some wider social work debates, but which, ironically, has been central to at least some religious perspectives for generations. This may be called the 'eco-spiritual' perspective.

An eco-spiritual perspective

Important though the community dimension we have been discussing undoubtedly is, it still falls short of a really comprehensive understanding of the full 'community context' of our spirituality discourse. Everything we have discussed up to this point has been very person-centred, which is unsurprising given the nature of the social work enterprise. Some recent theorists, however (Coates et al., 2005; Zapf, 2005; Crisp, 2008 in particular), have broadened and deepened the debate by raising some profoundly challenging issues not only about the context of all of our people-work, but also about the very environment in which this practice is undertaken. Furthermore, this environment, they argue, is not to be regarded as a mere context, or just the scenery and backdrop for our human drama, but as a crucial 'player' in the process, and therefore an important feature in the community dimension of all social work.

This deeper dimension finds echoes in the understanding of inter-connectedness previously discussed, in that many faith communities strongly believe in the accountability that human beings have for the well-being of the planet and its resources, both physical and human. This is located, they believe, in the relationship between Creator and creation which places human beings in the role of stewards, charged with the responsibility to take care of their complex environments rather than having a blank cheque for its exploitation. Zapf (2005) argues that most social work theorising has either ignored environmental consid-erations or presented them as merely 'modifiers or contexts'. In other words, these issues are to be taken into account in as far as they affect human behaviour but do not necessarily have value or significance in their own right. Zapf is unhappy with an understanding of spirituality that is 'limited in person-centred terms as an attribute of the individ-ual', and argues for a greater sense of interconnectedness. He poses the question,

> Can we come to understand our environment in spiritual terms, to appreciate and express and celebrate our connectedness? A simple yet profound question put forward by Haas and Nachtigal (1998) could serve as the starting point for rethinking social work's com-mitment to *person in environment:* what does it mean to live well in this place? We may never get to the profound spiritual dimensions of that question if we continue to constrain spirituality within the narrow boundaries of a person-centred approach. (p. 639)

In this context we are being encouraged to see the meaning and significance of the environment not just in terms of the meanings we ascribe to them for our own personal needs and welfare, but for the meaning and significance that they have *in their own right*. We might therefore wish to pose the issue not only in terms of our dialogue that we initiate with the environment, but also in terms of the dialogue that the environment initiates with us, where partnership is far more equal than we had previously been willing to recognise. Does the environment exist simply for us to exploit, or is a different relationship and world-view possible? And is the 'relationship traffic' one-way or two-way?

stop and think

■ What impact does your environment make upon your social work practice?
■ And what impact are you having upon your environment?

It is perhaps worth pausing at this point to pick up the threads from an earlier discussion and to recognise again that, from a religious perspective, this is very familiar territory. Many of the major faiths believe in a Creator, or a powerful life-giving force of creation, whether or not they seek to ascribe a name such as Adonai, God or Allah. They will argue strongly, therefore, that the physical world, which they believe owes its existence to a Creator or creative power, deserves to be respected in its own right as a precious, even sacred, place. Phrases such as 'stewards of the earth' capture the essence of this position: the earth's resources, living and inanimate, are to be used wisely and productively because they are held 'in trust' by each succeeding generation.

This is not to suggest, however, that this approach to the environment is held only by 'people of faith'; far from it. The contemporary concerns about climate change, environmental disasters, the diminution of natural resources, the decimation of rain forests and the huge impact of industrial pollution are shared by people of all persuasions, both politically and from many religious perspectives. These constitute perhaps one set of issues that unite people across a variety of world-views, as well as (paradoxically) highlighting those aspects of human nature that exploit greed and exploitation for personal gain, irrespective of the impact upon others. The economic crises that broke upon the world in 2008 highlighted both aspects of this in a very powerful way.

From an everyday social work perspective, however, these large-scale 'macro' concerns may seem far removed. Furthermore, to those whose lives are lived in (relative or absolute) poverty, these issues may feel doubly remote in that their first priority is simply surviving from one day to the next. Individual and global poverty are hugely complex issues, and talk of eco-spiritual concerns may simply not appear 'on their radar'. It would however be judgemental and arrogant in the extreme to assume that concerns for the environment and the planet are only felt and expressed by those who enjoy some degree of material well-being. We are all common citizens of the planet.

If this new emphasis upon the environment within social work practice is to take root, we need to find creative ways into exploring it, not least by a greater awareness and acknowledgement of the impact of the environment upon our well-being. The eco-spiritual approach to social work practice in effect places far less emphasis upon the centrality of materialistic approaches to human welfare, and represents a

> shift to post-materialist values which, while still valuing an adequate material standard of living, nevertheless gives priority to environmental protection and cultural issues, even when these goals conflict with maximising economic growth. (Coates, 2005, p. 9)

In short, it emphasises quality of life issues that include spiritual perspectives that move away from 'self interested competitive individualism to a much broader holistic understanding of our world and one more akin to that of traditional and indigenous societies and cultures' (Coates, 2005, p. 8).

It is important to stress at this point that eco-spiritual approaches are not advocating a 'one size fits all' approach by seeking to impose upon industrial post-modern societies ways of working that are more effective with indigenous, agrarian societies, or vice versa. It was such an approach by dominant western paradigms, which assumed that their approach was best for everyone else, that has been so strongly rejected, precisely because they failed to recognise the strengths and uniqueness of different communities and their distinctive understanding of well-being and belonging. What the eco-spiritual approach is advocating instead is an approach that really does celebrate diversity, and really does take seriously not only the human dimensions of social justice, but the powerful impact of the wider environment and our responsibility to it, as essential factors in our overall well-being.

Place and the self

Related to this, a growing body of scholarship is beginning to explore the importance of 'place' in communal and individual human existence, most especially around questions of identity. Crisp (2008) draws on the work of Sheldrake (2001) who talks about

> a vital connection between place, memory and human identity. The concept of 'place' refers not simply to geographical location but also to a dialectical relationship between environment and human narrative. 'Place' is any space that has the capacity to be remembered and to evoke what is most precious. (p. 43)

Perhaps this dialectical relationship may be less easily understood in the concrete and tarmac-covered landscapes of many industrial environments than in some other cultural contexts, not least because of western societies' apparent belief that 'humankind is separate from, as opposed to [being] a part of, the natural world' (Zapf, 2008, p. 638). Zapf, for instance, draws our attention to the ways in which Aboriginal cultural identities are

> 'tied so directly to the land and concepts of place', so much so that 'selfhood and "place-hood" are completely intertwined'. (p. 637)

Their spirituality, in other words, is deeply connected with land and place.

There are two contrasting implications for social work practice. First, the question about the extent to which people have learned, and are still learning, 'how to live well' in their present setting and context is an important issue for us as social workers to look and listen for in our dealings with people. For some people, issues around material prosperity may feature less highly than being able to enjoy and emotionally benefit from a sense of community, where people feel they belong, have a role to play and are cared for by friends and neighbours. Furthermore, the opportunity to work together to improve their immediate environment is evidence of their social cohesion and social capital. Secondly, but antithetically, the extent to which people feel uprooted, unsettled and unable to live well in their immediate setting and context is equally crucial, not least because the sense of loss and grief that accompanies such experiences of dislocation can be profoundly disabling and dispiriting. Work with immigrant populations, with travellers who are constantly harried and moved on from one locality to another, or with disadvantaged minority groups, are obvious examples. Similarly, the physical dislocation experienced by young or older people living in care settings, temporary accommodation, hostels, hospitals or hospices demonstrates how disconcerting and dis-orientating to their well-being this 'dis-connectedness' can be. The level of imaginative and creative care necessary in such settings is often underestimated, not least because workers fail to recognise the powerful sense of loss and disconnectedness that people can experience.

Example

Martha managed to leave Uganda at the beginning of Idi Amin's dictatorship. She says little about her experience just before she left except that she had been the victim of multiple rape and seen her whole family killed. She arrived in England with no possessions and only the clothes she stood up in. Martha considers herself lucky, however. She was allowed to stay, given a council flat and fairly soon found work as a cleaner at the local college. Nevertheless, the first few years were not easy. The flat is on a large, desolate estate and in the early years Martha experienced some nasty attacks on her property which appeared to have been racially motivated by people who thought she should 'go back to her own country'. Over the years many decent people have moved out and been replaced by 'problem' families which the council move in, supposedly temporary but usually replaced by others. Many of the older people are afraid to go out. Martha's health since her retirement has been dogged by angina and she recently ended up in hospital as a result of collapsing in the street. The social worker thinks that she would be better off with a ground floor flat in a warden-controlled complex – Martha's flat is on the second floor. Martha is adamant that she doesn't want to move. She says she has made the flat 'her place' after the terrible disruption she experienced when forced to leave Uganda. For some time she felt totally alienated in England and spoke to no-one outside of work. Then one day she ventured into the local Catholic church and re-discovered the faith which had always sustained her in the past. She also found a community of people who offered her friendship. Like all city centre churches, St Joseph's has seen declining attendances but a core congregation remains and Martha manages to keep going on a Sunday and have a coffee afterwards and she would not want to move out of the area. Besides, the other thing which helped her to recover her sense of self and place is that she planted up her tiny balcony with vegetable boxes after craving the small farm which she had left behind. She still manages to tend her vegetable patch, although she has to take it slowly, and is practically self-sufficient in fresh produce. Martha regards her balcony garden as a vital contributor to her physical and mental health and says she would die, spiritually, without it.

■ What does Zapf's question, *How can I live well in this place?*, mean to you, both individually and in your professional practice?

Conclusion

In our discussion of spirituality in this book we began with an individualistic interpretation, which places us as individuals in the centre of our world, and where we each choose a world-view that helps us make sense of the world and our place within it. In one sense, of course, the world-view that each of us chooses and seeks to live by *has* to be intensely personal and individualistic: it is, after all, our 'take' on life, and so long as it works for us, then that is all that matters, or so it would seem. Part of social work's response to this is to recognise the ways in which each person is a unique individual to be treated with dignity, respect and integrity.

However, in this chapter we have moved on to consider a range of community perspectives on spirituality which for social work can be encapsulated in the commitment to *celebrating diversity with social justice*. For social work, the issues raised by a contemporary understanding of spirituality sit comfortably with social work's fundamental values. But being comfortable is not what it is all about. Social work has a strong commitment to celebrate diversity with social justice; but this can only come at a cost. We have argued that it is the 'lived experience' of spirituality, whether from a secular or a religious perspective, that drives our commitment to social justice. Far from being a topic that belongs in a closet or represents the interest of just a 'quirky few', spirituality both captures and liberates the deepest desire within social work as a profession to see a more just, tolerant, fair and diverse society in which individuals and communities can flourish to their mutual advantage and benefit. Social work is strongly committed both to create and to cleave to a set of aspirational values that inspire and underpin all of its activities. Spirituality, as we have claimed throughout this chapter, occupies similar territory: it reminds us what the heart and spirit of social work is all about, and the vision that both beckons and sustains practitioners day by day as they seek to celebrate diversity with social justice. In this chapter, therefore, we have explored a wider community context where the relationship or connectedness between people are clearly an important aspect of spirituality. This may mean joining a community of like-minded people – religious or secular – which assists in their individual journey as they enjoy the company of some fellow travellers, but also provides a wider vision about how they are contributing to a greater purpose.

In a deep sense all of this has brought us back to the basic fundamental questions that we suggested lie at the heart of a contemporary understanding of spirituality. *Who am I? What does it mean to live in relationship with others? What meaning and purpose can I find/bring to my living?* Now we can add a further dimension, captured in Zapf's poignant question, *How can I live well in this place?* And, *what is my relationship to, and my responsibility for, my environment?* Zapf takes this further by suggesting that an even deeper understanding of spirituality would take us to the question of *'what does it mean to live well **as** this place?',* thereby rejecting the fundamental distinction between person and place in favour of a unifying spiritual connection (p. 238). As a 'gateway' word spirituality opens up all these questions for us, and suggests that a full answer – insofar as we will ever find one – must include community-based issues such as social justice and a care for the planet in whatever ways seem relevant in our differing contexts.

Our final chapter develops these discussions further. As we consider the global context of social work and the enrichment of both social work and understandings of spirituality which is to be found in non-western perspectives, we shall find, most excitingly, that spirituality is not the great divide that some people fear, but instead contains within it the potential and the challenge for authentic transcultural and environmentally sensitive social work practice. Once again we discover that a rich understanding of contemporary spirituality provides a powerful lens through which the full potential of social work practice can be viewed and understood.

taking it further

- Coates, J. (2007) 'From ecology to spirituality and social justice', in J. Coates, J.R. Graham, B. Swartzentruber and B. Ouellette (eds) *Spirituality and Social Work: Selected Canadian Readings* (Toronto: Canadian Scholars Press).
- Crisp, B. (2008) 'Social work and spirituality in a secular society', *Journal of Social Work*, 8, 363–375.
- Pierson, J. (2008) *Going Local: Working in Communities and Neighbourhoods* (London: Routledge).

chapter 8

Global and multicultural perspectives

Introduction

One of the most exciting developments in social work over the last 10 years has been the emergence of international social work as a common cause in which developed and developing countries participate on increasingly equal terms. Central to this development is the recognition that universal elements of social work – such as the upholding of basic human rights, advocating for social justice, recognising the unique value of each individual life and the goal of individual well-being – are informed and framed by markedly different world-views. Indeed, it is sometimes argued that, despite the International Federation of Social Workers' (IFSW) common definition of social work, contemporary social work itself is understood differently across cultures, variously affected by the processes of modernisation and its interface with tradition (Yip, 2005).

At the heart of these different world-views is the approach to spirituality. It is a mark of the impact of perspectives from social workers in the Global South, the indigenous peoples of Australia, New Zealand and Canada and the dialogue of 'East meets West' led by social workers from Hong Kong and China that spirituality has been afforded its rightful place in social work theory, ethics and practice. As we began this book let us remind ourselves as we approach its conclusion that the revised statement of principles of the IFSW affirms that social workers should uphold each person's 'spiritual integrity and well-being' (IFSW, 2004).

Various stages have been traced in the development of social work on the global stage. As the rest of the world became less inclined to simply import models from the UK and the USA, and countries such as Australia recognised their inappropriate application with aboriginal communities, it became necessary to tease out these fundamental differences in order to establish whether the global project of social work had sufficient in common to be worth fighting to retain. What becomes clear when this challenge to western 'professional imperialism' (Yip, 2005) is scrutinised is the extent to which western models of social work have incorporated a secular/religious divide which simply does not exist in other cultures and parts of the world. This difference in outlook has to be addressed if we are to make progress in both social work practice in multicultural contexts and the broader endeavour of global social work. It is this above all else which challenges social work in the developed world to engage with spirituality.

Such a quest moves the search for spiritually sensitive practice into a very different terrain from that which the western spirituality discourse commonly inhabits. The issue is less about how to identify and assess the spiritual need of the individual service user as about how to understand the relationship between individuals and their communities, and between communities of human beings and their natural environment. At root it concerns different ways in which we might understand the essence of being and how we stay connected with that, as well as how we can reconnect when disruptive influences distort and threaten to sever that connectedness.

This chapter is divided into two main sections. We shall start with the issue which first challenged western secular social work practice to take note of the significance of religion and spiritual beliefs – the context of multiculturalism in the developed world – before moving on to consider some of the ways in which global perspectives on spirituality are challenging hitherto dominant western social work paradigms.

Social work practice in multicultural settings

It was during the 1980s that social work practice in the UK began to be challenged by service user groups who claimed that social workers were so unaware of cultural differences arising from ethnic and racial diversity that their Eurocentric practice was in fact oppressive (Lloyd and Taylor, 1995). Similar arguments quickly developed in relation to social work's understanding of disability, the gendered nature of its interventions and ignorance or prejudice when it came to sexual orientation. In each of these examples, the case was pursued vigorously by social science academics and social work professionals; but in the case of race and culture, one aspect has been remarkably neglected in the theoretical analysis. This is the importance of religion and spirituality for the ethnic minority groups living in the UK, particularly first generation immigrants. Anecdotally, the authors can report that social work students from ethnic minorities point to the neglect of this topic as a 'blanking out' of a significant strand in their cultural background, even if they themselves are both westernised and secularised. Social workers engaging with service users from ethnic minorities have recognised their religion in certain contexts but too often in an entirely prescriptive way, noting, for example, particular practices and rituals which should be followed at the time of a death. This allows Henery to lay the charge that social workers in the west are interested only in the 'exotic otherness' of religious culture which is not Christian (Henery, 2003). Certainly, as we have already argued, few social workers are willing to engage with the *significance or content of faith and belief*. This means that social work in the Anglo-Saxon tradition is denying itself a significant opportunity to learn about other ways of engaging with the world, although the recent book by Furness and Gilligan (2010) makes an important contribution to redress the balance.

stop and think

■ To what extent do you take seriously the *beliefs* of a service user whose religion and culture are unfamiliar or even alien to your own?

Yip suggests that approaches to social work practice in multicultural contexts can roughly be divided into those which are 'culturally specific' and those which are 'culturally universal' (Yip, 2005, p. 594). Yip quotes Lee and Green's argument that *universal approaches* show sensitivity and openness to cultural difference, whereas culturally *specific* approaches focus on specific elements and practices (as in the example of traditions around death). Much of the training around cultural competence in fact contents itself with providing specific knowledge and awareness of situations in which such knowledge may be called for. Hodge agrees that familiarity with the norms characterising various spiritual traditions is helpful when constructing spiritual interventions (Hodge, 2008). However, Holloway argues that while we need knowledge and understanding of specific cultural elements, we need to go beyond that to interpret the *meanings* embodied in those practices and embedded in traditions. In short, while our knowledge must be *multicultural*, recognising specific differences, our approach must be *transcultural*, communicating across difference (Holloway, 2006). Torry also argues that practitioners need both 'generic cultural competence' and 'specific cultural knowledge' (Torry, 2005, p. 261), without which there is a danger of categorising individuals rather than responding to their unique needs in this particular situation. When the difference concerns religious beliefs and practices, the universal approach requires that we develop understanding of the spirituality embedded in and expressed through the institutional or cultural framework. Such understanding encompasses both the origins of particular beliefs and practices and the ways in which they interface with cultural traditions and social work models with which the social worker may be familiar.

Here again Yip's work is instructive. Yip points out that both 'static' and 'passive' models currently characterise much exchange across the global social work scene (Yip, 2005, p. 599). Static models, he argues, have been common, particularly in the importation of USA and UK models of social work in the development of social work elsewhere. This 'professional imperialism' continues to mark social work practice in the Pacific Rim and in the development of the profession and of social work education in the countries of Eastern Europe. Not only are attitudes and values fixed: the model does not allow for any degree of reciprocity; the imposing culture sees nothing to be gained from taking in elements of the 'other' culture. Such an approach characterised the attitude of western secular social workers to religion and spirituality (including their attitude to established Christian belief) and from Christian social work organisations to other faiths, during the first decades of professionalisation.

Passive models, according to Yip, assume that some cross-cultural *exchange* is inevitable, but it is limited to the accommodations and modifications which are necessary if the export and import are to work. There is no sense that a wider community might benefit from a genuine integration of ideas and understandings. Such a model might well be seen to apply to the current position of faith-based social work agencies in the UK and northern Europe, as well as to the attitude of secular social workers to individuals and families with firm religious beliefs. Struggles to accommodate different models of family life and child-rearing practices, for example, continue to be particularly evident in contemporary practice. Yip argues, however, that

> only a dynamic model of cross-cultural social work is suitable for the vigorous cultural exchanges taking place between western countries and Asian countries.... Every country can evolve their own practice wisdom and borrow other wisdom as well as transfer their wisdom to others. (Yip, 2005, pp. 600 and 603)

Surprisingly, only passing reference is made to the wisdom offered in Buddhism, Confucianism and Hinduism which might contribute to addressing the problems of contemporary life. Yet this dynamic cross-cultural model when applied to spiritual wisdom is both challenging and exciting. We shall return to this later in the chapter.

The notion of cultural competence

There is something of an irony embedded in the term 'cultural competence' in that it stems from the competency-led training models developed in the West (the UK in particular); the idea that in culture as in all else one should achieve at least minimum standards of competence could be seen as yet another instance of professional imperialism! The competency model is in marked contrast to the education and develop-ment model for training which is concerned with *where the student starts from* and how they, and their practice, develop – although the latter also concurs with the notion of achieving an acceptable minimum standard for qualification. This point is made not to be pedantic but because the whole tenor of this book has been about journeys – and the journey of the practitioner in feeling both willing and competent to engage with the service user's spirituality and spiritual need is something which we wish to hold onto.

However, Torry locates his discussion of cultural competence within reflective models of practice, suggesting that an essential part of reflec-tive practice is for practitioners to reflect on their own development in order to improve and achieve competence. Drawing on both stage and domain models of assessment, Torry argues that developing cultural com-petence is a process in which the practitioner gradually becomes aware of different types of knowledge (we might also add 'ways of knowing') and sensitive to the different ways in which these might appropriately be applied to their practice. Cultural diversity may be seen to operate at both the micro and macro levels of human interaction. So, for example, Giger and Davidhizar (1999, cited in Torry, 2005) point to diverse beliefs, values and behaviours operating in relation to phenomena as wide-ranging as the concept of time and communication behaviours. Micro-level aspects are frequently the behaviours and practices on which the culturally com-petent practitioner may focus, but it is the macro-level aspects from which these diverse practices stem. So for example, applied to the realm of spirituality, beliefs about what is sacred, and, moreover, about *what it means for something to be sacred*, will determine a whole cluster of atti-tudes and behaviours, including those of a ritualistic nature and those identified as specifically spiritual practices. The practitioner who comes 'from the outside' cannot achieve more than a superficial level of compe-tence without an understanding of that wider context, and their attitude will likely betray them. For example, the service user who declines a comforting cup of tea at a time of crisis because they are observing a religious fast may be admired for their abstinence but pitied for their deprivation, rather than the fasting being understood as a means of deep-ening the person's spiritual resources and hence their survival in times of trouble.

Moreover, achieving cultural competence should not be seen as a pro-cess which is in some way separate from or additional to the core skills of the reflective practitioner. Dean states,

 Our goal is not so much to achieve competence but to participate in the ongoing processes of seeking understanding and building relationships. (quoted in Furness, 2005, p. 255)

In cross-cultural social work practice these two processes cannot be independent of each other. Relationships cannot be built without, if not achieving complete understanding, at least demonstrating to the other person that you are genuinely seeking to understand. Such understanding will develop only as the social worker tries to find those points of connection intrinsic to any relationship. Thus cross-cultural practice might better be described as *transcultural*, the 'search for shared, accessible meaning instigated in those professionals who seek to help' (Holloway, 2006, p. 834). How can such a position possibly be reached when the spiritual and religious beliefs of the social worker and service user are poles apart?

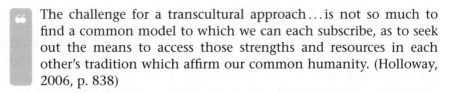

stop and think

- What are the obstacles in your practice to reaching shared meanings with the service user?
- What are the 'ways in' for you?

Transcultural approaches to spirituality

Writers who favour universal models which transcend cultural barriers do so through highlighting those elements in the various definitions of spirituality which relate to what it is to be human. Of note is the fact that no attempt is made to reduce different religious belief systems to common components, nor even to identify the shared characteristics of religiosity, since 'religiosity' makes no sense in cultures which do not share the Western mind's distinguishing of religious and secular. The potential for a transcultural approach stems from a perception that 'the spirit' is recognised by and in everyone, regardless of their culture or beliefs, and that 'spirituality' suggests how that spirit is expressed, including, but not wholly bounded by, such religious beliefs as may be held. Thus,

> The challenge for a transcultural approach ... is not so much to find a common model to which we can each subscribe, as to seek out the means to access those strengths and resources in each other's tradition which affirm our common humanity. (Holloway, 2006, p. 838)

We can do this through exploring the ways in which individuals construct meaning and re-construct meaning, for example, in the face of crisis or tragedy. The ways in which people do this within their own cultural, and sometimes cross-cultural, context are complex and unique – they constitute 'the weavings, comparisons and adaptations which individuals instinctively undertake in their personal meaning-making' (Holloway, 2006, p. 833). Another way of understanding this process is to utilise the idea of 'cultural frame' – that is, the identity, imperatives and assumptions – which shapes one's engagement with the external world. Individuals may internalise several cultural frames, and switch between them in their attempts to interpret their external world and find inner meaning (Yip, 2005). It follows, therefore, that it is likely that there are common reference points between different cultural frames. A broadly spiritual world-view may be one such common point of reference.

The above approach does privilege western notions of individualism, and it may be most appropriate when relating to people living in a multicultural context or those affected by cross-cultural differences. However, in her sustained critique of health care from an ethnic minority perspective, Gunaratnam has repeatedly pointed out that over-simplified assumptions about another person's culturally prescribed behaviour and beliefs do not take us very far down the road towards cultural sensitivity in the relationship between the service provider and the service user (e.g. Gunaratnam, 1997). Whatever the cultural context, we still know relatively little about the subjective experience of the individual within that context, including the extent to which individual differences arise or are insignificant in comparison with the common purpose of the community. Hegarty avoids this dilemma when she speaks of the spirit as the 'animating and vital principle' which leads to common spiritual resources and practices as a means of 'grounding a person in their own centre and *taking them beyond themselves*' (Hegarty, 2007, p. 43, our italics). Thus it is the individual's spirituality which is the source of connectiveness and the means to express those connections. It is also important to recognise the interweaving of spiritual bonds and meanings with other bonds and meanings – emotional, psychological, physical and cultural (Holloway, 2006).

Modifying practice

The point about the preceding discussion for the social worker practising in a multicultural context is that there must be some guiding framework for establishing a connection and developing a relationship between the worker and the service user. It is on this basis that social work intervention takes place. However, as was identified at the start of this discussion, the standard social work interventions themselves may not be appropriate without some modification which takes account of differences such as cultural style, assumptions, beliefs and accepted patterns of behaviour. This is no less so when it comes to spiritual care – recognising the significance of religion and spirituality in the service user's frame of reference is not of itself enough. In the following discussion we shall build on the material on assessment and intervention covered in chapters 3 and 5, particularly the work on spiritual biography and the construction of self-narrative.

Constructivist models offer a sympathetic way in to spiritual interventions with service users whose cultural background differs markedly from that of the practitioner. Greene et al. (1996) take as their starting point that 'a person's conception of reality consists of the meanings he or she has given to his interpretation of the world' (Greene et al., 1996, p. 173). Listening to the service user tell his or her own story – beautifully termed 'yarning' among Australian aboriginals (Lynn, 2001) – with knowledge of and sensitivity to their cultural frame combined with self-awareness of our own cultural assumptions and prejudices allows us to enter into that narrative and begin to see the service user's world through their eyes. This also gets over the problem referred to earlier (on a one-to-one basis anyway) of the value placed on distinguishing the individual from his or her community and cultural identity: if we listen with sufficient knowledge and understanding to appreciate the nuances of meaning, the service user will tell us what the comfortable balance is for them. However, the point about any therapeutic intervention is that its purpose is to address the problem(s) and achieve some positive change. Sometimes, and this particularly relates to spiritual issues, the problem is in the story which the service user has habitually told to themselves, or adopted from the 'versions of reality' told to them by others. Arriving at a modified story, which recognises the damage caused by the story but addresses this from within rather than from outside the service user's cultural frame of reference, is a skilled and sensitive process.

Greene et al. (1996) call this 'the co-construction of a new reality (or story)' (p. 174) and suggest there are two stages in this process: first, a slightly different version of the service user's story is fed back to them which is 'different enough from their situation, yet not too different, to further the conversation' (Lax, 1992, quoted in Greene et al., 1996, p. 174); second, the practitioner introduces – through questioning rather than advice – a 'novel' perspective, so that the worker and the service user jointly construct a new story which 'does not include the problem and the vicious cycles that maintain it' (Greene et al., 1996, p. 174). Of course this does not necessarily mean that the service user's situation is unproblematic, but that 'the problem' is newly defined and can therefore be approached without further reinforcement of the old damaging narrative. The social worker working with someone from a different culture, particularly if this is a marginalised culture, must be constantly alert to the danger of imposing their story instead of co-constructing a new story with the service user *from within their frame of reference*. In the processes of transcendence and transformation which we looked at in Chapter 5 this is particularly important.

Example

Ruth is a 42-year-old Nigerian woman who came to the UK 20 years ago. Ruth has ovarian cancer and has been admitted to the in-patient unit of the local hospice. She is receiving palliative care and the medical team are doing all they can to make her comfortable. However, Ruth's restlessness seems to go beyond her physical discomfort and the nurses are at a loss to know how to help her. They think perhaps she has unresolved issues with her family back in Nigeria and ask the social worker to talk to her. Ruth belongs to a local church and although she has had lots of visitors from the church, their visits seem, if anything, to leave her more disturbed. The social worker begins by asking Ruth whether she is in touch with her wider family. Ruth says that her parents and older relatives are now all dead. She has three sisters who are all in the UK. She says it would be nice to see them, but... The sentence is left hanging in the air. The social worker asks whether Ruth's husband has contacted her sisters and Ruth says that he wouldn't want to bother them to come from a distance. Seeing the social worker's puzzlement at this, Ruth explains that he doesn't believe she is going to die. As they begin to unravel this together, the story emerges that Ruth's church friends are all praying for her healing and she feels guilty that she is going to disappoint them and also God. In fact, Ruth feels that her illness is because her faith has not been strong enough all along, and now she is guilty of the ultimate sin because she accepts that her death is not far off and she wants to approach it peacefully rather than continuing to fight. The social worker finds herself struggling with this way of looking at things. She does not follow any religion herself but knows enough about the Christian story to recall the account in the gospels of Jesus in the Garden of Gethsemane and the disciple Peter's betrayal. She asks Ruth whether Jesus had not asked his friends to help him prepare for his death and whether Jesus had not understood Peter's moment of human weakness where Peter felt that he had let Jesus down terribly. A look of relief and understanding transforms Ruth's face. The social worker asks if she would like the chaplain to come and pray with her; Ruth accepts this offer gratefully.

Hodge looks at the challenge of using 'spiritually modified' cognitive therapy with service users from different ethnic and cultural backgrounds (Hodge, 2008). In some ways cognitive therapy, most commonly linked with cognitive behavioural therapy (CBT), might seem ill-suited to both these modifications. However, Hodge asserts that cognitive therapy has been found to be useful in dealing with existential problems as well as its common application in CBT, pointing out that most spiritual traditions affirm the importance of cognition. It is important to recognise, however, that cognitive therapy is not value-free. Acknowledgement of the underpinning values fostered by particular types of narrative is an essential prelude to the therapeutic intervention. Hodge points out that use of values which are incongruent with those of the service user may cause further harm, the intervention proving a negative experience from which they are most likely to withdraw. Conversely, Hodge cites evidence which suggests that where there is value congruence, the effectiveness of the intervention is increased.

It is precisely in the spiritual and religious domain that value incongruence is likely to occur for social workers from a western secularist tradition working with service users from ethnic minority communities where religious and spiritual traditions are embedded in everyday life. For such service users, Hodge suggests that some form of 'transcendent narrative' must be employed. This has very significant implications for social work interventions with people who affirm such a world-view to explain everyday events and provide meaning in their daily lives. Thus – and this is where it is essential to understand the service user's value system – the starting point must be to jointly recognise 'the engine which drives the change' (Hodge, 2008, p. 184). Hodge is insistent, however, that all individuals have the motivation and the capacity to 'engineer' change, regardless of whether they come from a culture which privileges communitarianism or individualism; but the goal and nature of the change will be determined by their particular cultural 'engine'.

There are two further points which we shall pick up from Hodge's very detailed and helpful discussion of this form and context for cognitive therapy. First, it is a mistake to assume that owning a particular religious identity implies acceptance of all its tenets of belief or complete adherence to its code of behaviour. Nor does high significance of religion and spirituality for the service user necessarily imply unwavering belief: 'clients' spiritual narratives may be nuanced, fragmented and even contradictory' (Hodge, 2008, p. 189). Second, people for whom spirituality is significant usually desire to 'grow' in this area of their life; therefore, to ignore or downplay this dimension in people who subscribe to a transcendent narrative is to bypass what may be the key to their achieving greater quality of life. Reflecting on current UK health policy with its objectives of achieving holistic and integrated care, Harrison (2007) recognises that the western models from which this stems may be way off the mark for many service users. She asks the question:

> What sorts of partnerships and collaboration do we need in health and social care to enable BME individuals and communities to achieve that sense of wholeness? (p. 6)

It is to diverse perceptions and experiences of wholeness that we now turn.

Spirituality and the challenge to western social work paradigms

In Chapter 7 we started to look at the eco-spiritual approach to the community aspect of social work. There are deeper implications of the eco-spiritual approach which take us to the very heart of the social work enterprise internationally. Coates et al. (2005) remind us that so much of what is deemed to be 'best social work theory and practice' is in fact westernised social work theory and practice, and that the struggle really to celebrate diversity with social justice is thwarted by social work's frequent

> preference for modernist, ethnocentric (i.e. European-American) paradigms which define rules for acceptable knowledge and practice. (p. 19)

These writers argue that the dominant western paradigms, such as anti-discriminatory and anti-oppressive practice, for all their good intentions, often 'make it impossible for minority cultures to lose or shake off their victim status'. This approach, they suggest, smacks of the well-intentioned 'powerful' trying hard to do something for the 'weak', while at the same time making the assumption that the 'weak' really are completely weak and unable to take any responsibility for their well-being. Westernised social work discourse, they suggest, has tended to emphasise

> the negative impact...of structurally limited life chances...an anti-oppressive perspective overlooks people's abilities to rise above their circumstances. Within the spirituality and indigenous social work literature, there is a greater recognition of the centrality of community, of 'individual 'agency', and of 'enhancing the capabilities of (vulnerable) clients to practise effective life-planning, find healing and gain mastery over their lives' (Ferguson, 2001, p. 41). These strength based approaches, while not denying the importance of structural factors, ... [see] individuals as self-governing agents rather than powerless victims of oppressive forces. (Coates, 2007, p. 5)

Clearly, many would want to take issue with this assertion. Anti-oppressive practice may not always, or even often, achieve its full objectives; the levels of disabling oppression may be more far reaching than we realise, and require drastic action sometimes at governmental levels for situations to be ameliorated. Sometimes the best that any social worker in any setting can hope to achieve is a creative accommodation to an unsatisfactory 'status quo', even at the risk of having the aspect of their role as 'social police' uncomfortably re-affirmed. Nevertheless, best partnership practice should always have a strengths perspective at its core (Moss, 2005; Saleeby, 2008), which the eco-spiritual approach strongly affirms.

Individual and community

One of the key differences often cited between Eastern philosophies and Western thought concerns the value placed on the individual or the community. Social work practice in the west has been strongly influenced by post-Enlightenment thought which privileges the individual and values autonomy. By contrast, Confucianism, Buddhism and Hinduism place the common good and communitarian values in higher esteem. In the history of western Christendom, the philosophical and ethical values of the Enlightenment converged with political and socio-economic influences to produce an emphasis in Protestantism on individualism and the 'Protestant ethic', which promised rewards for industrious individuals. At the same time, Christianity has also espoused the teaching of Jesus that it is in losing oneself that one truly finds oneself. Western religion therefore has traditionally had a somewhat ambivalent relationship with the importance of the individual. Western secularism, likewise, maintains fiercely individualistic thinking alongside socialist political aspirations. This focus on the individual is, however, dominant in contemporary western spirituality discourse. In the post-Christian era which fosters individualised customised beliefs over firm adherence to handed-down religion, self-fulfilment and actualisation are prized over belonging to a religious community.

Contemporary social work in the developed world also places high value on the individual; personalisation, individual choice, individual rights and autonomy are themes which resound across policy and practice guidance in the health and social care systems of the developed world. This is somewhat at odds with the theoretical basis for social work, which favours a social constructionist view of the world. Pitched into this uneasy tension is a branch of the contemporary spirituality discourse which social work has particularly promoted. This defines spirituality and spiritual care as *inextricably linked* to social justice and social responsibility. In Chapter 7, we explored some of the reasons for this. Indeed, Stewart (2002) argues for the inclusion of spirituality in the social work curriculum precisely because it has social and political as well as individual resonance. Liberation Theology, which we have touched upon throughout this book, also sees a concern with socio-economic concerns and social justice as the starting point for the nurturing of individual faith.

This perspective on spirituality has more commonly been applied in social work practice outside of the UK and the USA. For example, in a study of family violence in an aboriginal community in western South Australia, one perpetrator expressed his shame at having

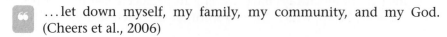 ...let down myself, my family, my community, and my God. (Cheers et al., 2006)

Social workers working with aboriginal communities in Australia have modified their individual family interventions to (as in this study) *mobilise the spiritual energy of the community to heal itself* through drawing on strongly held values of community justice and social responsibility. In an article comparing social work practice in Zimbabwe and Moldova, the authors argue that western social work models, ascribed to by both secular and faith-based organisations, have placed social workers in developing countries in an ideological stranglehold as they struggle with serious socio-economic problems on a daily basis (Moldovan and Moyo, 2007). Only by returning to the 'core social work value of social justice' (p. 469), the authors argue, can social work practice globally progress. Lynn (2001) agrees that confining community and social justice approaches to work with problematised aboriginal communities does not go far enough. Social work in the developed world should grasp the potential in other world-views for interventions in the developed world also. Understanding spirituality as a dimension of the social realm, with its twin axes of responsibility and sharing, opens up new possibilities for breaking out of the perennial dilemma for western models of social work of understanding problems from a social structural starting point, but, through the nature of its interventions, finding itself problematising the individual.

Example

Imran had started his social work training with high expectations. Born in the UK but with parents who had remained firmly within traditional Asian culture, he continued to loosely observe Muslim religious festivals but saw himself as someone who could move between both worlds. He had a strong sense of vocation to reach out to Muslim communities in particular. However, he soon found that his career as a social worker provided some huge challenges to his understanding of himself and society. He was appalled at the way some people behaved towards others which he described to his Asian friends as being animalistic and 'red in tooth and claw', and he often felt depressed by the thought that 'this was all there is to life'. He also found himself struggling with the way his student colleagues interpreted 'empowerment' and 'personalisation', realising, to his surprise, that his own values were somewhat different. One day, during multi-faith week at the university, Imran wandered into a prayer room and joined a group of Muslim students in their act of worship. He began to read and think more deeply about the religious and cultural traditions in which he had been brought up. As he did so, he began to find his capacity to cope was enhanced, and his belief that individual lives needed to be seen in a wider context helped him regain a positive focus on his life and career. Instead of feeling defensive about Asian family expectations, he gained the confidence to contribute a different perspective on relationships, choices and what makes for quality of life, which his class-mates found valuable.

The weight given to individual or social perspectives in any particular society can be seen to be determined by four factors: the ontological assumptions underpinning prescribed cultural patterns; attitudes to relationships and understandings of relatedness; the relationship between culture and identity; and cultural style (Holloway, 2007c). Each, although not solely concerned with spirituality, has an existential dimension.

In his discussion of use of narrative in social work practice, Hodge (2008) points out that about two-thirds of the world rejects the secular worldviews espoused by the global North in favour of 'transcendent narratives'. Moreover, within the societies of the global North, significant groups for social work practice, such as socio-economically disadvantaged immigrant and ethnic minority populations, adhere to spiritual values and belief systems. Social work is ever-mindful of its professional value-base and its impact on the way in which social workers understand and respond to the situations with which they work. In its recognition of differing cultural emphases between the individual and the community, it is important for social work to recognise the influence of spiritual values and the notions embedded in them about 'being', of whether 'I' am related to an 'other', be that some wider purpose or Divine Other:

 In Islam, self-actualisation is not viewed as the pathway to mental health. Rather, mental health is understood to be predicated upon surrender of the self to God. (Hodge, 2008, p. 182)

The lack of demarcation between the self and the other in Asian culture is frequently cited. Yip (2005) extends this to characterise Asian societies as 'relationally orientated', such that traditional values in which personal well-being and obligation are mutually dependent co-exist with modernisation. Thus, in Hong Kong, for example, over 80 per cent of the population say they have no religion, yet secular and transcendent narratives co-exist through this adherence to relatedness. Morice, outlining the 'Te Whare Tapa Wha' model of health care, which brings together physical, mental, social and spiritual dimensions of health and healing, reminds us that 'Maori health perspectives are wholistic, inclusive and relational' (Morice, presentation to MindBody Conference, November 2006). Where such culturally embedded assumptions are disturbed, as increasingly is the case between generations in immigrant populations or through the influence of western behaviours on aboriginal cultures, significant individual and community problems may result. Moreover, professional modes of interaction which rely on non-disclosure of the self may be counter-cultural (including for the worker themselves) and create barriers to the therapeutic process (Lynn, 2001). This has particularly been the case where the worker's own spirituality is concerned, where disclosure of their religious beliefs is regarded in social work at least as inappropriate at best and proselytising at worst. Interestingly, to declare that one has no beliefs is not usually seen as problematic, unless done in a way which is disrespectful to the service user. Lynn found that the aboriginal community expected a more 'friendly' engagement where 'sharing' included, if relevant, their spirituality; she challenges a concept of 'empathy' in which the worker gives nothing away about themselves yet expects to share intimate parts of the service user's life (Lynn, 2001). We may reflect here that a holistic approach implies 'whole person to whole person', as much as it means a comprehensive approach to the service user and their problem(s).

Person and environment

We began in the last chapter to think about approaches which are challenging social work's neglect of the environment; but to take this further we need now to delve deeper into contributions from parts of the world which employ a very different way of perceiving the relationship between the individual and the physical world. The traditional 'western' way of thinking about the person and their environment employed in social work theory stems from our favoured psycho-social model: *this* person in *this* situation, extended in more contemporary discourse to thinking about micro and macro levels of human interaction. In this model for understanding the person and their environment, the individual or possibly the group, is the focus, with the environment being seen as the context which influences their functioning. Indeed, Hollis, in her original articulation of psycho-social casework, identified five categories of 'direct methods' – all psychological interventions – and only one in the category of 'indirect methods', concerned with *'modifying* the environment' (Hollis, 1964).

The indigenous peoples of Australia, New Zealand, North America and the northern extremities of Europe have a very different way of understanding and experiencing their relationship with their environment: 'I'm not in the place but the place is in me'; 'Here nature knows us' (Suopajarvi, 1998, and Spretnak, 1991, quoted in Zapf, 2005, p. 637). This form of traditional knowledge derives from observations and experience of living in close association with the land, or nature, and is handed down from generation to generation. The 'sacred' is not set apart from the mundane but embedded in everyday life and practices. Aspects of this are also seen in Asian and African cultures, with many African languages having no separate words for 'religious' or 'secular'. In passing, we may note that it is not hard to see why, even if no other discrimination existed, the dislocation from this way of experiencing and understanding which occurs when people from 'traditional' and rural environments are transplanted into western urban environments is likely to create not only social problems but also existential crises.

It might be argued that contemporary western articulations of spirituality have bridged this gulf by their strong association with nature (Hegarty, 2007) and that all religions have understood the importance of creating and designating sacred spaces. Zapf argues that this misses the 'profound connection' to the environment in which selfhood and place are completely intertwined. Instead, place is used as a vehicle for our spiritual expression, and nature as a resource on which we may draw. Embedded in this understanding is a separation between human existence and the natural environment which we must somehow overcome. Indeed, in the Judeo-Christian tradition, the Genesis story sets up an oppositional relationship in which humankind must subdue and subjugate the natural environment and the animal world. Contemporary meditation practices adopted in the developed countries foster spiritual energy to re-connect and rediscover the sacred in 'our' world. The aboriginal notion of healing and wholeness draws energy from that land *of which we are an indistinguishable part*:

 ...a people rooted in the land over time have exchanged their tears, their breath, their bones, all of their elements...with their habitat many times over. (Spretnak, 1991, quoted in Zapf, 2005, p. 637)

Clearly there are important insights from this way of knowing to be taken into social work practice in multicultural contexts. However, what can we learn beyond that? As we discussed in Chapter 7, Zapf challenges us to consider the profound *spiritual* dimensions of the question 'what does it mean to live well in this place?' (Zapf, 2005, p. 639). Such a perspective might significantly enhance the approaches to facilitating and determining quality of life which we discussed in Chapter 4. It is interesting that one of the most popular rehabilitation therapies in learning disability and mental health services has been to utilise the resources of the natural world through gardening and horse riding activities, for example, since their calming and confidence-building effects have frequently been noted. Greater attention is being paid to the beneficial effects of bringing the natural environment into residential settings, particularly hospices, and we even (though occasionally) hear of pets in hospital wards. Interventions are designed which take young people from 'troubled' backgrounds out into the countryside; but the intention with those whose behaviour is disruptive is usually to pit them against a 'challenging' environment rather than to enable them to discover a oneness with their environment where their usual experience is one of alienation. This is not to rule out the possibility that experiencing the power and awesome scale of nature may be the path to allowing absorption and integration of the troubled self in some larger existence in the pursuit of wholeness.

So there are possibilities within what we do already, if social work is to take seriously the possibility that our physical world and spiritual worlds can be experienced as one. A greater challenge, however, lies in applying this notion of profound connectiveness to the alienating environments, many of them inner city, in which most social work service users live, certainly in the UK and the USA. Here we may draw on contemporary work from anthropologists, historians, cultural studies and the built environment which together is fostering connections past, present and future between people and their environments – the 'material culture'. This in itself is not the business of social work, but it is a growing movement which we do well to learn from and support. More directly, in our one-to-one interactions with service users and their families, this discussion returns us to the notions of transcendence and transformation which we looked at in Chapter 5. There are inspiring examples in history of how even the prison cell in a brutal regime can become a 'temple of the spirit' (e.g. Bonhoeffer, 1956). As social workers we need also to see beyond the 'dispiriting' material conditions of people's lives to the possibilities for growth, renewal, connectiveness and wholeness in communities and systems. It is not possible (or necessarily desirable) to lift people out of their environment of origin, but 'living well in this place' challenges us to facilitate transformation of those things which cause alienation into that which creates integration and connection.

- What in this discussion has challenged your models of social work practice the most?
- What idea can you take away as a starting point for expanding your vision and practice?

Conclusion

The IFSW has drawn up a definition of social work which it claims holds good globally:

> The social work profession promotes social change, problem-solving in human relationships and the empowerment and liberation of people to enhance well-being. Utilising theories of human behaviour and social systems, social work intervenes at the point where people interact with their environments. Principles of human rights and social justice are fundamental to social work. (IFSW, 2001)

There are those who question whether social work in some parts of the developed world looks anything like this (Wilson et al., 2008). Hugman, however, highlights four elements in the IFSW definition which he says are *shared aspirations* for social work across the globe (Hugman, 2007). These are *social change, well-being, human rights* and *social justice*. These four themes have run through this book's engagement with the relationship between social work and spirituality. We have taken a critical look at the ontological issues raised by the challenges within each and seen how so often social work's approach falls short. One of the reasons why this is so in the developed world is that social work itself has become increasingly oppressed by the rationalist, managerialist culture in which it operates. We have talked in this book about 'maintaining the spirit' of service users whose lives are marked by continuous hardship, pain and distress, whether arising from physical, emotional or socio-economic causes.

Throughout this book we have tried to show how by being open to spirituality, spiritual need and the challenge and potential which this dimension releases in spiritual care, social work practice might be enhanced for service users and social workers alike. We hope we have provided a model which is acceptable, accessible and appropriate for everyone, regardless of their personal beliefs. Religion is too often regarded as and demonstrated to be a dividing force, but authentic spirituality can never be a source of difference but rather the core of our shared humanity. Hegarty expresses it thus:

> Care transcending boundaries cannot happen where there is fear or defensiveness about beliefs or any religious or secular position. Care of the spirit requires openness and trust in the wisdom of the spirit. (Hegarty, 2007, p. 45)

Or to offer another take on this:

> A global social work movement true to the values of social justice and equality is one which is self-examining, one that is connected beyond culture, ethnicity and geography. (Moldovan and Moyo, 2007, p. 469)

The message of this book is that a sensitive, nuanced understanding of spirituality provides us with a connection which goes beyond those differences which frame our social work practice as much as they determine the everyday struggles of those users we seek to serve. Those values and skills which social work holds dear fall critically short unless they are imbued with this 'spirit'.

There is perhaps one final caveat to be lodged. We cannot get our heads round everything. Indeed, as Tracy (1994) suggests, spirituality (as well as religion) can also be seen as 'A massive act of resistance to the notion that everything can be explained' (p. 113). In spite of our best efforts, and at times because of our best efforts, a sense of mystery will remain. There will be moments when the deeply negative aspects of our work, indeed of human existence, threaten to overturn and crack open our carefully constructed world-views as we try to make new sense of it all. And there will be times when our sense of mystery will be tinged with awe and wonder as we contemplate the 'beyondness of things' and our apparent insignificance in the cosmos. Spirituality – whether secular or religious – is also about all of these wider, deeper and greater aspects to our living and working. In a poem which strikes at some of the fundamental dilemmas in contemporary social work, Michael Sheridan says this:

> If we nurtured the soul of social work, the spiritual would be recognised as an essential part of what we're about and would be reflected in all that we do – and the mystery would smile and be glad. (quoted in Canda and Furman, 1999, p. 185)

It is our very great hope that readers have journeyed with us in this book, that we have provided a helpful map in some of those areas which we all find perplexing or difficult, but that in so doing we have opened up exciting new possibilities for social work practice. This journey into the relatively unknown territory of social work and spirituality is, we suggest, a new way of 'knowing', fit for purpose when facing the challenges of contemporary social work.

taking it further

- Coates, J., Graham J.R., Swartzentruber, B. and Ouellette B. (eds) (2007) *Spirituality and Social Work: Selected Canadian Readings* (Toronto: Canadian Scholars Press).
- Hegarty, M. (2007) 'Care of the spirit that transcends religious, ideological and philosophical boundaries', *Indian Journal of Palliative Care*, 13: 2, 42–47.
- Holloway, M. (2006) 'Death the great leveller? Towards a transcultural spirituality of dying and bereavement', *Journal of Clinical Nursing, Special Issue Spirituality*, 15: 7, 833–839.
- Nash, M. and Stewart, B. (eds) (2002) *Spirituality and Social Care: Contributing to Personal and Community Well-Being* (London: Jessica Kingsley).
- Sacco, T. (1994) 'Spirituality and social work students in their first year of study at a South African University', *Journal of Social Development in Africa*, 11: 2, 43–56.
- Zapf, M.K. (2005) 'The spiritual dimension of person and environment: Perspectives from social work and traditional knowledge', *International Social Work*, 48: 5, 633–642.

References

Adams, R. (1998) *Quality Social Work* (London: Macmillan).

Akinsola, H. (2001) 'Fostering hope in people living with AIDS in Africa: The role of primary health-care workers', *Australian Journal of Rural Health*, 9, 158–165.

Anandarajah, G. and Hight, E. (2001) 'Spirituality and medical practice: Using the hope questions as a practical tool for spiritual assessment', *American Family Physician*, 63: 1, 81–88.

Attig, T. (2001) 'Relearning the world: Making and finding meanings', in R. Neimeyer (ed.) *Meaning Reconstruction and the Experience of Loss* (Washington, DC: American Psychological Association).

Australian Association of Social Workers (AASW) (1999) *AASW Code of Ethics* (Canberra: AASW).

Bailey, C. (2002) 'Introduction – 'The notion of implicit religion: What it means and does not mean', in E. Bailey (ed.) *The Secular Quest for Meaning in Life: Denton Papers in Implicit Religion* (New York: The Edwin Mellon Press).

Bauman, Z. (2007) *Consuming Life* (Cambridge: Polity Press).

Beckett, C. and Maynard, A. (2005) *Values and Ethics in Social Work: An Introduction* (London: Sage).

Beckford, J. (1989) *Religion and Advanced Industrial Society* (London: Unwin Hyman).

Beeston, D. (2006) *Older People and Suicide* (Care Services Improvement Partnership/Centre for Ageing and Mental Health: Staffordshire University).

Beresford, P., Croft, S., Evans, C. and Harding, T. (2000) 'Quality in social services: The developing role of user investment in the UK', in C. Davies, L. Finlay and A. Bullman (eds) *Changing Practice in Health and Social Care* (London: Sage/Open University).

Beresford, P. and Trevillion, S. (1995) *Developing Skills for Community Care* (Aldershot: Ashgate Publishing).

Bergin, A. and Jensen, J. (1990) 'Religiosity of psychotherapists: A national survey', *Psychotherapy*, 27, 3–7.

Biestek, F. (1961) *The Casework Relationship* (London: Allen and Unwin).

Biggs, S. (1997) 'Interprofessional collaboration: Problems and prospects', in J. Ovretveit, P. Mathias and T. Thompson (eds) *Interprofessional Working for Health and Social Care* (London: Macmillan), pp. 186–200.

Billings, A. (1992) 'Pastors or counsellors', *Contact*, 108: 2, 200–207.

Boddie, S.C. and Cnaan, R.A. (2006) *Faith-Based Social Services: Measures, Assessments and Effectiveness* (New York: The Haworth Pastoral Press).

Bonhoeffer, D. (1956) (edited by E. Bethge) *Letters and Papers from Prison* (London: SCM Publishers).

Boucher, D. and Kelly, P. (eds) (1998) *Social Justice: From Hulme to Waltzer* (New York: Routledge).

Bowpitt, G. (1998) 'Evangelical Christianity, Secular Humanism, and the Genesis of British Social Work', *British Journal of Social Work*, 28, 675–693.

Bradshawe, J. (1972) 'The taxonomy of social need', in G. McLachlan (ed.) *Problems and Progress in Medical Care* (Oxford: Oxford University Press).

Brierley, P. (2000) 'Religion', in A. Halsey and J. Webb (eds) *Twentieth Century British Social Trends* (London: Macmillan).

Brierley, P. (2000) *Religious Trends* (London: Marc Europe).

Brierley, P. and Hiscock, V. (eds) (2008) *UK Christian Handbook* (London: Christian Research Association).

British Association of Social Workers (BASW) (2002) *The Code of Ethics for Social Work* (Birmingham: BASW).

Bruce, S. (1995) *Religion in Modern Britain* (Oxford: Oxford University Press).

Burke, G. (2007) *Spirituality: Roots and Routes – A Secular Reflection on the Practice of Spiritual Care* (London: Age Concern).

Burkhardt, M. (1989) 'Spirituality: An analysis of the concept', *Holistic Nursing Practice*, 3: 3, 69–77.

Burnard, P. (1987) 'Spiritual distress and the nursing response: Theoretical considerations and counselling skills', *Journal of Advanced Nursing*, 12: 3, 377–382.

Burton, R. (2004) 'Spiritual pain: Origins, nature and management', *Contact*, 143, 3–13.

Butrym, Z. (1976) *The Nature of Social Work* (Basingstoke: Macmillan).

Campbell, A. (1981) *Rediscovering Pastoral Care* (Darton: Longman and Todd).

Canda, E. (2008) 'Spiritual connections in social work: Boundary violations and transcendence', *Journal of Religion and Spirituality in Social Work: Social Thought*, 27, 1–2.

Canda, E.R. and Furman, L.D. (1999) *Spiritual Diversity in Social Work Practice: The Heart of Helping*, 1st Ed. (New York: The Free Press).

Canda, E.R. and Furman, L.D. (2010) *Spiritual Diversity in Social Work Practice: The Heart of Helping*, 2nd Ed. (New York: The Free Press).

Cassam, E. and Gupta, H. (1992) *Quality Assurance for Social Care Agencies* (London: Longman).

Census (2001) *Ethnicity and Religion in England and Wales*. Available at www.statistics.gov.uk/cci, accessed 5 March 2009.

Chan, C. (2005) Keynote address, Towards Transcultural Spirituality conference, University of Hull, UK, 19 July 2005.

Channer, Y. (1998) 'Understanding and managing conflict in the learning process: Christians coming out', in V. Cree and C. McCaulay (eds) *Transfer of Learning in Professional and Vocational Education* (London: Routledge).

Cheers, B., Binell, M., Coleman, H., Gentle, I., Miller, G., Taylor, J. and Weetra, C. (2006) 'Family violence: An Australian indigenous community tells its story', *International Social Work*, 49: 1, 51–63.

Chile, L. and Simpson, G. (2004) 'Spirituality and community development: Exploring the link between the individual and the collective', *Community Development Journal*, 39: 4, 318–331.

Chopra, D. (2006) *Life after Death: The Book of Answers* (London: Rider).

Coates, J. (2007) 'From ecology to spirituality and social justice', in J. Coates, J.R. Graham, B. Swartzwebtruber and B. Ouellete (eds) *Spirituality and Social Work: Selected Canadian Readings* (Toronto: Canadian Scholars Press).

Coates, J., Grey, M. and Hetherington, T. (2005) 'An Eco-spiritual perspective: Finally, a place for indigenous approaches', *British Journal of Social Work*, doi: 10.1093/bjsw/bch391.

Coates, J., Graham J.R., Swartzentruber, B. and Ouellette B. (2007) *Spirituality and Social Work: Selected Canadian Readings* (Toronto: Canadian Scholars Press).

Coholic, D., Nichols, A. and Cadell, S. (2008) ' "Spirituality and social work practice", Introduction', *Journal of Religion and Spirituality in Social Work: Social Thought*, 27: 1–2, 41–46.

Coleman, P. (2006) David Hobman Memorial Lecture 2006 in G. Burke (2007) *Spirituality: Roots and Routes: A Secular Reflection on the Practice of Spiritual Care* (London: Age Concern).

Consedine, J. (2002) 'Spirituality and social justice', in M. Nash and B. Stewart (eds) *Spirituality and Social Care: Contributing to Personal and Community Well-Being* (London: Jessica Kingsley).

Cook, G. (2000) *European Values Survey* (Gordon Cook Foundation).

Cook, C. (2004) 'Addiction and spirituality', *Addiction*, 99, 539–551.

Cornette, K. (2005) 'For whenever I am weak, I am strong ...', *International Journal of Palliative Nursing*, 11: 3, 147–153.

Coulshed, V. and Orme, J. (2006) *Social Work Practice*, 4th edn (London: Palgrave).

Council on Social Work Education (CSWE) (1994) *Handbook of Accreditation Standards and Procedures* (Alexandria, VA: CSWE).

Coyte, M.E., Gilbert, P. and Nicholls, V. (2007) *Spirituality, Values and Mental Health: Jewels for the Journey* (London: Jessica Kingsley).

Crabtree, V. (2007) *Religion in the UK: Diversity, Trends and Decline*. Available at www. vexen.co.uk/religion.html, accessed 03 March 2010.

Cree, V.E. and Davis, A. (1996) *Social Work: A Christian or Secular Discourse?* (Edinburgh: University of Edinburgh New Waverley Papers, Vol. 3).

Crisp, B. (2008) 'Social work and spirituality in a secular society', *Journal of Social Work*, 8, 363–375.

Csikszentmihalyi, M. (1991) *Flow: The Psychology of Optimal Experience* (San Francisco, CA: Harper Perennial).

Culliford, L. (2004) 'Re: The heart of the matter', *British Medical Journal*, Rapid responses, 23 July.

Dalrymple, J. and Burke, B (1995) *Anti-Oppressive Practice: Social Care and the Law* (Buckingham: Open University Press).

Daniel, B., Wassell, S. and Gilligan, R. (1999) ' "It's just common sense, isn't it?": Exploring ways of putting the theory of resilience into action', *Adoption and Fostering*, 23: 3, 6–15.

Darlington, Y. and Bland, R. (1999) 'Strategies for encouraging and maintaining hope among people living with a serious mental illness', *Australian Social Work*, 52: 3, 17–23.

Davidson, R. (2001) *Visions of Compassion: Western Scientists and Tibetan Buddhists Examine Human Nature* (Oxford: Oxford University Press).

Davie, G. (2004) *Religion in Britain since 1945: Believing without Belonging* (Oxford: Blackwell).

De Boulay, S. (1988) *Tutu – Voice of the Voiceless* (London: Penguin Books).

Department of Health (2005) *Independence, Well-Being and Choice* (London: The Stationery Office).

Desbiens, J.F. and Fillion, L. (2007) 'Coping strategies, emotional outcomes and spiritual quality of life in palliative care nurses', *International Journal of Palliative Nursing*, 13: 6, 291–300.

DiBlasio, F.A. (1993) 'The role of social workers' religious beliefs in helping family members forgive', *Families in Society*, 74: 3, 167–170.

Dominelli, L. (2002) *Anti-Oppressive Social Work Theory and Practice* (Basingstoke: Palgrave Macmillan).

Doyal, L. and Gough, I. (1991) *A Theory of Human Needs* (Basingstoke: Palgrave Macmillan).

Dugan, T. and Coles, R. (1989) *The Child of Our Times: Studies in the Development of Resiliency* (New York: Brunner/Mazel).

Early, T.J. and Glenmaye, L.F. (2000) 'Valuing families: Social work practice with families from a strengths perspective', *Social Work*, 45: 2, 118–130.

Eliot, T.S. (1944) *Four Quartets* (London: Faber and Faber).

Ellis, M. (2000) *Revolutionary Forgiveness: Essays on Judaism, Christianity and the Future of Religious Life* (Waco, TX: Baylor University Press).

Ellison, C. (1983) 'Spiritual well-being: Conceptualisation and measurement', *Journal of Psychology and Theology*, 11, 330–340.

Emmons, R.A. (2005) 'Striving for the sacred: Personal goals, life meaning and religion', *Journal of Social Issues*, 61: 4, 731–745.

Etzioni, A. (1995) *The Spirit of Community: Rights, Responsibilities and the Communitarian Agenda* (London: Fontana).

Ferguson, H. (2001) 'Social work, individualization and life politics', *British Journal of Social Work*, 31: 1, 41–55.

Ferguson, I. (2007) 'Increasing user choice or privatising risk? The antinomies of personalisation', *British Journal of Social Work*, 37, 387–403. Special Edition.

Fonagy, P., Steele, M., Steele, H., Higgitt, A. and Target, M. (1994) 'The Emmanuel Millar Memorial Lecture 1992: The theory and practice of resilience', *Journal of Child Psychology*, 35: 2, 231–257.

Ford, D. (2004) 'The responsibilities of universities in a religious and secular world', *Studies in Christian Ethics*, 17: 1, 22–37.

Forgiveness Project, The (1993) *Exhibition: The 'F' Word: Images of Forgiveness*, held at www.theforgivenessproject.com/news, accessed 03 March 2010.

Fowler, J. (1981) *Stages of Faith. The Psychology of Human Development and the Quest for Meaning* (San Francisco: Harper and Row).

Fowler, J. (1987) *Faith Development and Pastoral Care* (Minneapolis: The Fortress Press).

Francis, L., Williams, E. and Robbins, M. (2006) 'The unconventional beliefs of Churchgoers: The matter of luck', *Implicit Religion*, 9: 3, 305–314.

Frankl, V. (2000) *Man's Search for Ultimate Meaning* (New York: Perseus Publishing).

Fraser, M., Richman, J. and Galinsky, M. (1999) 'Risk Protection and resilience: Towards a conceptual framework for social work practice', *Social Work Research*, 23: 3, 131–143.

Furman, L., Benson, P., Grimwood, C. and Canda, E. (2004) 'Religion and spirituality in social work education and direct practice at the millennium: A survey of UK social workers', *British Journal of Social Work*, 34: 6, 767–793.

Furman, L., Benson, P., Canda, E. and Grimwood, C. (2005) 'Comparative International Analysis of Religion and Spirituality in Social Work: A survey of UK and US social workers', *Social Work Education*, 24: 8, 813–839.

Furness, S. (2005) 'Shifting sands: Developing cultural competence', *Practice*, 17: 4, 247–256.

Furness, S. and Gilligan, P. (2010) *Religion, Belief and Social Work: Making a Difference* (Bristol: The Policy Press).

Garmezy, N. (1991) 'Resilience in children's adaptation to negative life events and stressed environments', *Pediatric Annals*, 20, 459–466.

General Social Care Council (GSCC) (2002) *Code of Practice for Social Workers* (London: General Social Care Council).

George, J. (1999) 'Conceptual meddle, practical dilemma: Human rights, social development and social work education', *International Social Work*, 42, 15–26.

Gibran, K. (1980) *The Prophet*, Pan book edition (London: William Heinemann).

Gilbert, P. (2007) 'The spiritual foundation: Awareness and context for people's lives today', in M. Coyte, P. Gilbert and V. Nicholls (eds) *Spirituality, Values and Mental Health* (London: Jessica Kingsley).

Gilbert, P. (2008) *Guidelines on Spirituality for Staff in Acute Care Services* (Care Services Improvement Partnership/National Institute for Mental Health in England: Staffordshire University).

Gilligan, P. (2003) ' "It isn't discussed": Religion, belief and practice teaching – missing components of cultural competence in social work education', *Journal of Practice Teaching in Health and Social Care*, 5: 1, 75–95.

Gilligan, P. and Furness, S. (2005) 'The role of religion and spirituality in social work practice: Views and experiences of social workers and student', *British Journal of Social Work*, 36, 617–637.

Gilligan, R. (1999) 'Enhancing the resilience of children in public care by mentoring their talent and interests', *Child and Family Social Work*, 4: 3, 187–196.

Gilligan, R. (2001) *Promoting Resilience: A Resource Guide on Working with Children in the Care System* (London: British Agencies for Adoption and Fostering).

Gilligan, R. (2004) 'Promoting resilience in child and family work: Issues for social work practice, education and policy', *Social Work Education*, 23: 1, 93–104.

Glendinning, T. and Bruce, S. (2006) 'New ways of believing or belonging: Is religion giving way to spirituality?', *The British Journal of Sociology*, 57: 3, 399–414.

Goldstein, H. (1990) 'The knowledge base of social work practice: Wisdom, analogue or art?', *Families in Society: The Journal of Contemporary Human Services*, 71: 1, 32–43.

Graham, J. (2008) 'Who am I? An essay on inclusion and spiritual growth through community and mutual appreciation', *Journal of Religion and Spirituality in Social Work*, 27: 1–2, 1–24.

Grainger, R. (1998) *The Social Symbolism of Grief and Mourning* (London: Jessica Kingsley).

Gray, M. (2006) 'Viewing spirituality in social work through the lens of contemporary social theory', *British Journal of Social Work*, 38, 175–196.

Greene, G., Jensen, C. and Harper, D. (1996) 'A constructivist perspective on clinical social work practice with ethnically diverse clients', *Social Work*, 41: 2, 172–180.

Greene, R. (ed.) (2002) *Resiliency: An Integrated Approach to Practice, Policy and Research* (Washington, DC: NASW Press).

Gunaratnam, Y. (1997) 'Culture is not enough: A critique of multiculturalism in palliative care', in D. Field, J. Hockey and N. Small (eds) *Death, Gender and Ethnicity* (London: Routledge), pp. 166–186.

Haas, T. and Nachtigal, P. (1998) *Place Value: An Educators Guide to Good Literature on Rural Lifeways, Environments and Purposes of Education* (Charleston, WV: Aalachia Educational Laboratory).

Harding, S., Phillips, D. and Fogarty, K. (1985) *Contrasting Values in Western Europe* (London: Palgrave Macmillan).

Harrison, P. (2007) 'Holistic thinking and integrated care: Working with black and minority ethnic individuals and communities in health and social care', *Journal of Integrated Care*, 15: 3, 3–6.

Hathaway, W. (2006) 'Religious diversity in the military clinic: Four cases', *Military Psychology*, 18: 3, 247–257.

Hegarty, M. (2007) 'Care of the spirit that transcends religious, ideological and philosophical boundaries', *Indian Journal of Palliative Care*, 13: 2, 42–47.

Henery, N. (2003) 'Critical commentary: The reality of visions – contemporary theories of spirituality in social work', *British Journal of Social Work*, 33: 8, 1105–1113.

Heyse-Moore, L. (1996) 'On spiritual pain in the dying', *Mortality*, 1: 3, 297–315.

Hirtz, R. (1999) 'Martin Seligman's journey from learned helplessness to learned happiness', *The Pennsylvania Gazette*, January–February, 22–27.

Hodge, D. (2000) 'Spiritual ecomaps: A new diagrammatic tool for assessing marital and family spirituality', *Journal of Marital and Family Therapy*, 26: 2, 211–216.

Hodge, D. (2001) 'Spiritual assessment: A review of major qualitative methods and a new framework for assessing spirituality', *Social Work*, 49: 27–38.

Hodge, D. (2005a) 'Spiritual lifemaps: A client-centered pictorial instrument for spiritual assessment, planning and intervention', *Social Work*, 50:1, 77–87.

Hodge, D. (2005b) 'Developing a spiritual assessment toolbox: A discussion of the strengths and limitations of five different assessment methods', *Health and Social Work*, 30: 4, 314–323.

Hodge, D.R. (2007) 'Social justice and people of faith: A transnational perspective', *National Association of Social Workers – Social Work*, 52: 2, April, 139–148.

Hodge, D. (2008) 'Constructing spiritually modified interventions: Cognitive therapy with diverse populations', *International Social Work*, 51: 2, 178–192.

Holbeche, L. and Springett, N. (2004) *In Search of Meaning in the Workplace* (Horsham: Roffey Park).

Hollis, F. (1964) *Casework: A Psycho-Social Therapy* (New York: Random House).

Holloway, M. (2005) *In the Spirit of Things … Social Work, Spirituality and Contemporary Society* (Inaugural Professorial lecture, The University of Hull, Hull).

Holloway, M. (2006) 'Death the great leveller? Towards a transcultural spirituality of dying and bereavement', *Journal of Clinical Nursing, Special Issue Spirituality*, 15: 7, 833–839.

Holloway, M. (2007a) 'Spiritual need and the core business of social work', *British Journal of Social Work*, 37: 2, 265–280.

Holloway, M. (2007b) 'Spirituality and darkness: Is it all sweetness and light?' unpublished paper, *Making Sense of Spirituality* conference, July 2007, University of Hull, Scarborough.

Holloway, M. (2007c) *Negotiating Death in Contemporary Health and Social Care* (Bristol: The Policy Press).

Holloway, M. and Lymbery, M. (2007) 'Editorial – caring for people: Social work with adults in the next decade and beyond', *British Journal of Social Work*, 37: 3, 375–386.

Holloway, R. (2004) *Doubts and Loves: What Is Left of Christianity* (Edinburgh: Canongate Books).

Holman, B. (1983) *Resourceful Friends: Skills in Community Social work* (London: Children's Society).

Holman, B. (1993) *A New Deal for Social Welfare* (Oxford: Lion Publishing).

Home Office (2003) *Restorative Justice: The Government's Strategy* (London: Home Office).

Home Office (2004) *Best Practice Guidance for Restorative Practitioners* (London: Home Office).

Horwath, J and Lees, J. (2008) 'Assessing the influence of religious beliefs and practices on parenting capacity: The challenges for social work practitioners', *British Journal of Social Work*, 40: 1, 82–99.

Houghton, S. (2007) 'Exploring hope: Its meaning for adults living with depression and for social work practice', *Australian e-Journal for the Advancement of Mental Health* (AeJAMH), 6: 3.

Howe, D. (1987) *An Introduction to Social Work Theory: Making Sense in Practice* (Aldershot: Wildwood House).

Hudson, B. (2000) 'Inter-agency collaboration – a sceptical view', in A. Brechin, H. Brown and M. Eby (eds) *Critical Practice in Health and Social Care* (London: Sage/Open University).

Hugman, R. (2007) 'The place of values in social work education', in M. Lymbery and K. Postle (eds) *Social Work: A Companion to Learning* (London: Sage).

Hunt, S. (2002) *Religion in Western Society* (Basingstoke: Palgrave Macmillan).

Hyde, B. (2008) *Children and Spirituality: Searching for Meaning and Connectedness* (London: Jessica Kingsley).

International Association of Schools of Social Work (IASSW) and the International Federation of Social Work (IFSW) (2004) *International Declaration of Ethical Principles of Social Work and International Ethical Standards for Social Work* (Bern, Switzerland: IASSW/IFSW).

International Association of Schools of Social Work (IASSW) and the International Federation of Social Work (IFSW) (2004) *Global Standards for the Education and Training of the Social Work Profession*, p. 6. Available at www/iassw-aoets.org/en/About_IASSW/GlobalStandards.pdf, accessed 03 March 2010.

International Federation of Social Workers (IFSW) (2001) *The Definition of Social Work* (Berne: IFSW). Available at www.ifsw.org, accessed 03 March 2010.

International Federation of Social Workers (IFSW) (2004) *Ethics in Social Work*. Available at www.ifsw.org.

James, A., Brooks, T. and Towell, D. (1992) *Committed to Quality: Quality Assurance in Social Service Departments* (London: HMSO).

Jevne, R. (2005) 'Hope: The simplicity and complexity', in J. Eliott (ed) *Interdisciplinary Perspectives on Hope* (New York: Nova Science Publishers).

Jones, K. (1993) *Beyond Optimism: A Buddhist Political Ecology* (Oxford: John Carpenter).

Joseph, S., Linley, P.A. and Maltby J. (2006) 'Positive psychology, religion and spirituality', *Mental Health, Religion and Culture*, 9: 3, 209–212.

Kellehear, A. (2000) 'Spirituality and palliative care: A model of needs', *Palliative Medicine*, 14, 149–155.

Kelly, J. (2004) 'Spirituality as a coping mechanism', *Dimensions of Critical Care Nursing*, 23: 4, 162–168.

King, M., Speck, P. and Thomas, A. (1994) 'Spiritual and religious beliefs in acute illness – is this a feasible area for study?', *Social Science and Medicine*, 38: 631–636.

King, M., Weich, S., Nazroo, J. and Blizard, B. (2006) 'Religion, mental health and ethnicity. EMPIRIC – a national survey of England', *Journal of Mental Health*, 15: 2, 153–162.

Kirby, L.D. and Fraser, M.W. (1997) 'Risk and resilience in childhood', in M. Fraser (ed.) *Risk and Resilience in Childhood: An Ecological Perspective* (Washington, DC: NASW Press).

Kissane, M. and McLaren, S. (2006) 'Sense of belonging as predictor of reasons for living in older adults', *Death Studies*, 30: 3, 243–258.

Koenig, H., McCullough, M. and Larson, D. (2001) *Handbook of Religion and Health* (Oxford: Oxford University Press).

Kung, H. (1984) *Eternal Life?* (London: Collins).

Leathard, A. (1994) *Going Inter-professional* (London: Routledge).

Ledger, S. (2005) 'The duty of nurses to meet patients' spiritual and/or religious needs', *British Journal of Nursing*, 14: 4, 220–225.

Liebmann, M. (2007) *Restorative Justice: How It Works* (London: Jessica Kingsley).

Lindsay, R. (2002) *Recognizing Spirituality: The Interface Between Faith and Social Work* (Crawlet: University of Western Australia Press).

Lloyd, M. [M. Holloway] (1995) *Embracing the Paradox: Pastoral Care with Dying and Bereaved People*. Contact Pastoral Monographs No 5 (Edinburgh: Contact Pastoral Limited Trust).

Lloyd, M. [M. Holloway] (1996) 'Philosophy and religion in the face of death and bereavement', *Journal of Religion and Health*, 35: 4, 295–310.

Lloyd, M. [M. Holloway] (1997) 'Dying and bereavement, spirituality and social work in a market economy of welfare', *British Journal of Social Work*, 27: 2, 175–190.

Lloyd, M. [M. Holloway] (2000) 'Holistic approaches to health and social care in the UK in the 1990s', Unpublished PhD thesis, University of Manchester.

Lloyd, M. [M. Holloway] (2002) 'A framework for working with loss', in N. Thompson (ed.) *Loss and Grief: A Guide for Human Services Practitioners* (London: Palgrave), pp. 208–220.

Lloyd, M. and Taylor, C. (1995) 'From Hollis to the Orange Book: Developing a holistic model of Social Work Assessment in the 1990s', *British Journal of Social Work*, 25, 691–710.

Lloyd, Murray (2005) 'Re: Secular and sacred spirituality', in response to 'Spiritual needs in health care' P. Speck, I. Higginson and J. Addlington-Hall, *British Medical Journal*, posted 24 August 2004: 329, 123–124.

Loewenberg, F. (1998) *Religion and Social Work Practice in Contemporary American Society* (New York: Columbia University Press).

Luckman, T. (1990) 'Shrinking transcendence, expanding religion', *Sociological Analysis*, 50: 2, 127–138.

Lymbery, M. (2001) 'Social work at the crossroads', *British Journal of Social Work*, 31: 3, 369–384.

Lynn, R. (2001) 'Learning from a "Murri Way"', *British Journal of Social Work*, 31, 903–916.

Maguire, K. (2001) 'Working with survivors of torture and extreme experience', in S. King-Spooner and C. Newnes (eds) *Spirituality and Psychotherapy* (Ross-on-Wye: PCCS Books).

Maslow, A. (1970) *Motivation and Personality*, 2nd edn (New York: Harper and Rowe).

Masters, W. and Johnson, V. (1996) *Human Sexual Response* (Toronto, New York: Bantam Books).

Mathews, I. (2009) *Social Work and Spirituality* (Exeter: Learning Matters).

Mattis, J. (2002) 'Religion and spirituality in the meaning-making and coping experiences of African American women', *Psychology of Women Quarterly*, 26, 309–321.

May, G. (2004) *The Dark Night of the Soul: A Psychiatrist Explores the Connection Between Darkness and Spiritual Growth* (San Francisco: Harper).

Mayers, C. and Johnston, D. (2008) 'Spirituality – the emergence of a working definition for use within healthcare practice', *Implicit Religion*, 11: 3, 265–275.

McClung, E., Grossoehme, D. and Jacobson, A. (2006) 'Collaborating with chaplains to meet spiritual needs', *MEDSURG Nursing*, 15: 3, 147–156.

McSherry, W. (2006) *Making Sense of Spirituality in Nursing and Healthcare Practice: An Interactive Approach*, 2nd edn (London: Jessica Kingsley).

McSherry, W. and Ross, L. (2002) 'Dilemmas of spiritual assessment: Considerations for nursing practice', *Journal of Advanced Nursing*, 38: 5, 479–488.

Ming-Shium, T. (2006) 'Illness: An opportunity for spiritual growth,' *The Journal of Alternative and Complementary Medicine*, 12: 10, 1029–1033.

Mohr, W. (2006) 'Spiritual issues in psychiatric care', *Perspectives in Psychiatric Care*, 42: 3, 174–183.

Moldovan, V. and Moyo, O. (2007) 'Constructions in the ideologies of helping: examples from Zimbabwe and Moldova', *International Social Work*, 50: 4, 461–472.

Moore, R. (2003) 'Spiritual assessment', *Social Work*, 48: 4, 558–561.

Morgan, J. (1993) 'The existential quest for meaning', in K. Doka and J. Morgan (eds) *Death and Spirituality* (Amityville, NY: Baywood).

Morice, M.P. (2006) *'Te Whare Tapa Wha'* A presentation at the MindBody Conference, November 2006. Available at www.mindbody.org.nz.

Moss, B. (2002) 'Spirituality: A Personal Perspective', Chapter 2, in N. Thompson (ed.) *Grief and Loss – A Guide for Human Services Practitioners* (Basingstoke: Palgrave Macmillan).

Moss, B. (2004) 'TGIM: Thank God it's Monday', *British Journal of Occupational Learning*, 2: 2, 33–44.

Moss, B. (2005) *Religion and Spirituality* (Lyme Regis: Russell House Publishing).

Moss, B. (2007a) 'Towards a spiritually intelligent workplace?', *Illness Crisis and Loss*, 15: 3, 261–271.

Moss, B. (2007b) *Values* (Lyme Regis: Russell House Publishing).

Moss, B. and Thompson, N. (2007) 'Spirituality and equality', *Journal Social and Public Policy Review*, accessed 1 January 2007. Available at www.uppress.co.uk/socialpublicpolicyreview.htm, accessed 21 March 2010.

Murray, R.B. and Zentner, J.B. (1989) *Nursing Concepts for Health Promotion* (London: Prentice Hall).

Narayanasamy, A. (1999) 'ASSET: A model for actioning spirituality and spiritual care education and training in nursing', *Nurse Education Today*, 19, 274–285.

Narayanasamy, A. (2004) 'Spiritual care. The puzzle of spirituality for nursing: A guide to practical assessment', *British Journal of Nursing*, 13: 19, 1140–1144.

Nash, M. (2002) 'Spirituality and social work in a culturally appropriate curriculum', in M. Nash and B. Stewart (2002) (eds) *Spirituality and Social Care: Contributing to Personal and Community Well-Being* (London: Jessica Kingsley).

Nash, M. and Stewart, B. (eds) (2002) *Spirituality and Social Care: Contributing to Personal and Community Well-Being* (London: Jessica Kingsley).

National Association of Social Workers (NASW) (2000) *Code of Ethics* (Washington, DC: NASW).

National Youth Agency (NYA) (2005) *Spirituality and Spiritual Development in Youth Work* (London: NYA).

Neimeyer, R. (ed.) (2001) *Meaning Reconstruction and the Experience of Loss* (Washington, DC: American Psychological Association).

Newman, T., with Yates, T. and Masten, A. (2004) *What Works in Building Resilience?* (Barkingside: Barnardos).

Nicholls, V. (2007) 'Connecting past and present: A survivor reflects on spirituality and mental health', in M. Coyte, P. Gilbert, and V. Nicholls (eds) *Spirituality, Values and Mental Health* (London: Jessica Kingsley), pp. 102–112.

Nichols, A., Coholic, A. and Cadell, S. (2008) 'Introduction to the special issue', *Journal of Religion and Spirituality in Social Work: Social Thought*, 27: 1–2, 1–3.

Nocon, A. and Qureshi, H. (1996) *Outcomes of Community Care for Users and Carers: A Social Services Perspective* (Buckingham: Open University Press).

Nolan, P. (2006) 'Spirituality: A healthcare perspective', *Implicit Religion*, 9: 3, 272–281.

Nouwen, H. (1972) *The Wounded Healer* (New York: Doubleday and Co).

Oliver, J., Huxley, P., Bridges, K. and Mohamad, H. (1997) *Quality of Life and Mental Health Services* (London: Routledge).

Orchard, H. (ed.) (2001) *Spirituality in Health Care Contexts* (London: Jessica Kingsley).

Ovretveit, J. (1997) 'How to describe interprofessional working', in J. Ovretveit, P. Mathias and T. Thompson (eds) *Interprofessional Working for Health and Social Care* (London: Macmillan).

Paquette, M. (2006) 'The science of happiness', *Perspectives in Psychiatric Care*, 42: 1 February. Available at www.wiley.com/bw/journal.asp?ref=0031–5990.

Paley, J. (2008) 'Spirituality and secularization: Nursing and the sociology of religion', *Journal of Clinical Nursing*, 17: 2, 175–186.

Paley, J. (2009) 'Religion and the secularisation of health care', *Journal of Clinical Nursing*, 18: 14, 1963–1974.

Parker, M. (2004) 'Medicalizing meaning: Demoralization syndrome and the desire to die', *Australian and New Zealand Journal of Psychiatry*, 38, 765–773.

Parton, N. and O'Byrne, P. (2000) *Constructive Social Work: Towards a New Practice* (London: Macmillan).

Patel, N., Naik, D. and Humphries, B. (1998) *Visions of Reality: Religion and Ethnicity in Social Work* (London: CCETSW).

Pateman, C. (1998) 'Democracy, freedom and special rights', in P. Boucher and D. Kelly (eds) *Social Justice: From Hulme to Waltzer* (New York: Routledge), pp. 215–231.

Payne, M. (2005a) *The Origins of Social Work: Continuity and Change* (Basingstoke: Palgrave Macmillan).

Payne, M. (2005b) *Modern Social Work Theory*, 3rd edn (Basingstoke: Macmillan).

Peberdy, A. (1993) 'Spiritual care for dying people', in D. Dickenson and M. Johnson (eds) *Death, Dying and Bereavement* (London: Sage).

Perlman, H. (1957) *Social Casework: A Problem-Solving Process* (Chicago: University of Chicago Press).

Perry, M. (1992) *Gods Within* (London: SPCK).

Pettifor, Ann (2008) 'Face to faith', *Guardian*, Saturday 11 October.

Pierson, J. (2008) *Going Local: Working in Communities and Neighbourhoods* (London: Routledge).

Pincus, A. and Minahan, A. (1973) *Social Work Practice: Model and Method* (Ithaca, IL: Peacock).

Pirani, A. (1988) 'Women: Psychotherapy: Spirituality', *Contact*, 95: 1, pp. 3–9.

Powell, A. (2003) *Psychiatry and Spirituality: The Forgotten Dimension* (Brighton: Pavilion/NIMHE).

Powell, A. (2007) 'Spirituality and psychiatry: Crossing the divide', in M. Coyte, P. Gilbert and V. Nicholls (eds) *Spirituality, Values and Mental Health: Jewels for the Journey* (London: Jessica Kingsley).

Priestly, M. (2000) 'Dropping 'E's: The missing link in quality assurance for disabled people', in A. Brechin, H. Brown and M. Eby (eds) *Critical Practice in Health and Social Care* (London: Sage/Open University).

Puchalski, C., Harris, M. and Miller, T. (2006) 'Interdisciplinary care for seriously ill and dying patients: A collaborative model', *The Cancer Journal*, 12: 5, 398–416.

Radcliffe, T. (2005) *What Is the Point of Being a Christian?* (London: Burn and Oates).

Rayner, M. and Montague, M. (2000) *Resilient Children and Young People: A Discussion Paper Based on a Review of the International Research Literature* (Melbourne, Australia: Policy and Practice Research Unit, Children's Welfare Association of Victoria).

Reese, D. and Sontag, M. (2001) 'Successful interprofessional collaboration on the Hospice Team', *Health and Social Work*, 26: 3, 167–175.

Rice, S. (2005) *The Golden Thread: An Exploration of the Relationship between Social Workers' Spirituality and Their Social Work Practice* (Unpublished PhD Thesis, University of Queensland, Australia).

Richardson, J. (1995) 'Minority religions ("Cults") and freedom of religion: Comparisons of the United States, Europe and Australia', *University of Queensland Law Review*, 18, 183–186.

Robinson, S. (2008) *Spirituality, Ethics and Care* (London: Jessica Kingsley).

Rolfe, G., Freshwater, D. and Jasper, P. (2001) *Critical Reflection for Nursing and the Helping Professions: A User Guide* (Basingstoke: Palgrave Macmillan).

Ross, L. (1997) 'Elderly patients' perceptions of their spiritual needs and care: A pilot study', *Journal of Advanced Nursing*, 26, 710–715.

Rumbold, B. (1986) *Helplessness and Hope: Pastoral Care in Terminal Illness* (London: SCM Press).

Rumbold, B. (ed.) (2002) *Spirituality and Palliative Care* (Oxford: Oxford University Press).

Rutter, M. (1985) 'Resilience in the face of adversity: Protective factors and resistance to psychiatric disorders', *British Journal of Psychiatry*, 147, 589–611.

Rutter, M. (1999) 'Resilience concepts and findings: Implications for family therapy', *Journal of Family Therapy*, 21, 119–144.

Sacco, T. (1994) 'Spirituality and social work students in their first year of study at a South African University', *Journal of Social Development in Africa*, 11: 2, 43–56.

Sacks, J. (2007) 'Chief Rabbi Sir Jonathan Sacks's lament on lost faith' as reported by Gledhill R. in the *Times* 29 July 2008, p. 15.

Saleeby, D. (ed.) (2008) *The Strengths Perspective in Social Work Practice* (NJ, Pearson: Allyn & Bacon).

Satterly, L. (2001) 'Guilt, shame, and religious and spiritual pain', *Holistic Nursing Practice*, 15: 2, 30–39.

Saunders, C. (ed.) (1990) *Hospice and Palliative Care: An Interdisciplinary Approach* (London: Edward Arnold).

Saunders, C. (1988) 'Spiritual Pain', *Hospital Chaplain*, March, pp. 3–7.

Schon, D.A. (1983) *The Reflective Practitioner: How Professionals Think in Action* (London: Temple Smith).

Sellar, W. and Yeatman, R.J. (1930) *1066 and All That. A Memorable History of England Comprising All the Parts You Can Remember Including 103 Good Things, 5 bad kings and 2 Genuine Dates* (London: Methuen).

Seligman, M. (1990) *Learned Optimism: How to Change Your Mind and Your Life* (New York, NY: Vintage Books).

Seligman, M. (1998) *Learned Optimism* (New York: Pocket Books).

Shardlow, S. (1998) 'Values, ethics and social work', in R. Adams, L. Dominelli and M. Payne (eds) *Critical Practice in Social Work* (Basingstoke: Palgrave Macmillan).

Shaw, M., Thomas, B., Smith, G. and Dorling, D. (2008) *The Grim Reaper's Road Map* (Bristol: The Policy Press).

Sheldrake, P. (2001) 'Human identity and the particularity of place', *Spiritus*, 1: 1, 43–64.

Sheridan, M., Wilmer, C. and Atcheson, L. (1994) 'Inclusion of content on religion and spirituality in the social work curriculum: A study of faculty views', *Journal of Social Work Education*, 30: 3, 363–376.

Sheridan, M. and Amato-von Hemert, K. (1999) 'The role of religion and spirituality in social work education and practice: A survey of student views and experiences', *Journal of Social Work Education*, 35: 1, 125–141.

Sinclair, S., Raffin, S., Pereira, J. and Guebert, N. (2006) 'Collective soul: The spirituality of an interdisciplinary palliative care team', *Palliative and Supportive Care*, 4, 13–24.

Skalla, K. and McCoy, J.P. (2006) 'Spiritual assessment of patients with cancer: The moral authority, vocational, aesthetic, social, and transcendent model', *Oncology Nursing Forum*, 33: 4, 745–751.

Smith, G. (2001) *Faith Makes Communities Work: A Report on Faith Based Community Development*. Sponsored by the Shaftesbury Society and the Department of the Environment, Transport and the Regions (London: DETR).

Smith, J. and Charles, G. (2009) 'The relevance of spirituality in policing: A meta-analysis', *International Journal of Police Science and Management*, paper submitted.

Special Interest Group (1999) see www.rcpsych.ac.uk/spirit and also www.rcpsych.ac.uk/college/SIG/spirit/publications/index, accessed 03 March 2010.

Sterba, J.P. (1999) *Justice: Alternative Political Perspectives*, 3rd edn (Belmont, CA: Wadsworth).

Stewart, B. (2002) 'Spirituality and culture: Challenges for competent practice in social care', in M. Nash and B. Stewart (eds) *Spirituality and Social Care: Contributing to Personal and Community Well-being* (London: Jessica Kingsley Publishers).

Stoll, R. (1979) 'Guidelines for spiritual assessment', *American Journal of Nursing*, 1, 1572–1577.

Stoll, R. (1989) 'The Essence of Spirituality', in V. Carson (ed.) *Spiritual Dimensions of Nursing Practice* (Philadelphia: W B Saunders).

Swain, J., Finkelstein, V., French, S. and Oliver, M. (1993) *Disabling Barriers – Enabling Environments* (London: Sage).

Tacey, D. (2003) *The Spirituality Revolution: The Emergence of Contemporary Spirituality* (London: Harper Collins).

Tanyi, R. (2006) 'Spirituality and family nursing: Spiritual assessment and interventions for families', *Journal of Advanced Nursing*, 53: 3, 287–294.

Teichmann, M., Murdvee, M. and Saks, K. (2006) 'Spiritual needs and quality of life in Estonia', *Social Indicators Research*, 76, 147–163.

Thompson, N. (2002) 'Social movements, social justice and social work', *British Journal of Social Work*, 32, 711–722.

Thompson, N. (2003) *Promoting Equality: Challenging Discrimination and Oppression*, 2nd edn (Basingstoke: Palgrave Macmillan).

Thompson, N. (2005) *Understanding Social Work: Preparing for Practice*, 2nd edn (Basingstoke: Palgrave Macmillan).

Thompson, N. (2006) *Anti-discriminatory Practice*, 4th edn (Basingstoke: Palgrave Macmillan).

Thompson, N. (2007a) 'Loss and grief: Spiritual aspects', in M. Coyte, P. Gilbert and V. Nicholls (eds) *Spirituality, Values and Mental Health: Jewels for the Journey* (London: Jessica Kingsley).

Thompson, N. (2007b) *Power and Empowerment* (Lyme Regis: Russell House Publishing).

Thompson, N. (2010) *Theorising Social Work Practice* (Basingstoke: Palgrave Macmillan).

Thompson, S. and Thompson, N. (2008) *The Critically Reflective Practitioner* (Basingstoke: Palgrave Macmillan).

Thorne, B. (2007) 'Awakening the heart and soul: Reflections from therapy', in M. Coyte, P. Gilbert and V. Nicholls (eds) *Spirituality, Values and Mental Health* (London: Jessica Kingsley), pp. 270–274.

Thurman, R. (2005) 'A Buddhist view of the skill of happiness', *Advances Fall/Winter*, 21: 3–4, 29–32.

Torry, B. (2005) 'Transcultural competence in health care practice: The development of shared resources for practitioners', *Practice*, 17: 4, 257–266.

Tracy, D. (1994) *Plurality and Ambiguity: Hermeneutics, Religion and Hope* (Chicago: University of Chicago Press).

Twycross, R. (2007) Unpublished paper to Dove House Hospice conference, Hull.

Ungar, M. (2006) 'Resilience across Cultures', *British Journal of Social Work Advance Access*, doi: 10.1093/bjsw/bc1343, accessed 18 October 2006.

United Nations Commission on Crime Prevention and Criminal Justice (2002) *Basic Principles on the Use of Restorative Justice Programmes in Criminal Matters* (Vienna: United Nations).

Wallis, C. (2005) 'The new science of happiness', *Time*, 165, 25–28.

Watts, F., Dutton, K. and Gulliford, L. (2006) 'Human spiritual qualities: Integrating psychology and religion', *Mental Health, Religion and Culture*, 9, 277–289.

Whiting, R. (2009) 'On reflection: Debating religion in social work education', JSWEC Conference, University of Hertfordshire, 8–10 July 2009.

Williams, C. (2007) 'On a path of most resilience', *Community Care*, 16 August 2007, 20–21.

Wilson, K., Ruch, G., Lymbery, M. and Cooper, A. (2008) *Social Work: An Introduction to Contemporary Practice* (Harlow: Pearson Longman).

World Health Organisation (WHO) (1995) *WHOQOL-100. Facet Definitions and Questions* (Geneva: Switzerland).

World Health Organisation (WHO) (1997) *WHOQOL, Measuring Quality of Life* (Geneva: Switzerland).

World Health Organisation (WHO) (1998) *WHOQOL User Manual* (Geneva: Switzerland).

Wright, S. (2005) *Reflections on Spirituality and Health* (London: Whurr Publishers). www.maydayhospital.org.uk, accessed 31 October 2009.

Younghusband, E. (1964) *Social Work and Social Change* (London: Allen and Unwin).

Yip, K. (2005) 'A dynamic Asian response to globalization in cross-cultural social work', *International Social Work*, 48: 5, 593–607.

Zapf, M.K. (2005) 'The spiritual dimension of person and environment: Perspectives from social work and traditional knowledge', *International Social Work*, 48: 5, 633–642.

Zapf, M.K. (2007) 'Profound connections between the person and place: Exploring location, spirituality and social work, Chapter 14', in Coates et al. (eds) *Spirituality and Social Work: Selected Canadian Readings* (Toronto: Canadian Scholars Press).

Zapf, M.K. (2008) 'The Spiritual dimension of person and environment: Perspectives from social work and traditional knowledge', *International Social Work*, 48: 5, 633–642.

Zohar, D. and Marshall, I. (1999) *SQ: Connecting with Our Spiritual Intelligence* (London: Bloomsbury).

Index

Gilbert, P., 19, 36, 111
Gilligan, P., 19, 69, 166
Gilligan, R., 108
Glendinning, T., 16
Glenmaye, L.F., 108
global financial crisis, 15, 148
Goldstein, H., 10
good and evil, 37, 43
Gough, I., 47
Graham, J., 11
Grainger, R., 4
'grand narrative', postmodernism's rejection, 13
Greene, G., 171
Greene, R., 108
Gunaratnam, Y., 170
Gupta, H., 74

Haas, T., 157
happiness
    and quality of life, 82–3
    and religion, 83
    scientific approaches to, 82–3
'Hard to Believe' (Powell), 86
Harding, S., 25
Harrison, P., 173
Hathaway, W., 69, 71
health and well-being, effects of religion and spirituality upon, 17–18, 90–3
Hegarty, M., 170, 179, 182
helplessness and hope, 105
Henery, N., 102, 166
Heyse-Moore, L., 50, 53
higher education, Ford's reflections on the role of, 8–9
Hight, E., 56
Hinduism, 167, 175
Hirtz, R., 88
Hiscock, V., 24
Hodge, D., 61–2, 67, 149–51, 166, 173, 177
Holbeche, L., 77
holistic care, 19
Hollis, F., 112, 179

Holloway, M., 5, 19, 23, 31–2, 34, 46, 50, 53, 59, 63, 65, 69–71, 97, 111, 124–5, 166, 169–70, 177
Holloway, R., 25–7
Holman, B., 152
'homeless humanism', 26
hope
    importance of, 104–5
    quality of life and, 83–4
HOPE questions, 56
Horwath, J., 127
hospice care, Saunders' original vision, 132
hospice, spiritual care in, 127
Houghton, S., 106–7
Howe, D., 47
Huddleston, Trevor, 78
Hudson, B., 103
Hugman, R., 143, 181
humanistic beliefs, 26
human rights, definition, 151
Hume, D., 10
Hunt, S., 12, 24–5
Hyde, B., 40

identity, 111
    Bauman on, 14
    Gilbert on, 111
IFSW (International Federation of Social Workers), 18–19, 150, 164, 181
'implicit religion', Bailey's concept, 16
indigenous/aboriginal perspectives, see aboriginal/indigenous perspectives
individualism, Bauman on the legacy of the New Right and, 15
inequality, 14
injustice, prophetic challenges to, 155
integrated community care, Beresford and Trevillion's challenge for the successful delivery of, 143–4
interagency collaboration, definition, 126
interprofessional, definition, 126

interprofessional working
background, 124–5
spectrum, 127–8
Islam, 10, 16, 24, 76, 155, 177

James, A., 74
Jensen, J., 25
Jevne, R., 106
Jewish Care, 11
Johnson, V., 82
Johnston, D., 34
joint working, 126
Jones, K., 155
Joseph, S., 87
Judaism, 10, 24
Judeo-Christian tradition, and quality of life, 76

Kant, I., 10
Kellehear, A., 100–1
Kelly, J., 84
Kelly, P., 150
King, M., 4, 92
Kirby, L.D., 108
Kissane, M., 54
Koenig, H., 17, 91–3
Kung, H., 52

learned helplessness, 87–8
learning disabled, spiritual care provision, 128
Leathard, A., 126
Ledger, S., 49, 59
Lees, J., 127
Liberation Theology, 101, 155, 176
Liebmann, M., 135
Lindsay, R., 3
liquid modernity, 14
Lloyd, M., 3–4, 19, 27, 46, 49, 51, 53, 60, 63–5, 71, 98–9, 103–6, 109, 115–16, 129, 143
Loewenberg, F., 70
loss of faith, 4, 32, 50, 52–3, 63, 115
Luckman, T., 25
Lymbery, M., 48, 125
Lynn, R., 171, 176, 178

McClung, E., 132
McCoy, J.P., 50, 66–7
McLaren, S., 54
McSherry, W., 34, 58
Maguire, K., 52
'maintaining the spirit', 51, 104, 106, 181
Maltby, J., 94
Mandela, Nelson, 79
Marshall, I., 88
Marx, K., 12
Maslow, A., 47
Masters, W., 82
Mathews, I., 19
Mattis, J., 61
Mayers, C., 34
May, G., 50
Maynard, A., 10
meaning making
Emmons' observations, 7
religion, spirituality and, 8
and spiritual narratives, 110–11
Thompson's observations, 7
mental health
importance of the 'search for meaning', 4
Islamic perspective, 177
and negative religious influences, 71
pragmatism of treatment, 86
and recognition of alienation, 50
rehabilitation therapies, 180
users' assertions of spirituality, 48
mental health teams, multidisciplinary approach, 128
Mill, J.S., 10, 75
Minahan, A., 102
Ming-Shium, T., 80
minority cultures, western social work paradigms' impact on, 174
Mohr, W., 57
Moldovan, V., 176, 182
Montague, M., 108
Moore, R., 70
Morgan, J., 32

social justice
  celebrating diversity with, *see*
    celebrating diversity with social
    justice
  as central social work value, 149
  demands for in religious works,
    155–6
  in the eco-spiritual approach, 159
  in Hugman's definition of social
    work, 143
social work
  philosophical and religious roots, 9
  psycho-social tradition, 12
  western paradigms' impact on
    minority cultures, 174
social work curricula, core themes, 7
social work education
  key questions for, 9
  spiritual/religious content, 20
social work practice, a conceptual
  framework for, 39–44
Society of Friends, 11
Sontag, M., 132
South Africa, 78
spiritual assessment
  biographical approach, 61, 65
  debates and dilemmas, 69–71
spiritual care, social work's difficulty
  with the notion of offering, 96
spiritual development, Fowler's model
  for, 99
spiritual identifiers, Brown University
  researchers' list, 59
spiritual intervention, secular *vs*
  religious perspectives, 97
spirituality
  as aspect of humanity, 29
  darker side of, 36–9
  defining, 3–4, 31, 33–5
  explosion of interest in, 30
  healthcare perspective, 34
  polarisation of religion and, 24
  relationship between quality of life
    and, 90
  relationship between religion and, 2

relationship between social work
  and, 1–2
social work's rediscovery of, 18–19
starting points for understanding
  the importance of, 7
therapeutic potential of recognition,
  97
vertical *vs* horizontal components,
  35
spiritual need
  categories, 49
  problems in identifying, 48
spiritual pain/distress, 49
  Burton on the origins, nature and
    management of, 50
  definitions, 53
  psychiatric perspective, 51
  relevant sources, 50–2
  and suicide, 54–5
spiritual pain/distress assessment
  approaches, 55
  domain approach, 65–9
  domain approach, 66–7
  identification, 55–7
  measurement, 57–60
  qualitative approach, 61–2
  self-narrative approach, 61
  tools, 56, 58–9, 61
Springett, N., 77
Sterba, J.P., 150
Stewart, B., 19, 47, 156, 175
Stoll, R., 35, 57
suicide, 53–4, 92
  spiritual pain/distress and, 54–5
Swain, J., 98

Tacey, D., 15
Tanyi, R., 62
Taylor, C., 48, 165
Teichmann, M., 85–6
terminal illness, 20, 54, 106
Thatcherism, 154
Third Reich, 43
Thompson, N., 7, 11, 13, 37, 47, 57,
  61, 84, 139, 141, 151, 153
Thompson, S., 139

Thorne, B., 116
Thurman, R., 81
Torry, B., 166, 168
Tracy, D., 182
transcendence, 3, 24, 27, 40–1, 100–2,
    104, 111, 116, 172, 180
'transcendent narratives', 173, 177
transcultural approaches, 169–70
transformation, 102–3
Trevillion, S., 143–4
Tutu, Desmond, 78
Twycross, R., 105–6

Ungar, M., 108

victim support schemes, 134

Wallis, C., 82
Watts, F., 87

well-being, faith and, 91–2
western social work paradigms, impact
    on minority cultures, 174
Whiting, R., 129
wholeness, 103–4
Williams, C., 108
William Temple Foundation, 83
Wilson, K., 181
Wittgenstein, L., 33
Wright, S., 28

Yeatman, R.J., 24
Yip, K., 164, 166–7, 170, 178
Younghusband, E., 11
youth work, 40

Zapf, M.K., 35, 157, 160, 163, 179–80
Zentner, J.B., 34
Zohar, D., 88